You Were Here Before Why Are You Here Now?

—〜〜—

Experiences of A Past Life Regression Therapist

Barbara Pisick RN,PMHCNS-BC

"To meet the challenges of our times, I believe that humanity must develop a greater sense of Universal Responsibility. Each of us must learn to work not just for our own individual self, family, or nation but for the benefit of all mankind."

~DALAI LAMA

To all seekers on their spiritual path who freely shared their hopes, dreams, fears, anxieties, and feelings with me and want their experiences to serve as an inspiration to others. Your courage to explore other dimensions continues to be an inspiration to me and all of the people with whom I've worked.

~BARBARA PISICK

Dedicated to Victoria McNamee, whose support and encouragement inspired the totality of this work and who has traveled with me through many lifetimes.

Table of Contents

"But never forget that you came from the Lower World for a purpose. Only those who forget why they came to this world will lose their way. They will disappear in the wilderness and be forgotten."

~GOGYENG SOWUHTI (SPIDER GRANDMOTHER—A CREATOR DEITY OF HOPI MYTHOLOGY)

Introduction

Do you ever wonder about your life purpose or question why you are here? Have you ever had a deja vu experience or the feeling that you intimately know a person who you have never met before? Or found a foreign place instantly familiar? The search for meaning and life purpose was dramatically heightened for many Americans by the confluence of national and worldwide events after September 11, 2001. These experiences dramatically increased people's concerns about world problems and spirituality. They began to ask themselves the timeless questions: Who am I? Why am I here?

Many people living in the New York City area as well as throughout the world began to search for these answers through past life regression therapy (PLRT). The foundation of this alternative psychotherapeutic technique is based on reincarnation, the central underpinning for precepts of birth, death, afterlife, and rebirth in Eastern religions. It is predicated on the understanding that we continue to reincarnate because of the necessity for increased soul development as well as the need to understand and fulfill our soul's life purpose. The soul evolves through many lifetimes. Inherent in this philosophy is an acceptance of the universal connectedness of all people.

The goal of my past life regression therapy is for people to heal their problems and to understand their life purpose as they work on furthering their soul development. Tragic events that occur in our lives show how suddenly life can change, leading people to rethink the direction of their careers and relationships.

A surprise for me and others I have worked with is the awareness that a life purpose doesn't always require setting lofty, personal goals. It can be as simple as self-healing, self-acceptance, and self-love, while allowing your loving energy to go out into the world. Through PLRT, many people have become more aware of their life patterns, and they were able to recognize that their current focus was self-oriented and materialistic, which resulted in a lack of connection with others or not making a world contribution.

My own search for life purpose and meaning began during my student-nurse experiences while I worked on a pediatric unit in a New York City major medical center. Many parents had asked me why their child was picked to suffer. As a young 17-year-old, I had no answers, but simply tried to comfort them.

However, that nagging question continued to resonate within me. Why would God let a little child suffer? My question was not answered. In those days, the 1960s, spirituality was not widely acknowledged within the healthcare system. My pediatric and hospital-wide experiences motivated me to search through my immersion in Eastern philosophy teachings for an understanding of life's purpose, my purpose, and why little children suffer.

Although growing up in a nonreligious family, I believed in God, but I had no awareness of the concept of reincarnation. My parents told my brothers and me that we all had a contribution to make to the world and that we had to "give back." Our mother participated in tireless volunteer work that she derived great pleasure and satisfaction from. She reminded us that we should treat all people equally, never discriminate against anyone, and that name-calling hurts. In short, we should treat others with great care.

That's probably why my brothers and I are all contributing members within the health-care field.

I worked as a registered nurse in the surgical and critical-care areas for more than 17 years as part of a team—a "family"—of nurses, aides, and doctors caring for patients. Our rewards came from working with people, seeing their responses to our care, and the camaraderie we enjoyed. We pulled many patients through some very harrowing experiences before the invention of the modern-day Intensive Care Units. The teamwork was special, and the synergy was extended to the entire ward of patients. I loved my work, which was highlighted by patients who chose to entrust me with their life stories. Those fulfilling exchanges inspired me to further question my own life purpose.

While working in administrative positions, I found that the time-consuming, day-to-day bureaucracy kept me from what I loved and was inspired by the most, direct patient care. So I began my search for answers through the study of the mind-body-spirit interactions at the Alfred Adler Institute and became a psychotherapist.

What attracted me to Adler's theory was his pivotal belief in social interest, or *gemeinschaftsgefuhl*. This belief acknowledges a way of addressing life through our own contributions to the greater good within a community. Adler describes the importance of interconnections in the world. My exposure to Adlerian theory allowed me to examine my own outdated perceptions that had been based on Freudian theory. Freudian theory did not recognize or encourage a person to have a world view or to take on the responsibility to make change in the world. Adlerian theory is a more holistic concept than self-absorption. As a result, I began to change my own world view and also began teaching this idea to patients. I saw that Adler's focus on social interest was echoed in Buddhist spiritual beliefs.

While in a psychiatric/mental-health nursing program that focused on systems theory and family therapy, I gained an expansive understanding of individuals and their dynamic interactions within their families and the world. My rapidly changing perceptions enabled me to view the universe from a larger perspective. Therefore, I was able to shape a more holistic and spiritual approach to my psychotherapy work. This led to newer possibilities as I began to use a variety of techniques while gaining a broader understanding of my role as a facilitator.

The belief that we are all here on earth during this lifetime for a greater purpose was a new idea for me. This idea could only be understood through personal searching and questioning. My own consciousness began to evolve while working through my own personal issues. These experiences highlighted the importance of my acknowledgment of all people as interconnected souls, and these changes transformed every part of my life.

During that time, while struggling with spiritual issues, my mother called sounding very upset and worried. She said the sweater that she was knitting for me would not be ready for the December holidays. Her deep concerns surprised me, since things like this had never bothered her before. Upon awakening one day a few weeks after her phone call, I said out loud, "D-day the 6th," but I didn't understand what that meant.

One afternoon while I was sitting in a classroom, a breeze flashed past my face. Since the window was closed, I thought that was odd. Upon returning home that evening, I was told that my mother had died during that afternoon at the exact time I felt the breeze. I can still feel that vivid moment to this day. It was D-day, December 6. At some unconscious level, I believe my mother knew that she wasn't going to be around to finish the sweater. But how could she or I know she would die on December 6th? I instantly realized that there were so many more dimensions to my life than I could have imagined.

Beginning Hypnotherapy Work

This was the beginning of many experiences resulting in my increased awareness of the multiple dimensions of consciousness. I became more open to the possibility of the soul's existence after death and the belief that things happen for a reason. It was obvious to me that those occurrences were coming from another level of consciousness. As a result of these events, I acquired an enhanced view of spirituality.

While I learned alternative modalities within a holistic program for healers, my ideas about life purpose continued to expand as well. I began to integrate the mind-body-spirit interactions into my daily personal and professional life; I identified the broader spiritual reason why events happened and what I could learn from these experiences. Then I changed my solutions to situations, which resulted in outcome changes. I then introduced these ideas to my patients and used hypnotherapy with them to enhance their experiences. Their total relaxation, which occurred in a very short period of time during the trance state, an altered state of consciousness, totally surprised me. While people worked on their problems in relation to weight, smoking, and self-esteem, they responded and were able to access deeper levels of consciousness.

Through this process, they were able to tap into their deep-seated, internal desire to help themselves. It was amazing to see that the suggestions I made to people while they were at altered levels of consciousness made a tremendous difference in their ability to successfully follow a course of treatment for their chronic problems. The use of these techniques often led to greater self-empowerment. These changes were also much more rapid than the changes people usually made during the psychotherapy process.

Somehow, the harnessing of their minds led to physiological body changes such as decreased blood pressure, increased relaxation, and an amelioration of their chronic pain. As a result of these cathartic experiences, people began to deal directly with their stress and anxiety rather than masking their discomfort with drugs and alcohol.

Some people experienced early childhood memories that they had no conscious recollection of. Others who had asked to experience hypnotherapy to explore their childhood memories spontaneously described a past life regression during their altered state of consciousness. They found this to be puzzling, since they had never heard of reincarnation. These regression experiences affected their unconscious mind, resulting in behavioral changes while they transcended their conscious difficulties. As a result, they reexamined their current life experiences in a different way, using the concept of reincarnation as a framework while making life-pattern changes.

In the beginning, it was difficult for me to integrate a belief in reincarnation and the soul's evolution into my professional work, since my early nursing-school education was based on the "scientific method." An important realization for me was that people's emotional and spiritual experiences are descriptive and anecdotal; therefore, they should not be treated like the hard sciences. Most importantly, even though these experiences had not been quantified by scientific measurements, that did not mean they did not exist.

Unfortunately, the lack of measurement has been and continues to be one of the major reasons why the American scientific community continues to devalue spiritual experiences. The anecdotal experiences as evidenced in this work demonstrate that a large number of people make life changes as a result of PLRT, reflecting its powerful effect.

During the late1980s, I met and spoke with Dr. Brian Weiss, the renowned author of *Many Lives, Many Masters*. Since I was a psychotherapist who was performing similar work, he referred many people to me for PLRT. At that time, I became one of the first psychotherapists in New York City to be recommended by him for PLRT. I am grateful for his support of practitioners like me and applaud his courage for documenting the past life experiences he encountered with his patients. A powerful result was the opening of the field for all of us who were privately using this work.

Past Life Regression Therapy (PLRT)

My interest in using past life regression therapy (PLRT) grew as increased numbers of people from throughout the world expressed interest in their life purpose and soul journey. As they began to reenact past life experiences, I found that their stories were quite compelling. This work was a natural transition for me, since people's experiences led them on a spiritual quest. Accelerated personal growth was an added bonus.

These explorers functioned normally and came from all walks of life and age groups throughout the world. My examination of people's past life regressions included those who traveled from China, India, England, France, Japan, Spain, South America, and throughout the United States, demonstrating a consistency of universal patterns regardless of nationality. They were blue-collar workers, psychiatrists, actors, housewives, lawyers, nurses, chiropractors, judges, doctors, college students, and professors.

Most wanted to understand their troublesome relationships with current partners, friends, parents, siblings, and business associates. People reexamined long-held beliefs through their past life regression experiences. They were able to gain insight into their complex relationships as well as problems with their panic attacks and phobias. A common goal for them was to determine the meaning of life—their life purpose.

While I helped people to work through the accessed information, I saw immediate changes. Through multiple-case studies of individuals' regressions, the continuity of the soul's evolution over time can be seen.

Differences From Other Modalities

PLRT differs from other psychotherapeutic modalities because it demonstrates people's abilities to rapidly find the crux of their chronic mind, body, and spirit problems. This work was performed while they were in an altered state of consciousness—the level of consciousness similar to the hypnotic trance or meditative state. During the regression experience, people spoke about specific information that was germane for an understanding of their current life stresses while learning how to make life changes. Often, their individual traumas, which may have originated in this lifetime or in a past lifetime, could be viewed as the underlying cause of their current distress. The regression findings were then integrated into their current life situations as they made the necessary changes to find their life purpose.

A 2011 Gallup poll finding reported that 90% of the population believes in God and prays daily. I found that many people described their dismay regarding the lack of discussion about the importance of spirituality and religion during their prior psychotherapy experiences. They were happy they could finally discuss this during the regression work. These results give credence to people's concerns about the omission of these topics in relation to a very important part of their life.

As a result of their regression work, people told me that their need for a personal commitment was awakened. This was manifested by their desire to make a contribution by "giving back" and to make a difference in the world. When they recognized their own unproductive interactive patterns, they began to change. Some with terminal illness or suffering the loss of a loved one felt uplifted when their beliefs in reincarnation were validated. Affirmation of the everlasting soul was a comfort to them. People were now able to transform their fears of death while acknowledging that the soul continues to evolve over time.

However, through all of these reenactments, I found that a belief in reincarnation is not quite the same as the experience of a tangible, palpable past life regression. Some individual regressions were very loud and dramatic. Many people were frightened (as was I) by their screams, especially when they included terrifying events. In fact, one of the psychotherapists in my office suite was worried that something terrible was happening in my office when she heard someone screaming during a regression. Within these regressions, people often experienced intense emotions and severe physical vibrations as you will read about in their detailed regressions.

Discussions in relation to their regressions often resulted in the healing of current life fears that had been resistant to traditional treatment. These powerful experiences allowed people to clearly see their problems while making the necessary changes. This resulted in their increased personal fulfillment. Some with chronic disabilities from medically resistant panic attacks and phobias experienced dramatic changes in these conditions. As a result of the regression work, they were now able to face their fears with freedom from anxiety and emotional paralysis.

The Purpose of This Book

The purpose of this book is to present some of the PLRT experiences of individual seekers on their path of greater spiritual understanding while showing the impact that this information had on their lives.

This book's personalized, experiential work is built on only a small percentage of hundreds of examples of individual regression experiences. It illustrates the tremendous personal growth of those who have undergone PLRT.

This work is enlivened by the documented, word-for-word, detailed expressions of selected regressions, reflecting how a search for answers to current problems can affect people's overall search for a life purpose. The detailed regressions allow readers to understand their own interpretations as they read participants' regressions. It then becomes clear how a person derived lessons from his or her experiences.

A large percentage of people believed the past life regression experiences they reenacted were truthful accounts of their past lives. The reliving of those past lives illuminated their current life experiences, resulting in a greater understanding of the broader dimensions of race and religion. People described what happened to their souls at the time of death in that lifetime and afterward. At the same time, they reported information relayed from their spirit guides in regard to how they should make life changes. This affirmed a belief in reincarnation, which led to their broader spiritual journey.

My purpose is not to "prove" that these regressions are actually past life regressions. For some people, they may simply be a metaphor for their current life problems or a storytelling vehicle that allows them to translate current problems in a safer, more distanced way. This technique can help someone to see his or her problems more clearly. People do not have to believe in reincarnation in order to experience a clearer understanding of their current dilemmas through this work. If people with binge-eating problems can be helped by confronting those issues more easily when they see themselves starving through the Irish potato famine, the end result is what matters the most.

Some may view people's altered states of consciousness as wanderings of their imaginations. The end result, however, is that these experiences liberated them from their chronic problems. Hopefully, this book and some of the therapeutic exercises included here will encourage people to begin their own search for their past lives and their life purpose.

Within these writings, the client's stories reflect each individual's life changes, resulting in a greater appreciation for his or her own personal contributions. This includes a reexamination of values, especially in a world that appears to reward self-focus and materialism. These stories highlight the fact that all people are interconnected and must take more responsibility for their paths while recognizing that there is a universal consciousness. The individual's search for a life purpose, like Spider Grandmother's belief, affirms the importance of spirituality and is an integral part of this book. As people read about others' regression experiences, I hope they will be encouraged to begin their own life search.

For the record, all of the reported regressions through-out the book are included word-for-word from the taped recordings. They have not been changed for grammar. Likewise, the regressions have been approved for inclusion by the individuals. Changes have been made to protect the identity of the individual.

I believe this book differs from others in the field because of my own belief in reincarnation as the structural underpinning for my PLRT work. Most writers of this type of work have hesitated to acknowledge reincarnation as a belief system. They tend to treat the regressions as stories that have metaphoric implications for life, so they often do not base their work on the spiritual concepts of Buddhism and/or other beliefs. I integrate the findings from the past life regressions into a spiritual context, which is then intertwined with the psychotherapy.

The personalized, experiential work includes people's detailed explorations of their search for answers to current problems. In the process of working with others, my own spiritual beliefs were deepened. And I personally have made life changes as I learned to accept the spiritual dimensions of my own life.

Namaste (I bow to the divine in you.)

1

A Shocking Beginning

"Everything can be taken from a man but one thing: the last of the human freedoms—to choose one's attitude, to choose one's own way."

~VIKTOR FRANKL

Throughout my 38-year psychotherapy practice, I witnessed shifts in the health-care practitioners' attitudes in relation to their professional practices. This changed from a Western medicine view toward one that includes a more holistic view. The result was a multidimensional health-care model.

Broad levels of transformation in the area of health care have led the average person to gain a greater understanding of the importance of treating the underlying causes of a disease instead of just the symptoms. Public beliefs are also changing as people take increased responsibility for their own health. Upon receiving an "untreatable" diagnosis, people become more proactive. They search for the most up-to-date medical information through the Internet, outside sources, and consultations with other physicians. Patients have become more informed and involved in their care as they take physicians off their pedestals as the final arbiters and decision makers.

It has been shown that when traditional health care does not address their problems, more people actively seek the care of alternative health practitioners. The PLRT work is one of the modalities they choose to explore. This work acknowledges a mind-body-spirit connection while recognizing the importance of the quality of life and spirit.

Some people believe that their current lifetime experiences on earth are similar to that of a school. They learn how to make changes in their lives by working on issues that they believe they came into this lifetime to heal.

While searching for the root of their problems through past lifetime reenactments, people recognized that their life purpose was to continue to work on their current unresolved life patterns as well as make changes in and contributions to their communities. A 2007 government survey reported that people spent more than $33.9 billion out-of-pocket on complementary and alternative medicine. This reflects people's beliefs in alternative forms of treatment.

Religious Beliefs and Reincarnation

Reincarnation acknowledges that the soul enters human form at birth, on earth, during different time periods. Within this belief system, individuals choose to incarnate into each lifetime with a purpose. That purpose is to allow a person to experience a multifaceted life while working through spiritual and experiential lessons.

The Hindu and Buddhist beliefs are that the soul continues on after death to evolve through many lifetimes until it reaches nirvana, the elimination of desire and suffering. We all have a soul purpose, the reason why we are here on earth. These beliefs mandate that we take responsibility for our lives by engaging in a direct dialogue with God or a Higher Power instead of communicating through spiritual intermediaries (e.g., clergy) who claim they are the only "direct channels."

The ultimate goal for those who believe in reincarnation is to achieve the highest attainment of "Godlikeness," so eventually there is no need for the soul to continue to materialize in human form. It is important for people to work toward evolving themselves as well as to make changes in the world.

Karma is a "natural causal law that involves each person's intentions, leading to a particular action" (*The Essential Dalai Lama: His Important Teachings*, 2006). *Karma* is the part of the belief system acknowledging that each person is born into this lifetime with a residue of influences from previous lifetimes. Thus, our current karma is an accumulation of our thoughts and actions arising from all of our previous lives. The soul is believed to continue to return to a new lifetime until past karma is worked through and enlightenment occurs. At that point, there is no longer a need to reincarnate.

The PLRT focus is on the transformation of karmic patterns within our current life situations. This can be accomplished through life examination, as some people search for their life purpose and begin to evolve their souls. According to reincarnation concepts, each individual's incarnation lasts a short time in the universal life span. There is a continuity of a stream of consciousness over successive rebirths, which must be worked through in this lifetime in order to permanently escape the birth, death, afterlife, and rebirth cycles known as the "wheel."

Right actions in this lifetime can allow a soul to evolve to a higher level in the next lifetime. As the soul merges with the cosmic consciousness, the ultimate goal of nirvana is reached, and there is no longer a need to return to an earthbound life. This is the height of spiritual growth. Thus, enlightenment occurs as the individual is completely freed from the cycle of craving and all attachment and material desires.

During my extensive reading and exploration, I found that for centuries, both Christians and Jews believed in reincarnation until it was forbidden by religious leaders. As a central underpinning for Buddhism and Hinduism, reincarnation acknowledges an interconnection of all peoples throughout the world. More than 1.2 billion people accept reincarnation as a part of their religious beliefs and the means for the soul's growth and development over time. For Buddhists, the concept of the soul in a cycle of everlasting renewal can be viewed as similar to a reparative process or the continuous death and regeneration of body cells within our physical body.

The concept of change dates back to Heraclitus (540-480 BC) who stated that, "We cannot step twice into the river." He meant that both the person and the river can never be the same as both are always transforming. More than two thousand years ago, the philosopher Plato described the soul as existing before entering human form. We can see that the idea of the soul's existence before coming into the body at birth without any memory is not a new concept.

Hindus accept all religions as a way to reach God. For them, the cycle of births and deaths is called *Samsara*, when the soul passes from one life to another. Eventually, the soul can break away from the cycle of birth and death by becoming an eternal servant of *Krishna*, the incarnation of the Supreme Being.

The traditional beliefs of Judaism address life's meaning with its belief in "tikun halom," a responsibility for repairing or making a contribution to the world. Judgment occurs after life. Advanced seekers of wisdom, through the Hebrew mystical teachings of *Kabbalah*, believe in reincarnation.

Kabbalah study usually occurs at age 40 when individuals spiritually mature and begin to question their life purpose. Up to that time, they are seen as accumulating life experiences and wisdom. The Hasidic masters believed that the knowledge of past lifetimes helped a person to gain insight into the repairs that must be made from previous incarnations. The repairs are their life purposes, and as a soul evolves, death is viewed as a door into another realm. There appear to be two levels of teaching within Judaism: one for the masses, and the other for advanced seekers within Kabbalah.

Christianity's traditional tenets do not acknowledge reincarnation. Christianity teaches that at death, the souls of believers go to heaven, which is eternal life. Souls of nonbelievers or sinners go to purgatory or hell. Many Christians view non-Christians as residing in limbo.

The *Nag Hammadi* writings, which were found in Egypt in 1945, are believed to be the secret teachings of Jesus to his disciples. Included is the Gospel of Thomas, which has been dated to the first century. The translation of Jesus's 114 sayings has resulted in interpretations that differ from those included in the Bible. They raise questions about the essence of Christianity. These writings focus on the individual's self-examination from within, without the influence of others. The first teaching is, "Whoever finds the meaning of these sayings will not taste death."

One can perhaps interpret this as a message alluding to reincarnation. In the New Testament, Jesus Christ's message was, "Follow me and you will find eternal life." This may suggest that the awakening of an individual's spiritual life results in overcoming death, or perhaps, to the soul's continued reincarnation. The Gospel of Mark includes descriptions of two levels of teaching: one for the masses, and the other for Jesus's disciples.

For those interested in reading about the *Nag Hammadi*, there are two books that clearly demonstrate those findings. They are, *The Gnostic Gospels* by Elaine Pagels, Professor of Religion at Princeton University, and *Insights from the Secret Teachings of Jesus: The Gospel of Thomas*, by Christan Amundsen.

What Is Past Life Regression Therapy (PLRT)?

Past life regression therapy (PLRT) combines psychology and spirituality, using an altered state of consciousness as the vehicle through which past life traumas are accessed. This work has been used by holistic mental health practitioners since the 1970s. People who are searching for their current life meaning and life purpose actively seek PLRT. Past life regressions can elicit information that helps people analyze their chronic problems.

The regression sessions that I have conducted often highlighted a person's unproductive life patterns, which may have persisted throughout many lifetimes. Most people acknowledged a belief in reincarnation. Through the integration of that information into their current lifetime issues, people were eventually freed from their dysfunctional habits. This cathartic process led to life changes. The past life regression experiences demonstrate their importance by allowing us to understand the everlasting movement of each soul toward greater spiritual growth and awareness.

Altered State of Consciousness

The hypnotherapy experience is an altered state of consciousness. I leave a wide berth for individuals' explorations. They are instructed to keep the problem they chose to examine in mind as they go back to another time or another experience that might be important to look at for healing and for their highest good. At that time, people are able to determine why a past experience happened to them.

The therapist *must not shape* patients' experiences during the exploration of their regressions. When using hypnotherapy, I never suggest that anyone go back to a specific time period or what they might be seeing or hearing. This is important in order to maintain neutrality while avoiding the introduction of any new information.

During the relaxation part of the hypnosis process, I ask people to surround themselves with white light, sunlight, or God's light for protection. I suggest that they keep their minds open to whatever is presented to them visually or physically while in an altered state of consciousness. In most regression sessions, after people experience a past lifetime, I usually recommend that they go to their time of death in order to bring them to closure.

I found that the reported experiences were as varied as being burned, drowned, mutilated, or dying peacefully in bed surrounded by their family and loved ones. Most people described their souls rising out of their bodies and going up to a place of light.

While in that place, they were able to transmit messages to help themselves in this lifetime. These messages often reflected an understanding of what people believed would be relevant to assist them to understand and heal their current problems. As a result, they were then able to view their lives in a more meaningful way. Also, people were able to gain an understanding of a more broadly defined global life purpose. Some also began to understand how soul mates function in their lives.

I used each individual's spontaneously accessed information from these sessions to further assist in the healing process. I was very careful to acknowledge people's vulnerability during the hypnotherapy in order to avoid jeopardizing the validity of the findings.

The word-for-word regression experiences that I have included literally demonstrate the actual sequence of patients' regressions, their own interpretations, and how the integration of that information transformed their life problems. This provided an opportunity for psychotherapists to replicate the work and to critically interpret the findings.

Their experiences usually resulted in an alleviation of their symptoms. Patients began to understand that their symptoms and the illness itself might also be lessons to evolve their soul purpose.

People evolved more spiritually through this process, which I believe is a reflection of their ability to apply the spiritual implications gleaned from these past lifetimes to their current lives. They were able to gain a greater understanding of how to deal with their issues by learning the greater spiritual lessons. However, each person must always take the lead in describing all of his or her experiences.

Why People Choose Past Life Regression Therapy

I found that an interest in spirituality across all groups of people usually begins during a time of life shifts such as physical ailments, disability, great personal tragedies, professional disappointments, or the senseless deaths of loved ones. These events often force us to slow down until we are able to become more "open" to other beliefs.

During this exploration, people say they are searching for "deeper" meaning within their lives. Many people do not become aware of their life purpose until their late 30s or early 40s, when they search for meaning and become more "conscious." Most people I have worked with believe that their souls chose to incarnate in this lifetime to work on their life purpose. For them, the goal of this work is not only the past life regression experience, but also a personalized approach to recognize their current life purpose.

One of the most frequent reasons people chose to explore this work with me was due to their "stuck," long-term psychotherapy experiences.

They often described their lack of success in accessing the underlying causes of their chronic emotional problems. To many of my patients, it became immediately apparent that this therapy is different from other treatment modalities. Through PLRT, origins of current life traumas were more rapidly facilitated. This information has helped people to have an "aha" experience, resulting in their ability to integrate findings from their past life regressions into their current lives. Many describe dramatic changes within their chronic relationship problems as they overcame difficulties managing their weight, self-esteem, panic attacks, and abuse problems.

Spirit Guides

During this process, many people talked about their spirit guides. The information that some people channeled from their spirit guides usually described their current life purpose, which continually wove its way through many of their regression lifetimes. People often called their spirit guides and guardian angels their "spiritual protectors." They believed everyone had spirit guides.

I have also come to believe in the existence of spirit guides who I believe are there to watch out for us. Spirit guides are often described by some as "angelic beings" that reside in a different realm and are there to "guide and protect" people. Others visualized their guides as an Indian spirit, a white-veiled essence, or an ethereal spirit. During this work, I was told by some Catholic school graduates that their teacher-nuns told them to leave enough room on their classroom seats for their guardian angels.

Many seekers believe that the messages they received during PLRT came from a Higher Source. One example of how these beliefs have become a part of the public consciousness was demonstrated in a *New York Times* article (June 2005). A rabbi noticed that his PSA level (a test for prostate cancer) became slightly elevated from 2.4 to 3.4. Even though his physician told him that these numbers fell within the normal range, the rabbi was concerned that he might have prostate cancer. His physician told him that he did not have to worry until the results were above 4.

Out of the blue, however, the rabbi remembered a strange incident that had occurred three years before as he was leaving a Center for Religion and Health. A stranger had said to him, "Are you here for the prostate cancer support group?" He said no. The man proceeded to say to him, "I want to give you a piece of advice; don't pay attention to the absolute PSA number, but if you see it rising, that's a cause for concern."

The memory of that conversation led the rabbi to persist by voicing his concerns with his doctor who finally referred him to an urologist. A biopsy was performed, and a small cancer was found. It consisted of cells that are usually associated with an aggressive form of cancer. The rabbi believes that as a direct result of that encounter with a stranger, he became more insistent with his physician. He said, "It was a 'message from God.'"

Throughout my PLRT work, so many people told me about their beliefs in relation to their spirit guides or what they variously called their intuitive hunches or their gut experiences or mentioned things that "just happened out of the blue." Some, like the rabbi himself, will choose to believe that his spirit guides or guardian angels made sure that the information was passed onto him; others might not and will just say he was persistent and he's a rabbi, so of course he's going to believe that. But I believe it is important for us to be open to the possibility.

Past Life Regression Therapy Experiences

I began to use PLRT as a treatment modality more intensively with the many people who sought to experience it in the 1990s. I could evaluate the reliability of the people who were seeking this type of experience. These individuals were normal, alert, honest, and fully functioning in the world of relationship and work. In fact, there was no motivation on their part to invent stories about their experiences. People described their past life regressions as invaluable since these experiences helped them more clearly understand their current life situations. As a result, they were able to integrate these new findings into their lives.

When other psychotherapists and health-care professionals heard about their patients' results from the PLRT, they referred themselves. Their primary interest was in the use of PLRT for their own personal and spiritual explorations.

A PLRT session begins with a discussion about the individual's problem areas. Then, attention is focused on specific areas of vulnerabilities that need to be resolved during this lifetime. Sometimes, I describe the regression work of other individuals to give them a greater understanding of what other people have experienced. This also gives them an idea of the work's dimensionality. People never described an experience similar to what I had talked to them about. I was surprised that they were often emotionally affected by other peoples' regression experiences. Through their regression reenactments, they connected their current pain and suffering to prior lifetimes while discovering the reasons for their current discomfort.

Mary was one of the first patients to experience the PLRT with me. Her interest in this work came about as a result of her desire to explore conflicts surrounding her long-standing health-care career. Formerly an outstanding nurse-practitioner, she took a $20,000 per year pay cut to work in a secretarial job. She could not understand her vehement opposition to continuing to work in the medical field. Mary told me that nurses were being asked to take increased responsibility for patient care without proper training and supervision.

During her regression, Mary talked about the importance of past life regression experiences. She said the following to me while in an altered state of consciousness:

M: Do not concentrate on the traumas or the negative or the black, because it will contaminate you. Keep yourself clear and a flowing channel and fill yourself with light and laughter. You will be ready for what's beginning to happen. People are waking. Like a lightness, walking together into the future. If they're concerned about negative things, they will get pulled down or weighed down, like baggage. It's hard to turn one's eyes from darkness or negativity. We must help put ourselves in a state, washed with light, love, and laughter. People are going to have to leave the darkness. If they can keep the light of love and laughter, they will be needed in the future. Look at past lives, for it will be beneficial for what's coming. If you provide the space (she implies me) and open the door, it's up to them to walk through or not. What is past you are bringing to the now, with them.

While Mary was in a trance, she talked about the concept of past lives as if she were a teacher preparing me for the work I was embarking on. She channeled the following information to me:

M: We so often look at past lives as linear and they aren't. We are part of this center, and the rays coming into the center are past lives. Simultaneous experiences come to make up the whole. Some will be ready, some will not. Some will misinterpret, and some will not. Some will create to please, some are on a sincere journey, don't take it to yourself. You're simply a catalyst. For some it's a fad. Just release it—let it go—it is energy—don't waste your energy, put it where it needs it. There will be different levels of learning. All levels. All will get some stimulus to grow. You'll sense those who are just trying it, like a sea that might open and close.

These were good teachings for me at the beginning of my PLRT work. Mary was letting me know that some people would appear for a past life regression as a fad in order to see who they were in another lifetime. I did find that others were ready to take the next step by finding a way to heal their problems and to ascertain their life purpose. Among the hundreds of seekers of this work, only a few people displayed an interest in the regressions as a fad. Most saw it as a stimulus toward their spiritual work and growth.

Then, while Mary was still in an altered state of consciousness, a powerful experience emerged that shocked both of us. I nearly jumped out of my chair during her first past life regression session. An intense feeling of fear and shock came over me despite her calm description of being burned alive at the stake. Mary's hand was gently draped on the arm of the sofa in my office as she softly described the horrific situation she had just seen. In low tones, she quietly described her charred hands and body as she was being burned at the stake. She said that members of the healing community in which she lived during this past lifetime realized that she had a "special healing ability" with birds. She used an ancient hands-on healing technique that at that time was considered witchcraft. If a bird had a broken wing, she could see where the break was, and her fingers "seemed to help it knit faster." So, when a wealthy landowner asked that she heal his dying young son, the healers asked her to perform the healing.

M: My guides are with me—but the Sage Femme, Wise Woman and the Wolf, aren't with me. (She is referring to her spirit guides.)

I was supposed to put my hands on the child. The other healers had used herbs and they didn't work. I didn't know people's bodies. It was very confusing. Head or chest. I guess I put my hands on both. They tried other things and they thought maybe this would work. I don't know people—bodies. I thought I had to at least make-believe that I was doing something, because that's what I was brought there for. So, I moved my hands up and down from the head to the chest.

The person who took me there was an older woman. The father brought him down to the shore. They took me back over to the island and I knew it wasn't right because there wasn't any power there. I couldn't feel anything. Like with the animals, you can feel something. I could almost visualize a wing, the inside of a wing. You could almost visualize what had gone wrong. Then I put my hands on the chest and head. It was like I didn't know what this was. I was wrong, because instead of saying I can't do this, I don't know what this is, I moved my hands up and down to make-believe that I was doing something. [I wanted] to please or not to embarrass the woman in front of the man; make it look I like I was doing something. It was almost like I felt they had a reputation to keep up.

I get this image...men didn't come on that island. I got this feeling of some men actually invading the island and that pit in the center. (She drew a picture of the fire pit.)

I think that's where it happened—where I got burned. They came on the island because nobody had helped his son. Those who had given herbs didn't help and I was the last one. They didn't touch anything in the village, but they wanted, he wanted vengeance.

He demanded my life for his son's. It was like a sacrilege, that's the "now" word.

The other men were there to stick a pole down into the fire pit. They cut a tree, put it down into the ground, and I got tied to it. There is a feeling of standing back away from this and watching this, 'cause I was asking myself, "Why am I not reacting? I'm over." I know exactly where I'm standing. I'm up from it, actually. This is like devastation to the community. It's like they were almost helpless.

B: Why couldn't they do anything to the men? Weren't there enough of them?

M: No, there were plenty of them. I get a feeling of five-six men. They tied me to it. Some of the women had taken the younger children and moved them to the lower part of the island, 'cause they didn't want them to see this. 'Cause they knew what was happening, and it was like this was not the place to burn someone. This was a ritual ceremonial fire pit, and it was desecrated by them wanting to do this. The men gathered. There were pine needles. They gathered branches and they threw it all into this fire pit.

B: What did you do?

M: I don't feel like I'm awake. All I know is I am outside of my body watching this going on. I'm on the post and my head is down on the post. It's like dangling. It's like I'm not there.

B: Is your spirit outside your body?

M: No, I'm still there. I'm not dead, but it's like the me, now. Cannot put myself in there so I'm sort of hovering back up in the woods, watching this. But the me, then, is not consciously there.

B: What is it you have to learn about this experience to bring into the here and now to learn about yourself?

M: Think about a piece that I'd never think about before. I tried faking it, knowing how much it meant. They had tried with herbs and nothing worked, and I was like their last hope. Because I'd shown so much promise, I had sort of a mystical connection with animals. They thought I might be able to do it with this child. I tried faking it to save them, protect them. To please her.

B: So what do you want to take out for yourself for now? To learn something for yourself in the here and now, from this experience?

M: Be real, be honest. Say when you don't know how to do something. Know what you can do and when there's a special skill. Use it only in that area. Don't try to carry it over into something else, like animals to humans. Learn to say no. Don't offer more than you can do. Know your limitations. Don't lose the "Wolf" part of me. And learn when to say no.

When Mary came out of the regression, she described the healing of a bird:

M: It's like I could see through the feathers. It's like I was getting this image of a wing and it had actually been broken like this. And with my hands I could, without upsetting the bird, pull it together so that it was approximated. And then I would just put my hands over it. And it wasn't like it magically healed and became perfect, but it was like you could almost see something starting in here, so that it adhered and then it took time. But it was a distinct image of a bird's wing. But it's like if you had x-ray vision and could see through this hand, but you went over to the desk and you tried applying our x-ray vision to the desk and wasn't anything you could see. I mean, that was like what the contrast was. I tried looking. I see this child lying on the beach and I tried putting my hands on. It was like nothing. The woman who I was apprenticed to had shown me and I had watched.

Mary believed that the power came to her from her metaphorical "Wolf" side. The pressure to perform the healing was so strong, that even though she did not feel ready, she faked it. The healing did not work, the son died, and the landowner had her burned at the stake. She believes that her failure to heal the son was a direct result of her not being allowed to have her "Wolf" come with her when she went to heal the boy. Mary told me that she saw me there as a member of the healing community who had encouraged her to perform the healing.

Now in this lifetime, a situation offered her an opportunity to stand up for herself. The dilemma resulted in her feeling compelled to leave her profession permanently. Perhaps this was an emotional overreaction since she could have worked in another health-care agency. However, Mary was so upset about this specific work incident that she felt forced to leave the nursing profession. She wanted to understand her strong feelings and to make sure this was the right path for her to follow.

In hospitals, there may be severe repercussions for a nurse who refuses to perform a procedure when directed to do so by a supervisor. In fact, nurses have been held liable when following a supervisor's orders if they knew that what they were being asked to do was not safe and went against their own judgment. Mary's conflict was a consequence of an authority figure telling her to do something that she believed was clinically wrong. It could result in a job loss if she did not follow orders. She could also be held responsible for malpractice and jeopardize her nursing license if she didn't follow her professional judgment. So, her concerns were warranted in this *Catch 22* situation. She decided to resign rather than continue to fight those issues. Obviously, she was angry at the nursing profession for not supporting her. This was symbolized during her regression when her community did not stand up and protect her from the men who burned her at the stake.

Mary said that this past life regression experience illuminated the importance of her standing up for herself by not performing inappropriate procedures. After discussing the regression, she recognized that this was a test. It would help her to determine whether the lessons she learned from that lifetime could be implemented.

She felt immediate relief as she recognized the magnitude of her current decision. In that past lifetime, she was unable to say no to something she did not feel capable of performing, and she faked it. At this time, she is finally able to acknowledge her limitations and to verbalize them, especially when she feels the work is not safe.

Mary thought it was interesting to see me as a member of that healing community, especially since I was now facilitating her current lifetime healing. Did we come together in this lifetime to heal something for both of us? Did I feel guilt in that lifetime if I had encouraged her to perform a healing that she did not feel ready to do?

The important message for her was to understand her limitations, feel good about her decisions, and to learn to say no when it was appropriate. She allowed herself to trust that whatever she experienced was for her highest good. Her original problem was solved, and she now understands why she no longer chooses to work in the medical field. Mary affirmed this is part of her life purpose.

My gut feeling was instantaneous that I was there during that lifetime. Ironically in this lifetime, I am involved in using this alternative healing modality, PLRT, to help her in this lifetime although I didn't help her in that past lifetime we shared together.

In her PLRT session, Mary was burned at a sacred altar for practicing a healing technique that was viewed as an unusual practice during that time. Clearly, the punishment was inappropriate. Perhaps this memory imprint reverberated while she was reacting to a current lifetime situation: she was again asked to perform a procedure that she was inadequately prepared for. This incident may have occurred during this lifetime to serve as a karmic lesson to free her from the trapped feeling of not being able to say no. In that lifetime, it resulted in her death, while in this lifetime, it resulted in her freedom.

Mary's experiences in the regression served as a metaphor for her current work situation. The distancing from her current lifetime experience allowed her to see her problem with less emotion. As a result of that lifetime experience of healing, she made a decision to follow another life path direction. Her belief in spirituality and her understanding of reincarnation have added multiple dimensions to her life. She now believes things happen for a purpose and always for her highest good. Currently, she is happy at work and in a loving relationship.

Mary's regression affected me in a very powerful way. This was the first PLRT session I had conducted with a patient who was working with me for awhile in ongoing psychotherapy. However, I was now able to understand the power of the past life regression work as I watched how it transformed her daily life. Her rapid growth in relation to this chronic problem encouraged me to continue this work with other clients. I don't know whether I was a healer during her past lifetime. However, it felt good to be able to help her heal during this lifetime.

In 2009, I had an unusual intuitive experience while re-reading Mary's regression. I could still remember the feelings I experienced as she described being burned alive at the stake. I decided to e-mail her and simultaneously discovered her house had been struck by lightning and she had sustained minor burns. Her town was having a fund-raising drive to help raise money for her. Once again, there was fire in her life as a destroyer, but she was pretty much spared by the experience. Thankfully, this time she was untouched, and her house was insured, but some of her possessions were burned. In this lifetime, she did not suffer, and her community rallied around her.

Some people chose to explore past life regression work because they were searching for answers to their unresolved, lifelong, emotional shocks. They described themselves as immobilized around old, conflicting issues. Others were not able to understand their feelings or make any breakthrough in their therapy. Many people's regressions elicited experiences that were not recognizable to them during this lifetime. For others, the trauma of a sudden, violent death in another lifetime seemed to keep their souls stuck in that lifetime. The PLRT experiences resulted in their reliving that lifetime trauma. As a result, they were now able to focus on their problems more clearly, make decisive changes, and were no longer plagued by feelings of immobilization or emotional shock.

Charles was lying on the sofa visibly trembling during his regression, which was not his usual demeanor. His decision to work with PLRT resulted from his extreme dissatisfaction at the lack of movement in his life. He had spent many years living within a strained marriage that marital counseling had not helped. He remained within his marriage because of his concern for his children. Charles felt trapped and was still very unhappy, and he decided to make a life change.

While at home, he would click through the television channels and invariably stop at WW II documentaries and start crying for no apparent reason. Charles had not been a soldier, so he could not understand the spontaneity of his responses. He became tearful at images of Kamikaze fighters. To this day, I vividly remember his past life regression sessions because of the intensity of his physical reactions during his regressions.

C: I feel anxious. I feel like I'm on a ship waiting for an attack. I'm wearing Navy coveralls. It seems very peaceful on the water. I'm looking out at the horizon, and I feel very anxious. I'm just assuming it's the Pacific. It's a quiet ship, a real big ship like a football field. Beautiful sunset, sky-blue, but darkening. The planes on the deck are American. Is it toward the end of 1944? October. My name is Ralph, like Schmidt. And the sky begins to get darker.
(He begins to breathe harder.)

C: It's morning a few days later. It's very noisy with guns. People are running—back and forth.
(He is still breathing heavily.)

C: Planes are taking off. Pilots get in the planes. I'm not a pilot. I use a signal directing the planes. I'm scared.
(He is now experiencing heavy abdominal breathing.)

C: I'm just trying to relax. I just saw planes coming. I just tried to back away (he talks excitedly) and keep them from—I think these are...(he screams out loud): *They're not ours! They're Japanese planes!* I don't know. They're just Japanese planes. It's just so noisy. It's raining bombs. I just want to be somewhere else. I don't want to be here. A lot of bombs are falling everywhere. A lot of guns are going off all over the place. I just don't know what to do. I just want to go and run some place. Like I wait to watch; I don't think there's anything for me to do 'til the fliers come back. The loudest noises are the antiaircraft guns. I feel like it's just the beginning, and this is going to keep on. How long am I going to be stuck here? I feel like I want to go home. My chest and hands and neck feel like they're buzzing, like a strong vibration. An electronic buzz goes through my stomach to my neck and up to my hands and palms. It's calmer now, quieter. People go around their business doing stuff. I think our planes are coming back.

When the session ended, Charles's hands were buzzing and his fingers were shaking. He talked about the event like a person who was actively involved in a bombing with all of the attendant fear and anxiety. After the regression, he talked about what he had just experienced.

C: It was my job to guide planes on deck with flags or cones of some kind in my hands. I was very scared, because I knew that our planes were going to intercept an attack. After about 20 minutes, Japanese bombers came in and the sky rained bombs. It was deafening, and I was near some antiaircraft guns. I was scared out of my wits and wanted to hide, but I knew that I couldn't and that it wouldn't do any good. I also didn't want to miss anything. I wanted to see it all. I was petrified and just kept thinking that I wanted to go home. Then my stomach and chest started buzzing and it spread to my neck, arms, and especially the palms of my hands. It felt like a very strong electronic vibration. It was very weird, because it was a strong, really physical sensation. It got calm again after awhile and our planes started returning. I knew it was over for the time being, but I had an overwhelming sense of dread. I knew that this was just the beginning and that there was much worse to come, and it might be years before I could go home.

Sitting through this experience, I felt his fear and anxiety, which was quite palpable. Charles was very surprised by his regression. The following week, he said: "Last week's session was just the tip of the iceberg." He began to describe a series of events that had occurred following our session.

The day after the session while watching television, he felt teary as he watched the airplanes taking off from the flight deck of an airplane carrier. That same night, he went to a play with a friend, not knowing it was about a family dealing with the aftereffects of war. He sat there crying. Then he received a newspaper magazine section that he had not ordered, highlighting a WW II copilot's firsthand account of his experience aboard a bomber. At the same time, Charles's mother spontaneously began to talk about her brother, who died during WW II. This was very unusual, since she never talked about him. His mother described how his uncle had been pestering his mother to allow him to join the navy because he was not of age. His parents refused to sign the papers permitting him to join, so he stopped talking to them and joined the navy anyway. Charles was surprised at the coincidence of all of the events that occurred immediately after his past life regression experience.

As the next regression began, he said:

C: I feel the vibrating. I'm on a bunk down below. I'm more upset and crying and writing home. I'm not really writing about what is happening. I'm very homesick and very upset about being here and in such danger. I can't write home about it. I want to write home and write a pleasant letter. Don't want to get my family upset. I'm seeing an image. Is it somewhere in the South or the Midwest? Just like, I'm scared out of my mind.

He began to squeeze his eyes tightly while in the regression. He continues.

C: Just like an explosion and everyone is running. I'm down inside of the ship and run up onto the deck. A surprise thing; skies are clear, no attack, and an explosion on the deck. People at that end of the ship are dealing with it. Everyone on deck, planes are leaving. I'm involved in the preparation and help them to go. In my hands are cones to help direct the planes. They're all gone and I'm done.

Loud sirens. An air raid. I think we're going to eat. I can't eat. I have to find out what's going on. I go back up. Nothing yet. Just planes coming. I think they're Japanese planes. The same place I saw last time. I don't see our planes. I wonder where the planes are. Antiaircraft guns and bombs being dropped. I don't see anything yet. I am writing a letter. I wanted the letter to sound upbeat and not worry anyone. It was addressed to "Marge," somewhere in the South/Midwest.

He described being on deck and preparing planes for take-off while guiding them.

C: After that, a friend and I were talking and joking. There is an air battle far in the distance, 10 or 12 specks and lots of smoke. One plane has gotten through and is approaching at about 100 feet. We watch it as it slowly gets larger, but none of our planes are near, as the distant battle continues. We quietly watch for a long time, not even shooting until it gets well in range. It's being hit, but it keeps coming. When it's about 50-100 feet away, part of it gets blasted off and the bulk of it sails 20-30 feet over our deck and crashes into the ocean. I'm OK. No one is hurt.

B: Move forward to your death in that lifetime.

C: I see a lot of blood. There's a lot of destruction that I see from water level. The water is oily and full of debris. There's a lot of fire and smoke from ships and on the water. There are still planes crashing and guns firing, but it's the end of the battle. I don't feel any pain, but I am floating with a life jacket, and I'm not very aware or fully conscious. My right elbow to head is buzzing again, and it's hanging limp to the side. I can feel the buzzing up the back, the back sides of my neck, and on the left, back side of my skull. I can move my left arm, but now that hand starts buzzing, too. Nothing else happens. I die in the water from my injuries.

B: Bring yourself forward in time.

C: I see some bright flashes and a vague, angelic form. I feel that intellectually, it made sense at the time to do what I did, but I'm angry and frustrated that I let myself get in that kind of situation again—mortally wounded and waiting, trapped, to die. I've failed in letting this happen to me again.

Charles said that his past life regressions were the opposite of what he had expected. At first, he thought he was a pilot and not on the boat. To this day many years later, he still feels the vibrations that he felt while on the boat. When he writes about WW II, he still has physical feelings related to his experiences. He envisions that 19-year-old guy in the Pacific during the war, gets tears in his eyes, chills go up his back, his heart starts pounding, and he can remember every little expression. These strong, emotional responses, which continue to affect him, are very powerful. He now has more of a belief in reincarnation, which he said, helps him.

Releasing his emotions during the regression and afterward gave Charles the ability to evaluate his life experiences. He relived the terror of being trapped on the boat and waiting to die. This was similar to a prior regression he had experienced as a knight, when he was "mortally wounded, waiting, trapped, to die." Charles believes his feelings of anger and frustration in those two lifetimes keep him currently trapped. He recognizes that events happen that are beyond his control, so he has stopped blaming himself for being trapped in those situations.

The integration of the information that Charles accessed through the past life regression experience helped him to mobilize his life. As a result of this reenactment, he changed his career, relocated to another state, and eventually dissolved his unhappy marriage. Today, he recognizes that he can make life changes and no longer feels "trapped and waiting to die."

At the present time, he is happily remarried in a loving and creative relationship. While using his teaching and art skills, Charles found a new career. The unfinished business from that lifetime was completed during his current life. As a result, he gained a greater level of spiritual awareness. Working through the images of that lifetime and others has allowed him to make life changes that he believes are for his highest good.

The experiences of Mary and Charles demonstrated to them the continuity of life as their souls progressed through each lifetime. The lessons to be learned from these regressions demonstrate the importance of working through "stuck" patterns. They can show us how to be true to ourselves and become more evolved through making our life purpose a more integral part of our lives.

These are just two examples of the hundreds of regressions I have witnessed in which people's experiences resulted in life transformations. Both learned that they could choose their attitudes, their reactions, and how to interpret events and implement a plan of action in response to dire circumstances.

Many people have asked me for help in learning how to get out of stuck patterns on their own. I have included basic exercises at the end of some chapters to help you, the reader, to begin to access your own truths. They will allow you to come to a quiet, still place and understand more clearly what's important for you to know for your highest good. Hopefully, you will be able to gain a clearer understanding of your life patterns and your life purpose.

The following exercise is a basic one. Over time, this simple meditation will change in its dimensionality as your transformation continues.

Exercise

You can make your own CD, which will allow you to enter a deep state of relaxation. Speak slowly so that you can follow a rhythm, which will allow you to go deeper and deeper into a state of relaxation.

1. Prepare yourself to be undisturbed for at least 30 minutes. Sit in a comfortable position. With your eyes closed, picture yourself in a safe place. Visualize pure white light, like sunlight, totally surrounding your body in peace and love and harmony.

2. Breathe in to the count of three and hold it, then let it out to the count of three. Breathe in to the count of three and hold it, and let it out to the count of three. With each breath in and each breath out, allow yourself to come to your deepest level of relaxation.

3. Allow yourself to stay in that safe place and bring yourself to a deeper and deeper level of relaxation where all that's important is the breathing in and the breathing out. All that's important is the breathing in and the breathing out. Stay quiet and listen to your breathing in and breathing out as your body comes to its deepest level of relaxation.

4. Then say the following "I AM" prayer.

"I AM"_____ (insert your name); "I AM"_____ (insert your name).
    "I am surrounded by the love, wisdom, and healing power of a higher power for my protection."
    "I am always surrounded by the healing light of the universe."
    "I am always surrounded by my guides and angels, which allow me to see, hear, and feel what's important for my highest good."
    "I will honor my own intuition on a regular basis."

5. Let all thoughts come to your mind. Watch them and hear them. Some may have no meaning; some may be profound. Allow yourself to learn how to begin to listen to your inner voice, and recognize your innate wisdom. Appreciate your feelings and intuition.

6. Think about a current life experience that is difficult for you to overcome and that seems to have no current lifetime experience. Give yourself some time to honor all the information that comes up whether in a visual or cognitive way.

7. Bring yourself back to the here and now by allowing the energy to come up your legs to your knees, to your heart, to the top of your head.

8. As you continue to breathe in and out, let all energy come back to the here and now and allow yourself to be very alert, focused, and vibrant. Count to three, and when you're ready, open your eyes and remember all that you experienced.

Practice this exercise on a daily basis, and you can learn how to still the mental chatter and allow whatever is for your highest good to emerge. Eventually, you will be able to come to a level of quietness and awareness more quickly. This is a good way to become much more relaxed and centered.

Keep a journal and write about the thoughts and images that come to you.

Also, pay attention to your dreams at night. Leave a pad or an electronic recorder at your bedside so that when you wake up, your thoughts can be readily accessed.

2

Why Am I Stuck?

"Remember, you are on your special journey. Those who cannot remember the past are doomed to repeat it."

~SANTAYANA

How often do you realize the repetitive pattern of your problems? Many people often told me that was one of the reasons they chose to explore PLRT. Through this work, I witnessed many people's PLRT sessions come alive with dramatic descriptions of their past lifetimes as members of a different gender, religion, race, sexual orientation, and national origin.

A young Black mother described her lifetimes as a wealthy Asian woman and later as an Irish man. A Jewish woman was quite upset while she talked about her experience as a nationalistic, WW II German soldier. A Catholic man, who questioned why he was very sensitive and cried easily during movies, described giving birth as the baby was torn from "her" by Polish Nazi soldiers.

Many people's regression experiences left me speechless, especially when one religious Jewish man depicted his lifetime in a convent as a Roman Catholic nun. Imagine the surprise of a young woman as she experienced her day-to-day life as a German resistance worker during WW II. After she was arrested for distributing leaflets to her neighbors depicting the atrocities that were being carried out throughout Germany, she was taken to a concentration camp with her daughter. She believes that the daughter she was incarcerated with at that time is her ex-husband in this lifetime. Both of us were stunned as she revealed that information. This helped her to more fully understand her current relationship with her ex-husband. People's regressions often led to further discussions of their current life problems, which were subsequently healed by the new findings.

Throughout the hundreds of regression experiences, most people highlighted relationships as their primary area of concern. This is not surprising, since relationships are such an important part of our lives. In fact, chronic, problematic relationships were the most common reasons people sought this work. And one of the most common outcomes of PLRT was the enhancement of their interpersonal interactions as well as dramatic relationship changes. Many began to understand how soul mates function in their lives. Weight, self-esteem, and abuse issues were additional areas that were successfully healed.

These are important findings, which prompted me to implement the more extensive use of this type of work into my psychotherapy practice. The reliving of their experiences enhanced people's abilities to view their lives in more meaningful ways and to fully comprehend their global life purpose. In fact, life purpose exploration was an outgrowth of this work for many. The most important focus of the work was to help seekers in their search for a clearer understanding of why their relationships became stuck or did not grow. Throughout their search for a greater understanding of their long-term-relationship commitment fears, some common problems were often revealed. These problems often highlighted relationship difficulties with unavailable partners, intimacy issues, or sexual problems.

Many people who came to experience PLRT described their dissatisfaction with years of working within the psychotherapy model. Many were searching for a different way to make progress in the healing of their chronic problems and to effect life changes. An important finding was that many people felt stuck in the traditional ways of accessing information during traditional psychotherapy. Some described the absence of discussions regarding the role that spirituality and life purpose play in their lives as a tremendous void. Most were surprised at the past life regressions that they recounted, since these situations were not based on any current lifetime experiences. Yet through the regressions, people were able to translate and integrate the experiences from that lifetime into their current life and move forward.

Within my traditional psychotherapy practice, people revealed their innermost thoughts and feelings about relationships. As they described meeting someone they really liked, felt a "click," and the immediate question was, "Is this the one I am going to marry?" They often began to frame the relationship in the context of marriage with a constant focus on the future. Their inability to be present in the moment resulted in their missing out on the spontaneity, fun, exploration, communication, and uniqueness of meeting a new person. This occurs when meeting someone who has different, innovative, and creative ways of viewing the world. They often felt bombarded by intense cultural pressures to marry early and have children, which was ever present in their thoughts. People tend to measure their movement through the yardstick of their friends' engagements and marriages and become frantic until they do the same.

Some people decided to explore current or former romantic relationships, especially those that were intense and passionate when they first met. A common experience that was described by many was their first meeting with a person that resulted in an intense deja vu experience. These were accompanied by feelings that they had known this person before, shared similar values, were on the same wavelength, and could read one another's minds. They shared a mutuality of feelings that they both found to be very overwhelming. An extremely emotional experience began, even though they did not know each other well enough to warrant that intimate level of response.

Some people tended to interpret this type of connection as a soul-mate relationship. They recognized that the intensity of that meeting sometimes kept them in an unhealthy relationship too long. During their past life regression experiences, they often reenacted a past lifetime with this person. People recognized that they felt so comfortable with each other because they had experienced prior relationships together. As they realized that, they were able to deal with the relationship in a more realistic way. The consistency of these findings prompted me to begin documenting their experiences.

Samson's relationship revolved around his girlfriend's sexual problems, resulting in their dramatic "on and off" states. He is amiable and active in his field of work, with many friends. He couldn't understand the problems that were occurring for him and his girlfriend. After attending a workshop, he came to see me to explore whether he could unearth the causes of his problems. His perceptions about his girlfriend changed after his past life regression in which he visualized himself as a young girl who was being molested by her father in that lifetime. Samson immediately recognized his current girlfriend as his father. Through this awareness, he realized that the relationship was not working, could not be healed, and decided that it had to end. The information he gained through his regression experience helped to transform his formerly ambivalent and stuck feelings. He believes that they both came together in this lifetime to heal their past relationship. Now, he was able to assert his power by ending this unfulfilling relationship.

Helyn decided to explore PLRT because of her boyfriend's concerns about the lack of sexual intimacy in their relationship. She is a quiet-spoken, successful businesswoman and had no idea why this problem was happening to her. She acknowledged that she loved him very much and had never experienced a problem like this before. It was interfering with the furthering of their emotional intimacy, and the relationship was deteriorating. Traditional marital therapy failed to help them, and they felt that PLRT was a last resort. They did not feel very hopeful.

During a past life regression, Helyn described a lifetime as a Native American. While her tribe was raided, her husband and child were taken from her and killed. The moment in which she saw the experience, she re-experienced the anguish, suffering, and guilt she had felt as a result of her inability to save her family. She realized that she was currently avoiding intimate relationships that might lead to her having a husband and a child.

As a direct result of her past life regression experience, Helyn experienced a profound change in her ability to freely communicate with her partner in emotionally intimate ways. Upon recognizing her old patterns of fear and guilt, she was able to break free from the shackles of her past unhappiness. In a short period of time, this breakthrough resulted in a profound change in their relationship.

Dolores is a strong, dynamic, professional woman in her mid 30s who works in the financial world. She is very outgoing and is able to compete productively in a world usually dominated by men. During the course of her psychotherapy, she developed skills and tools that enabled her to overcome the emotional baggage she had carried into adulthood. Her improved ability to handle daily life stresses resulted in her feeling happier while also becoming more self-sufficient. She created a life that brought her the added dimensions of joy, creativity, and companionship.

As Dolores created a newer and more functional reality, her relationships changed and were transformed into more fulfilling, powerful experiences. She realized that she was continually looking to friends and family for their opinions and decided that this behavior was draining her energy. She wanted to take her power back, and her ongoing goals were to become increasingly more centered, internally focused, and able to evaluate life situations on her own.

Through her increased interest in spirituality, she became aware of the concept of reincarnation and believed it would be important to experience her past lifetimes. Finally, as she explored healthier love relationships and searched for the genesis of a neck problem, she felt ready to seek an awareness of her soul's development.

Dolores easily went into a trance.

D: I don't want them to take it away, and I see myself in that cell, struggling to hold onto the castle. I'm alone. It's cold in there. Concrete stone. Weird shoes like grey—like the knights wear—mesh and leggings. I have a beard and grey hair.

B: What is your name?

D: Lucas.

B: Do you have a last name?

D: Augustine—an old man—70s? Gaulle, France. Maybe early 1500s, 1600s. I'm just very alone. I don't want them to take it away. My home. I feel something bad. I see a sword in my neck. I can see it going in. I think I was in the house, and someone stabbed me from behind.

Dolores visualized herself as a strong, wealthy man in medieval times, perhaps of nobility. This man was having a difficult relationship with his brother, whom Dolores instantly recognized as her current sibling. She watched as she was stabbed by another person who she believed is her current mother with whom she has a problematic relationship.

Through these lifetime regressions, Dolores accurately described her current relationships with both family members. Her visualizations led her to cut through stuck and unproductive family patterns. One result of the resolution of her patterns was her ability to experience a newfound openness and freedom. This enhanced her ability to search for a life partner.

Dolores was also now able to transcend and free herself from her chronic dysfunctional familial patterns. Her neck problem totally disappeared after the regression. It could be interpreted that her "stuck" energy from that lifetime was released as a result of the regression. Another way of interpreting her experience is to say that she projected her current family relationship problems onto an external source. This was manifested by her developing a stiff neck instead of her addressing her difficult family problems; that is, her unhappiness was transferred to a neck problem, which she could care for. However, she chose to affirm her past lifetime experience with helping her move forward in her life.

Sarah is an extremely successful Asian woman who worked in the financial field. She was searching for the origins of her short-term, problematic, romantic relationships. As she began coughing very forcefully while in the trance, she described a scene of herself as a young wife and new mother dying of a pulmonary embolism. A young child and husband whom she deeply loved were left behind.

S: I'm a woman. A fire's burning. An old stone house with a thatched roof. One-room house, fire burning—room orange. I'm very happy. An easy life; a long time ago. Longer ago than last life. Loving husband and a baby. It was as if we had just finished making love, and he loves me very much, and he has to get up and go out, and I feel contented. He goes to work, but I'm very happy. A very happy moment—baby asleep. We're very common people but very happy. I stare into the fire. The fire served as the center of a lot of what we did—eating—and is in the center of the house. We weren't rich—nothing much. I die in the same house. Not too old. Those days you didn't live long. Not an accident. Actually, I died soon after that.

She started to cough again while in a trance in the session.

S: I died alone, and he wasn't with me. I died of an embolism in my sleep. I saw him come back, but I was dead. He was horrified, because there was no reason.

While in a trance state, she was teary and crying for some time in the session.

S: I'm very upset. I left him alone. I didn't mean to. It just happened so suddenly. I didn't want to go, and I was very young—in my 20s. I wasn't sick. Child was a year old.

I didn't want to go. How could I leave him? I didn't want to leave them. It was not my choice. I lingered a long time for him; my spirit. I so wanted to stay. I'm supposed to leave. We have other things to do.

I was told they'd be OK. Even though they suffered, it was not my purpose to stay with them. I miss him terribly (she began to cry). I was rushed away fast. I finally left them. He's still kneeling. I felt how brokenhearted he was. How shocked. He didn't understand. I wanted to let him know about things out of [our] control. He is sad—he couldn't hear me. He was too overwhelmed. He never forgot me. He never remarried. He's someone I will meet. He's the one I will meet by accident, purely by chance. Suddenly, just as suddenly as I left.

B: What is your life purpose?

S: Sometimes, things happen that you don't want to happen. It may seem unfair, but really there's a greater reason and purpose. Sometimes, we're part of a bigger, grander scheme of things that have to do with many other people. He had to understand loss to appreciate life today. He's alive today. If he didn't lose me then, he wouldn't find me now. The lesson was for him; that's why I was ushered away, with a purpose that we meet again sometime later. So I said I understand after looking at him for a long time, and I followed the calling of who was calling me away.

B: Where does the soul go?

S: It rests.

B: What was the message for you?

S: That I can't waste any time doing things that don't matter and are other people's causes and not mine. I was following other people's battles and not mine. I was determined to come back and do more things, and be more productive.

Don't worry about things that may seem important to others. You know what's important for you. You know what matters and not other people's causes.

Sarah believes that she must heal her current relationship problems while continuing to work on her spirituality issues. The information that she received during the regression is vitally important for the work she has to do within her current relationships. As a result of this past life regression work, she is now pursuing newer career opportunities that are dramatically different from her financial career. And if she does meet him again, that would be wonderful!

Sarah's regression was one of a few times people described their own deaths when their partners were away while performing their daily activities. People never returned, having been killed, or simply disappeared. The traumas from sudden-death experiences often resulted in a state of shock for the soul. When people are reborn into another lifetime, they often have to heal from those traumas.

Lenore described multiple trust issues, which were manifested by her difficulty becoming emotionally intimate in romantic relationships. She was a woman in her mid-30s and worked in the art world. Lenore is very spiritual and believes in reincarnation. In a past life regression, she envisioned herself wearing a long ball gown during a 19th century party, dancing with her current life partner. As the clouds came forth, she couldn't see anything, as the action was suspended.

L: I know that he dies, and I don't want to look at it, because I already know. I don't have to look. He did bail out before me. One night in this lifetime, I started sobbing and saying to him, why did you leave me? As I said that, I realized it was totally out of context to anything that happened during this lifetime. Obviously, he didn't understand what I was talking about.

She described her angels talking to her while she lay in the altered state of consciousness. They said:

L: She's scared, so we have to put her down in the right place.

The reenactment of this experience helped Lenore to more clearly understand her current intimacy conflicts. She allowed herself to become closer with her partner. The conflict she experienced came from her fear of committing to someone she thought would leave her, as "he" had done in a prior lifetime. Her partner in this lifetime was totally unaware of her experiences, and he was confused by her reactions toward him. When she told him about her past life regression experience, he understood her earlier reactions more fully.

Alison is a very bright, outgoing woman who was working in the area of business communications. She was not happy with that type of work. She was born in Europe and has been a New Yorker for many years. Describing herself as a spiritual person, she is strikingly tall, attractive, energetic, and quite verbal with a flowing communication style.

Alison believes her pattern of quick, sexually intimate relationships allows her to be in control of her romantic relationships. Unfortunately, she had difficulty maintaining long-term, intimate relationships.

During one PLRT experience, she saw herself as a 13-year-old peasant Egyptian girl, "being used with other young girls by people of the rich aristocratic society." Her job was to "fan them so they can be cold if it's hot." Also, "to clean for them and be used as a sexual object or sexual whore, by whomever wanted her."

They were young girls with skinny brown bodies. In that culture, girls "weren't worth much." If their families didn't have money, they were sent into slavery because their fathers couldn't pay for them. Alison realized that she continued her sexual patterns to this lifetime and the devastating impact it has had on her relationships.

As a result of our further conversations, she developed an awareness of how to become more emotionally intimate and still feel in control. She did not have to be sexually intimate too quickly. "I had a hard time with the tightening around my heart, and the tightness is no longer there."

Her anger at the abuse by these wealthy people also resulted in her ability to more clearly understand why she mishandles money. Even though she does fairly well financially, she does not allow herself to accumulate money. Alison believes this may be her way of avoiding financial prosperity or identifying with wealthy people because of her former abuse. In a telephone conversation, she told me that her work in her new field is increasing. She believes this is a result of her past life regression experience. Today, Alison is happy about her increased prosperity and new ability to hold onto money.

Eric entered therapy to work on relationship problems, adjust to his new career, and explore spirituality. A former Wall Streeter, he left the field to become a writer. He began a spiritual and physical cleansing, which included donating his expensive suits, his other clothing, and assorted material goods to homeless people. He derived great pleasure from people's responses to their newfound treasures.

However, his focus now shifted to his own physical ailments. This led to a decrease in the amount and types of food he could eat, and he was suffering greatly. Even though Eric persevered by eating healthy food, doing yoga, taking herbs and vitamins, his body focus persisted. During this process, he became more intuitive. When a dream prompted him to begin taking acidophilus, he did so and felt better. He began to pay more attention to his intuitions, trusting them for the first time. As the focus on his physical symptoms came and went, his interest in socializing with women was nonexistent.

I thought he was stuck in his explorations, so I asked if he might be interested in using PLRT as another way for him to work on his problems. His immediate response was that past life regressions were usually explored by women who ended up claiming they had been Cleopatra. He said he did not believe in reincarnation, but he decided to think about it.

That night, he had a dream, circa 1800s, and the characters in his dream seemed very true to life. This dream had a similar quality to a past life regression experience. This prompted him to decide to try a past life regression session with me the following week.

Eric went into a trance easily. He saw himself as a severely depressed Louisiana plantation owner circa 1836. He had shot himself in the head because of his inconsolable losses. This was two years after the death of his twin daughters and wife through typhoid fever. He described the violent act of shooting himself in the head, and told me that his soul remained stuck in the room where he shot himself.

E: The soul gets stuck and he can't get outside to be with his wife and kids. He just wants to be with them and lie down in the plot.

He described the soul being like pure gelatin, banging into the corner of the room at the ceiling where the walls meet. I spontaneously said to him: *"Let's free the soul up."*

E: I'm opening the window in the bedroom, and the soul goes into the plot, and I'm lying under the earth like Alissa and Ernestine.

This was an unusual experience. We both knew intuitively and spontaneously that the soul had to be physically freed up. While returning from his altered state of consciousness, Eric said:

E: Because you're gonna lose them and not be with them in the afterlife.

During the regression, he saw a person who he said was his spirit guide Norris, who said to him:

N: You have no idea how much this means to me.
(Because Eric helped free up the soul.)

E: He wants to bestow something upon me. It's hard to say what he's doing.
He says, "Don't look at the body, and don't look at the gun."
I wanted to ask him something about being shot through the temple. He said, "Forget about that. Let's go outside. He introduces me to the children, and they both curtsy to me.

While talking further about the Louisiana life, Eric said:

E: The slaves are in the fields, and I'm feeling more empathy in my house, but I don't want to be in the room where I killed myself. I'm on the front porch alone, and Norris is on the porch with his pipe. He said:

N: How have you been?

E: I've been battling health problems.

N: Why don't you ask for help?

E: I don't know how to ask for help.

N: What do you want?

E: I don't know what I want.

N: Then I'll give you something you haven't chosen. A new place to live, a woman of your dreams, and two beautiful children. Ernestine and the children said how they love you very much.

E: Norris goes back into the house. I walk out to the slaves, and I walk to each and every one and tell them to take a rest. They don't think I'm the plantation owner. They think I'm drunk. People are in a different position. They don't know how to accept help. There's a white light over the field. They feel better. I look back at the house and Ernestine and the children are at the window.

After this experience, Eric started to examine all of his relationships, especially those with women. He recognized that his patterns of avoidance were due to his fear of being left again by someone he loved. He said that he felt that he had been punished in that lifetime and didn't understand why his wife and children were taken from him. As he talked about this regression experience in his subsequent sessions, he was able to translate the feelings he experienced within the regressions into his current-day avoidance of romantic relationships.

After further discussion about this past life experience, Eric began to be more outwardly focused, socializing in a more comfortable way. He became more open to meeting women, allowing himself to be interested in the possibility of a relationship. He began venturing out into the world, and he began focusing less on his body.

However, what became even more pronounced were his reactions to African American people he came in contact with. He had described them as arrogant and hostile, and he reciprocated in kind. Eric definitely had a problem with African Americans. He didn't understand why they weren't "nicer" to him since he had been a slave owner on a plantation who was friendly "with his slaves." He said, "I didn't beat them the way other plantation owners did." Eric recognized his current, arrogant attitude toward African American people and began to work on that part of his belief system.

Eric's life has changed to a degree; he now has a deeper belief in God and continues to become more spiritual, which is manifested in the way he lives his daily life. He also pays much more attention to his intuition. "I feel like I'm getting these illnesses because I'm supposed to heal and get more knowledge."

Through PLRT, most people were able to recognize similar patterns within their relationships. It is important to examine the relationships with the significant people in your life and to review whether these relationships include respect, love, and trust and are in harmony with your beliefs. Remember, a person we view as a soul mate may not be the one we should be in a long-term, romantic relationship with. Sometimes, people come together for a short time to help one another acknowledge their current life purpose and remind one another that purpose is important to everyday life.

Elizabeth's "insane jealousy" over the actions of her current boyfriend and her inability to understand his reaction motivated her to explore PLRT. In her rational mind, there was nothing her boyfriend was doing except for a little innocent flirting when they were in social situations. She knew that he loved her and they would eventually be married. However, her jealous feelings were driving him "over the edge." Elizabeth was actively searching for her spiritual path and was very interested in PLRT. She easily went into deep relaxation and an altered state of consciousness. She quickly came upon the following scenes.

E: I see vague pictures or outlines. The setting and clothing were different from current times. It's older. Like the time period is something you would have seen in the 1800s. Men were debonair with big mustaches. Women had big dresses and flowery and broad umbrellas. Like English. I think the 30s or that era. I'm part of the upper echelon.

Something seemed "off." I think we were going to be engaged. We're at a ball, dancing. Lots of friends around. My good friend is there with someone else. He didn't seem happy. He has a cool hat on. Dancing, people change partners, and I went with a good friend.

We had drinks out of a large bowl and drifted out onto the balcony. Going outside to get some fresh air. Huge, balcony, green grass. I see him with that friend. He's close to me, but we see them down in the bush making out and going at it. We both see our mouths drop and my heart breaks. I felt everything fall apart after that. I don't think I ever said anything to him after that. I broke it off. Said nothing to him or her. My friend said something to the girl. A big sadness. I don't think I ever loved anyone again in that lifetime. I became a hard person, lonely. I never married.

Elizabeth immediately realized that she should have addressed the situation at the time. She told me that the person she loved was not the person she thought he was.

E: The friend who was next to me cared a lot about me and saw how low I had sunk. I still feel a slight mistrust of people. I keep envisioning that moment when I saw him; it keeps flashing in my mind.

Elizabeth had an earlier romantic relationship with a man in this lifetime. Her friends told her that he had been "fooling" around with other women. At that time, her mood dramatically changed from total happiness to feeling totally depleted and devastated. This replicated her reaction again during this lifetime. In her current lifetime, she fears relationships. She was constantly fighting her feelings of mistrust as she tried to love her boyfriend and allow herself to become emotionally closer. While at a social event, she was dancing with him and having a good time, when a flashback occurred. Something clicked that she couldn't put her finger on.

E: I withdrew from him and said I wanted to go and get a drink. He saw I was pulling away from him and I wanted to be in my own quiet space and be withdrawn. I said to myself I didn't want to make the same mistake.

After her past life regression, Elizabeth was able to make a connection from her past feelings to her current, irrational feelings about her boyfriend. She no longer has "crazy jealousy dreams" and feels more calm and relaxed. Elizabeth believed she was on a good path. This past life regression experience helped her to recognize the genesis of her current lifetime fears. She decided to talk with her boyfriend about her past life regression as well as how she feels about his flirting. He instantly understood her current reactions and feelings and changed his flirtatious behavior since he knows how much it bothers her.

Sometimes, two people perhaps meet as a soul lesson for one another and for others, while at other times they might serve as reminders that they are straying off their spiritual paths. If we keep this in mind when we meet new people, it can only enlighten us and enhance our world view. Each person must learn how to be present in the moment and to focus on the quality of these moments. Then, we can find out another person's values, hopes, and aspirations. Other people can help us gain a greater appreciation of the multiplicity of world views, of the events that happen in people's lives, and how they handle them. Learn how to be in the moment. As the American spiritual leader Ram Dass says, *Be here now.*

Most people believed that their regressions were true recounts of their past lives since they affirmed their belief in reincarnation. Others told me of psychics who had revealed their past lifetimes to them or that they had an intuition about where they might have lived or where they expected to appear, so they were completely surprised when they experienced lifetimes that were very different from what they had expected or completely out of character for their lifestyle. In fact, they could not understand the genesis of these regressions. When I explained PLRT to patients, they were thrilled to add this spiritual dimension to their explorations.

I believe the past life regressions were quite real for most of the clients who were exploring their nonproductive patterns. Individuals' regressions also could be interpreted as a metaphor for problems or a storytelling vehicle that allowed them to take a safer, distanced view of their problems.

Chronic Problems

I was surprised at the way past life regression experiences allowed patients to address their chronic problems more rapidly. Throughout the years of my traditional psychotherapy work, I found the rapidity of change to be unusual. Through PLRT, people began to understand the reasons for their previously unresolved disabilities; they connected their current pain and suffering to that regression lifetime. As they began to unearth the reasons why that experience happened to them, they were also able to focus their attention on why the discomfort was present in this lifetime. The discomfort was usually in a current area of vulnerability that needed to be resolved. As a result of this process, they were able to keep the problem from recurring. They could then determine which areas of their life needed their attention, work on them, and begin to evolve more spiritually.

While I continued with my work in PLRT, I found that certain patterns began to emerge within people's experiences. The clinical part of me was skeptical that this work could have such a rapid effect on an individual's problem. However, the facts were there. People suffering with crippling fears and phobias began to rapidly release their fears and lead more active and freer lives. This was for real, and I recognized the importance of using this work with larger numbers of people.

Some people talked about soul-mate relationships. They described these as sharing a lifetime with a person they felt intricately connected with. These relationships were described as a coming together to encourage mutual, spiritual growth; a way to heal past karmic relationships; and a spiritual teaching opportunity for both partners. This is different from the current, cultural view that a soul mate is supposed to be the romantic love of your life. Ironically, that concept often keeps people in unloving and destructive relationships.

During past life regressions, many people experienced lifetimes in which they were connected to their current partners. The integration of the PLRT session findings into their current situations allowed many to make dramatic changes in their current, chronic relationship problems. For some people, their chronic problems were also intertwined with difficulties managing their weight, problems with self-esteem, panic attacks, and abuse issues. This work helped them to work through their problems and transform their stuck patterns.

My Personal Past Life Regression

As I watched people reenact their profound experiences, I decided to explore my own past life through regression work. The first two times I tried, I could not relax long enough to experience a deep, altered state of consciousness. It was hard to quiet my mind.

However, since my clinical experience with patients had been so powerful, I persevered. During my first regression, I saw myself as a male Native American, naked from the waist up, leaving my wife and young son as I went on a spiritual quest with other tribe members. We left our families behind. While on this quest, we were ambushed by a neighboring, jealous tribe who viewed us as a people who were happy and fulfilled and never fought with others. We were at peace and one with nature, and they believed that the essence of our happiness resided in our physical hearts. They assumed they could attain what we had by cutting out our hearts. They didn't "get" it.

At the moment of my death within the regression, I thought we had been ambushed by White men. I saw my spirit hovering "outside" my body with an arrow sticking out of my chest. What pained me the most was the realization that I had been killed by another Native American. That revelation was too shocking for me to believe.

It was revealed to me that in that lifetime, my wife was very unhappy with my continuing spiritual quests. These trips entailed my leaving her behind for long periods of time. I talked with my current partner who told me this was a problem that I apparently had been totally oblivious to. Ironically, this was a recurring problem and theme in my relationship this time around, too as I had often worked late hours.

However, the intensity and regression of that lifetime quickly awakened the seriousness of the problem. This awareness dramatically highlighted my current lifetime personal relationship issues. I had to do something immediately, and I did. It was amazing that my past lifetime regression demonstrated a current problem that I was not even aware of. It had continued from the past into the present.

Another surprise was an image of "our son" in that lifetime, who is currently my youngest brother with whom I've always had a close bond. Because of our eight-year age difference, I felt like a "mother" to him when we were young. As young adults, he finally told me that he had felt abandoned at eight years of age when I left home to attend nursing school. That was also the age my son was in my past lifetime when I was killed on my spiritual quest. I told my brother that my current partner was his mother in that lifetime. He looked at me as if to say, "What is my sister up to now?" Within the regression, I could feel the intensity of the experience that clients had described to me. The power, richness, and vibrancy of the regression experience were pronounced for me. I felt impassioned to further this work.

During that past life regression, there was a young Native American in the tribe receiving his feather, symbolizing a coming of age, around the time I was killed. This person is someone who is currently active in the past life therapy field and who has helped me with PLRT work. Since he paved the way during this lifetime, this gave me the opportunity to once again go out onto my spiritual path and not be afraid that I would be killed.

Eric, who I had mentioned earlier, had worked on Wall Street for many years and had become disenchanted with a variety of negative practices. Through his spiritual search, he changed his career to one that he found to be more creative. However, he did not believe in reincarnation and was reluctant to try PLRT. Both of us were very surprised as he spontaneously began his PLRT session with a channeled message for me from his "Healing Guide" as follows:

E: "You want to know some information about writing. You want to know about the soul. Everyone knows their purpose in life but spend their lives avoiding it. The first reason is laziness, not willingness to surrender, arrogance. Which is why people continue to live 80 years because it takes so long. You may have more than 80 years. Even your profession is not what you're supposed to do. Sometimes, everyone is supposed to help. But such a small percentage do that many must return many times to taste what it's like to help people. That's the way you should write a book. *Your purpose is just to help people.* Explaining the soul is a dictionary. The way to help people is to link their problems to what they don't know; to show them their petty problems can be fixed if they see a higher purpose. Show them their past life to end their petty problems. Convince them that they have a higher purpose. It will help them. The problem with your patients is that they are concerned about themselves. They must get over themselves to help others. The soul is a transparency—a trace. It is energy that has to be directed. On its own, it can become confused. It doesn't die, and it doesn't live, that much I can tell you. It's better to sell 10 books to 10 people. That's why it must be specific problems that you have every day. Your patients are a microcosm. Extrapolate. Be specific. Have a section for marital problems. Show how past lives get in the way of someone getting along as a couple. Show single people why they're afraid to be alone. Teach them the joy of being alone. Just make sure you don't write for the masses. Don't include things a lot of people would hold onto. Be specific, give a lot of examples. List problems that people commonly have, not just for one person, but list all the problems. You can describe past life therapy in your book. Most don't describe it. It is a search for the truth. If they don't believe, they should try it, anyway. Because they don't believe in the wind, it's still there. They can't see the air they breathe every day. People want to change. No person should leave your office just worrying about them. Make them realize that a car is metal and money is just paper, and all these are insignificant, and all can burn and crumble. The soul doesn't."

We were both totally surprised by this information coming through Eric, since he did not usually use language in that way. And he would never have brought forth that information on his own. I assumed that his spirit guides were speaking through him and decided to keep that message in the fore-front of my ongoing work.

Through the witnessing of hundreds of individuals' regression experiences, I realized that these reenactments gave people an avenue to talk about their emotional difficulties in a way they could not through traditional psychotherapy. As a result of the regression work, they were able to talk during their psychotherapy sessions about their experiences within a spiritual framework at multiple levels. They understood the broader reasons things occur, and they had the will to change. Even though PLRT is not currently widely used, I believe it will continue to become a widespread treatment.

The rapid transformation of people's problems was most interesting for me as a psychotherapist. At that time in the late 1980's, I had worked more than 10 years using traditional psychotherapy. During the next 30 years, I also worked with PLRT, which helped people heal their problems. These regressions led to the seeking, finding, and living out a life purpose becoming more important for many people. They could now embrace a belief in reincarnation and not be afraid of death. People were able to gain a broader perspective of their current "stuck" life patterns, which clarified their life purpose. A clearer awareness of the origins of their fears became apparent, and they were usually unrelated to current life experiences. I found that many people were surprised that their past life experiences were often reflected in their current lives. It was the beginning of a spiritual awareness for many. An important outgrowth of these regression experiences was the reminder that we are on our current spiritual paths.

Since many people had only come for a few regression sessions, and others came from abroad, I was not able to follow up with some of the insights they had experienced and how it impacted their lives over a period of time.

Exercises

One way to gain a greater knowledge of your relationships is to begin the deep relaxation technique from chapter 1 and allow all thoughts that come to your mind to be acknowledged.

Begin to search for patterns and common themes in all of your close relationships, old and new.

List the most significant relationships in your life.

1. What was significant about it?
2. What was good or bad about that relationship?
3. Is there a theme in this relationship that repeats itself in other relationships?
4. Were your needs being fulfilled? Was the relationship one of respect?
5. Acknowledge whether each relationship served you, nourished you, or drained you.
6. Did you grow in each relationship?
7. Were you an equal partner?
8. What was it about a significant relationship that continues to keep you questioning, "What was that about?"
9. What was your most emotional/tempestuous/ difficult relationship?
   a. What were the highlights of that relationship?
   b. Examine the good and bad aspects of that relationship.
   c. Are there prevailing themes from this relationship that recur in other relationships

After these explorations, your relationship patterns with friends, family members, and romantic partners should become so much clearer for you.

Remember to continue recording all of your thoughts, dreams, and experiences in your journal. I am sure that many readers who are interested in reincarnation would like to access their own past lives. Throughout my work with PLRT, I have found that it was quite easy for most people to experience a past lifetime. It took a bit longer for others to practice "letting go." Many people I know have also been accessing their past lives through their dreams as well as with spontaneous thoughts or images.

Begin by becoming more aware of all of your dreams, whether they seem significant or not. Be aware that your dreams are presented in your own private logic and language. You are the best one to analyze these messages. Often, people believe they aren't dreaming because they cannot remember their dreams. Most of us dream, but because we aren't interested, we don't focus on our dream life. If you want to take notice of your dreams, here are some suggestions that I have used throughout my practice.

Start by placing a recorder or pen and paper by your bedside. Say to yourself, "I want to remember all of my dreams," or make a suggestion to yourself that you want to access information from within about a specific problem. As you awaken and before you get out of bed, record the dream into your recorder or write down any thoughts or memories that come to you. Sometimes, even one word can be used later to try to access the rest of your dream.

Try to understand the underlying message of your dream by asking yourself what significance each aspect of the dream has for you. See if there is any relevance to current events. Sometimes, people will have very real dreams about circumstances that occurred during another lifetime, and stories unfold for them. They often realize that they have been having similar, recurring dreams throughout their lifetime.

The most often reported dreams are "chase" dreams. People describe being awakened in a panicked state feeling as if they escaped just in time before being caught. If this is your experience, you can use that feeling and imagery while in a relaxed state. Instruct yourself to go to another time or experience that will help you more clearly understand the origins of this information.

As you think about reincarnation, keep in mind the following questions:

1. Are there people in your current life that you feel you've known before?

2. Is there a person whom you view as your soul mate? What is it about the relationship that you think makes this person your soul mate?

Think about people whom you have met and instantly felt so comfortable and at ease with you felt like you knew them before. That feeling may not have made sense at the time since it was the first time that you met. If you have had that experience, remember that feeling, and while in a relaxed state, see if any thoughts or images come up in relation to this person.

Think about places throughout the world that you feel drawn to or where you have an unrecognizable yearning and urge to be. There may be no family members or friends who come from that place, and yet you know that it is familiar to you. You may have an affinity for the language of that country or an intense dislike. Plan your imagery around that place and see what information comes up for you.

A certain type of dress or preference for wearing grey over blue has often been described by people who experienced lifetimes during the Civil War.

These are some ways for you to access what seems very natural and familiar to you despite the fact that there is nothing in your current life to warrant that familiarity.

Think about hobbies, avocations, desires, and interests that seem to have no origins in this lifetime. This is just the beginning of your path in determining who you were and understanding how that knowledge can help you solve your problems today while gaining an understanding of your life purpose.

3

I Can Fly Again!

"He who has a why to live with can bear with any how."

~NIETZSCHE

People often suffer from chronic conditions—such as panic attacks and phobias—that are usually unresponsive to traditional treatments. The treatments usually include combinations of antidepressant medications with behavior modification and/or psychotherapy. Some research studies recognize that antidepressants may help some people face their panic attacks. However, up to one-half of the subjects relapsed when the medication was discontinued. Their anxiety levels decreased, but the symptoms were not permanently eradicated.

Patients told me that they did not know of any current life experiences to warrant their severe phobias. In fact, during traditional psychotherapy, the core issue for their panic attacks and phobias was never found. Most mental health practitioners acknowledge that phobias and panic attacks are chronic conditions warranting the long-term use of medication. Unfortunately, there are many people suffering from phobias and panic attacks who continue to search for treatment. Perhaps the use of PLRT may help them heal their fears and anxieties.

In my psychotherapy practice, many people vividly described their chronic suffering from the crippling afflictions of panic attacks and phobias. They found these conditions to be persistently unresponsive to their traditional psychotherapeutic treatment. Their feelings of exasperation with these chronic conditions were often manifested as inexplicable bouts of jealousy, insecurities, and other chronic, irrational fears. I found that many of their fears were related to being in the physical realities of water, heights, enclosed spaces, or in public areas. These conditions resulted in their feeling trapped and in a psychologically crippled condition for life. Patients told me that they could not identify any current life experiences that warranted what they described as irrational fears.

These poignant discussions led me to review the psychotherapy literature. I found it troublesome that the problems of panic attacks and phobias have not been resolved satisfactorily through the use of medication or psychotherapy. So 30 years ago, after recognizing that other therapies were not effective treatments for these conditions, I decided to focus on these and other areas of people's lives that they were dissatisfied with through a more extensive use of PLRT.

Many people who chose to explore PLRT reported their current fears of being trapped in all enclosed spaces, such as cars, buses, subways, elevators, bridges, planes, in water, at heights, and in public areas. They were overcome with severe anxieties, resulting in their being psychologically crippled for life. These anxieties kept them from traveling, working, or socializing, which often resulted in *agoraphobia*, a fear of being in crowds or publlc places where they do not feel safe. This is often accompanied by anxiety attacks and may result in avoidance of those places. Their reports depicted chronic panic attacks and phobias, mirroring problems that are experienced by many.

As I implemented regression work into my currently 38 year psychotherapy practice, I was quite surprised at the findings. Patients who had been suffering from the crippling afflictions of panic attacks and phobias demonstrated immediate and dramatic responses. I was surprised the most by the number of patients who experienced vivid lifetimes, including incidences of drowning, violent death, or being trapped. They responded to these regression encounters positively. I don't know whether I was more surprised by people's vivid past lifetime regressions or the fact that their problems were resolved as a result of these experiences.

During their past life regressions, those with panic attacks and phobias often experienced drowning, being thrown from high places, public stoning in the public arena, and other humiliations. They saw a correlation between the origins of their current life fears and the negative outcomes they had suffered that came from another lifetime. These past life regression experiences afforded them opportunities to face their chronic and complex problems within a short period of time. As a result, their fears, levels of anxiety, and emotional paralyses greatly diminished. People experienced an *immediate* healing of chronic phobic patterns and fears. They viewed the recurrence of similar experiences in this lifetime as their being challenged again to stand up for themselves.

Joseph could not understand why it was so frightening for him to be alone at home since nothing significant had ever occurred there to warrant his fears. During a past life regression session, he saw images of his abduction as a woman from a Middle-Eastern home. He was a young woman with a baby who never saw her husband or family again. One result of his reliving of this experience was his loss of his tremendous fear of being home alone.

Other patients immediately lost their current lifetime irrational fear of water through their past life regression incidents of drowning. Another person searching for answers to her chronic problems experienced a past life regression and reported the spontaneous elimination of her persistent fears of riding in the subway.

When Lois came for regression work, she described her agoraphobia problem. It was manifested by her chronic fears of leaving her house and being alone in public. During a past life regression lifetime, she reported that people of Rome were throwing stones and rocks at her as she was stoned to death. The message for her to learn during this lifetime was to be careful about how she told people about her beliefs. Lois acknowledged she often hesitated to tell people "who she is," and now she knows the underlying reason. While she was in this altered state of consciousness, her guides told her that she must ask for forgiveness in order to have a better understanding of her life today.

Lenore was eager to explore her long-term feelings of panic that arose while she traveled in the subway and aboard planes. She was able to explore her persistent phobic feelings while in enclosed places. Her list included fears of bridges, tunnels, subways, elevators, bathrooms, and rooms without windows. Because of her paralyzing thoughts of being trapped in an elevator, she walked up and down many flights of stairs at work. Lenore also experienced feelings of panic during her dreams, often awakening in a total panic.

Her anxiety was beginning to increase because of an upcoming cross-country train trip; she was fearful of being stuck in the "Midwest." (One of her past life regression sessions is described in chapter 3.) Talking with this very attractive, 40-something, outgoing woman, you would never guess the dimensions of her fears. Lenore was on a low dose of an antidepressant that was gradually being reduced. Determined to find the origins of her problems, she did not want to take the medication. During her regression, she described the following:

I just see rock, like a cave. It's big. Though I feel alone, I'm not afraid. I don't know if I'm wearing pants or a dress, but it's old-fashioned. I don't see anything but the rock. I'm just standing there. I'm not afraid, though I may be hiding. I'm just standing and waiting. I think I'm in darkness, and I think I'm suspended again. It's all so melodramatic. Don't want to say it's wild. I'm in the cave, and I can see daylight, and I think somebody blocks the cave with a rock. I haven't done anything. I feel innocent. I think it must be a big rock. It had to be two men. I can't imagine I can leave the cave. Now there's ringing in my ears. Of course, I think I'm going to panic. It's just me. I'm standing and wondering why they would do that. Can't tell if I'm a man or a woman. I can't go there.

She felt trapped, so I verbally talked her out of that situation. I said to her, "Lenore, go to your death in that lifetime."

It's very dark. I thought it would be light. It looks very funny. The soul looks so funny, as it just walks away. It just gets up and walks away. I was so innocent. It was in Western culture—American, 1600.

That image after death. My body was tense, while looking at this white image. So funny, how funny. Death is a release.

Afterward, Lenore said she felt panicked by these experiences and was haunted by the image of the cave. She felt that she was confronting the frightening part. The night after the regression, she felt very anxious. However, after a week, she felt her anxiety had decreased by 30%. Her experience highlights the importance of going slowly during the regression, which can allow each person to judge his or her own pace. She said to me:

> In the cave, I saw myself as a young man, standing with the rock and saying, "Why me?" I'm worried about the agoraphobia, and I woke up in a total panic.

During the next session, she said:

L: I think I have to go into the cave again. (And she easily went into a light trance.) I'm looking for a way out. I don't know what to do. If I go farther and farther, there may be a way out, but I have a feeling there won't be. I think I run, just trying to find a way out. I don't think I'm going to. I'm in a blind panic still wondering why. What I don't understand is why I don't move the rock. I think I return to the big chamber. I don't think there's far to go. I think if I'll wait, maybe somebody will come. First, I try to entertain myself. I just sit and wait. It's starting to look worse. I look disheveled, then thinner, and I look older. Nothing to eat. I couldn't be there very long. I think I just wanted to die.

B: Lenore, go to the time of your death in that life.

L: I see myself fall over backward. I was sitting on a rock. I can't tell if I'm watching me fall over or standing outside the body. The body looks so small and pitiful. I look bigger than the body.

B: What message did you get from this experience that can help you in your current life?

L: I see why my fear is so bad. I learned to be trapped in the cave. Even after death, there isn't an escape from the cave.

B: How can that help you with your fears today?

L: I get the words to write. I've got to feel the soul escapes the cave. First, I have to see the soul escape the cave. But I still feel trapped. I rise, but I don't let go completely. I have trouble reconciling that I can leave or rise. That the body isn't me. I've left it.

Maybe I don't want to leave a wife. I think hard. I think the land is important. Maybe it is spirit that left. It's the land that holds me. I love it so. It's my responsibility. I don't know who'll take care of it. I don't want to leave the trees and grass—my farm. To learn to let go. Look at what's ahead. What's past, leave behind. What's ahead, is less than what's behind. *It's all about leaving. I couldn't foresee what was. What's ahead is less than what's behind.* What's ahead being unknown? Not just trapped. An issue to leave and not want to leave.

The feelings that Lenore described kept her stuck during that time. She was then able to transform her anxieties about her upcoming vacation by choosing to use positive thoughts about how much she was going to enjoy her time. We worked together on a plan for her to begin to practice meditation and relaxation techniques. She was to visualize herself being free from fear while reminding herself that she always carries her safety zone with her wherever she goes. She said afterward:

> I eventually have to go into the cave and see my soul rise through that rock and surround it with a lot of light. My thoughts held my soul in the cave.

This metaphor highlights the way a person's thoughts can bind up the person's ability to function in the world. Lenore now believes her regressions took her back to someplace in Europe between the 1400s and 1800s.

L: The rock, but transcending all of that. Just growing bigger and bigger. The cave is so small, I think of being trapped for eternity, and that I can get out. The fear is that I won't be able to get out. To see the spirit as it leaves the body. I have to learn what it means to be free. I think I'm supposed to go try it. I have to see that the spirit is bigger in the cave. The cave is really small. That it's not a matter of going through it and insignificant. The cave is so small and the spirit gets bigger. I think like my fears, they just go with the cave. As the soul grows bigger and bigger, the cave gets smaller and smaller.

The overwhelming shock of this experience kept Lenore from being able to look at the entire regression experience all at once. In subsequent sessions, she worked through the feelings of being trapped while experiencing less anxiety. She didn't feel as phobic and had more confidence and less fear.

Upon returning from a wonderful vacation, her fears of panic in closed places had once again decreased by another 30%. As she said, thoughts told her to "trust my own intuition." She said, "What is ahead is **not** less than what is behind." This transformed her prior assertion that, "What's ahead is less than what's behind," a significant shift in her thinking. As her feelings of claustrophobia greatly diminished, we continued to work further on other more personal issues. Her next regression follows:

I'm getting the silliest messages. I'm silly to say this: "Do what you want, do what you can, and you'll always be a happy man." I always feel comfortable on cobblestones. I think it's taking me to Munich, and if I'm there, I'm just wandering and looking. I wonder if I'm that man in the cave. The same images. The brown knee breech pants, vest and white shirt, and cloth coat. It feels like I'm new to the city. It all seems beyond me. I'm amazed. I just came from the country. It's the same street that I saw in this area when I was 17 years old, on vacation in Munich with my family during this lifetime. I had a major deja vu in Munich. I knew what was around the corner in the old section. I think I'm being taken advantage of by people who saw my innocence. They're giving me a big hearty welcome. I'm so innocent. I think I'm back in the cave again. I think they must've shut me in there. I think it must be connected to money, but it isn't a lot. I'm in that damn cave again and it seems so far away. Don't get stuck. "Do what you want, do what you can, and you'll always be a happy man." I was naive letting others enslave me.

As she expanded further in this session, she was able to see the larger purpose of that lifetime without panicking. By the next session, she reported her overall anxiety had decreased by 60%, and this level was being sustained.

My anxiety in relation to elevators began to change. Before I'd see an elevator while watching television and have a lot of anxiety. My anxiety has much reduced. I'm surprised I still cannot go into elevators yet. In regard to subways—a year ago I couldn't get over my fear, and now I'm considering it. I still feel bigger and I feel more solid. A year ago, I would have been anxious 24 hours/day when thinking about elevators.

During her next regression, Lenore asked to go back in time to an experience that would be for her "highest good." As the regression began, she talked about the experiences she had with her "angels." She believed in angels before this work.

L: I'm hearing, "Where fear is put love." First my own main angel who wants to throw me around spins me around, and lets me fly so I can fly. He's trying to teach me to break free and fly. I think I see the trees. There's a tunnel. I guess I'm supposed to go down the tunnel. I wonder if this is the way. When in there, I see it is not black, it's grey-blue. I can see the atoms.

B: What is the lesson for you?

L: *Strength*—to learn to be stronger. Softness is a basis for strength. Of course, maybe that's why they took me through the tunnel. It's safe. They're teaching me how to get my bearings. Maybe they're desensitizing me. By seeing a tunnel is just part of everything else. That it's not like a solid and impenetrable rock. It's like dancing atoms...life...my photographs. I'm supposed to go into the tunnel again. I think it's going to be like water. To take a deep breath going in. It's part of everything else and there's light here, too. It's very funny. We have a little tunnel, and my higher self pops up and goes into this tunnel, and I'm supposed to do the same thing. You can, you can, you can, if you want. They always repeat everything three times.

I have trouble visualizing getting this. There's a force that keeps me from entering it, as if I have to push through that force. So physical. Like energy running at me. Only way to get through it was to swim through it. I feel like I'm reentering it. I think they're saying this is energy, and I don't know if it comes from the tunnel or it comes from me. I think I'm so sensitive I can feel it, and they throw me off. I think I'm in. I don't really like it. I think I'm supposed to see again. So funny. They make me practice this. I have to move forward and let the energy carry me along. I never liked that. It's so funny. A split screen. I see trees—like a tunnel. They just want me to sit on it. I feel like I can almost smell the subway. You never know where they are going to pop up, and my higher self popped out of my forehead, and this huge vortex of energy around my chest. And my soul popped out. They're telling me to go along with the energy. I don't want to go along with the program.

B: Why is it important to experience past life regressions?

L: You go back and you are your own witness. I've always wanted to go back and change the past.

For Lenore, each regression helped her through her fears of becoming stuck. She talked about waking up depressed after the two past sessions. She felt she was always caught in a dream.

That's tragic. I'm afraid I'll get caught in it. My panic attacks have subsided, but I still feel 50% anxious. The phobias are not felt as much.

She decided to get on an elevator with a friend along with a maintenance man and felt fine. Now, she talks about wanting to fly on her next trip since she hasn't flown for so many years because of her phobias.

> The claustrophobia is about being out of control and trapped. These guides threw me around. The first time I had six angels, three on each side of me. Gradually, over time, the numbers reduced to 2-3, and they held me closely. I was in their arms, and I was worried they were gonna drop me. Now, they toss me around, and faster, and I was disturbed. They said to me you're not stuck anymore, in relation to my situation at home. They said, *"Got the message can you L?"*

Lenore went on a second vacation and called me while on vacation. She told me that she was so shocked by her experiences that she had to call and tell me. She said the "little" lesson about practicing going into tunnels was very helpful to her and allowed her to enjoy that day "with little or no anxiety, and just pure joy and pure fun." Lenore was able to spend an entire day at an amusement park with relatives. She went on every ride, something that she was unable to do for 20 years.

She also said that the three sessions that were related to her early childhood allowed her to understand the issues with her family. In addition, she said to me, "So at least on my part, I'm having a most wonderful time, and I just have to tell you how important the last few sessions were in making all the difference in my having a wonderful, wonderful time!"

Lenore returned from the trip and told me she got "stuck" (metaphorically) on a few rides, but the important part was that she didn't panic. Originally, she feared that she would panic and not be able to get out. Her previous focus on fear and negativity kept her distracted and stuck in a box. These fears were a thought form consisting of stuck energy, which stood in the way of her getting where she wanted. Through PLRT, those thoughts were transformed to self-love and self-acceptance and the idea of being open to all new possibilities. She was able to get herself "out of her box"—or the cave—in which she was trapped by her own thoughts about the cave. In this way, she replaced fear and negativity with love and self-acceptance.

> My heart is still open, and I'm not so nice, but my heart is open. I keep thinking of replacing fear with love.

During all of Lenore's regressions, she described how her spirit guides turned her around. She didn't think that she was important enough to ask her spirit guides for help, and she couldn't believe they would help her the way they did. After her last session, she felt her vibration was "up."

> I have to learn how to ask and accept it. That they're there for me when I'm in trouble. I can see what I want and it manifests. I was focusing on the fear and the negatives, of traveling on a plane, and now my new job is bicoastal and travel is paid for, so I can go back and forth, overcome my fear of flying, and prepare my professional work. For me, the eight sessions have made an amazing change within me and in my life.

During this session, she began to talk about her angels:

> You know what they're doing? Turning me around and they call me, "Lenore the Drill," turning me like this. They're unwrapping me

like a mummy. They want to free me up more and more. They've unwrapped me three times now, like a heavy bolt of fabric. It always starts at the same place. I think they want me to get it, as if I'm all wound up. The only thing that comes to mind is my friend. I think it is about me feeling that I'm loveable. I'm embarrassed to say this: they say you're a blessed divine soul that matters. So joyous. Childhood issues were not known and not understood and I was not cared for in the way I needed to. Carrying them around is silly. They're unwrapping me again. Unwrap and unveil who I am. Unveil myself. It's kind of scary. They're showing me with a veil over my face. I have to lift it up. Gotta get rid of some of that hurt. Fears from tears, tears release fears. You are blessed.

After the session, she said that the information that came through was all verbal and not visual, and her spirit guides said:

We love you and we like Barbara. In three sessions I got better, in four sessions I get grounded, and now I feel love.

After this session, she left a message on my machine: "Amazing things are happening. My development is so rapid that I get scared."

Lenore's deja vu experiences in Munich are similar to occurrences that have been reported by so many people. Lenore's visualizations within the cave reminded me of Plato's cave allegory of being trapped in a cave of misunderstanding. The images were of her being trapped in a cave, not being able to turn her head, and unable to see anything surrounding her. This was a metaphor for her experience of feeling trapped in her body with unchanging, panicky thoughts. They helped to keep her trapped in place, immobilized, and unable to logically review those thoughts. These patterns continued in a circular motion. Through her visualizations during the past life regressions, she was able to picture herself transcending the confines of the cave. As that occurred, she was able to let go of her chronic panic attacks and phobias and leave the cave, so to speak.

Throughout the regression experiences, Lenore recognized the intensity of her trapped feelings at her current job. She acknowledged that she has to be the one to make the next move to change her career. As a result, she and her fiancé made a decision to move cross-country to follow new careers.

It was such a fulfilling experience to see this woman let go of her shackles of fear and anxiety as her life transformed. It was a privilege to be part of her journey as she changed her life perceptions in order to be free. Her final career path changed in a totally different direction than she could ever have imagined while living and working in New York City. Her current path is working as an energy healer and assisting others to transform their lives. Through PLRT, many people have allowed themselves to take risks and ride new pathways, trusting that whatever happens is for their highest good.

In Lenore's case, she made increasingly more complex changes that occurred within eight sessions over many months. However, her symptoms had been firmly entrenched in every activity of her daily living for many years. This is important for people to understand when seeking this treatment for chronic conditions. The alternative may be a lifetime of phobias and panic attacks.

For some sufferers of treatment-resistant panic attacks, the reliving of one or more past life regressions explained the reasons for their claustrophobic fears. The emergence of these powerful past lives not only helped people to heal their current life fears but also to change their behavioral patterns. Some were able to overcome chronic phobic patterns immediately or within a short period of time. Without fear, they were now able to ride in elevators and subways, cross bridges, fly on airplanes, and swim. Their joys with their newfound freedoms were real, while their anxiety, emotional paralysis, and fears were greatly diminished.

As people transcended their phobic patterns, their rate of improvement depended on the degree to which the phobias had been chronic as well as the degree of impairment. As a psychotherapist, I know these are important findings. Perhaps, like Nietzsche, their understanding of a past lifetime experience helped them to transform their current life patterns.

Through the continuation of this work, certain patterns began to emerge. The clinical part of me was skeptical that the regression work could have such a rapid effect on an individual's problems. However, the facts were there. People with crippling fears and phobias were letting go of their fears and were able to lead more active, freer lives. This was for real.

Many people who experience similar fears and phobias can learn how to utilize stress management techniques in their quest to understand their fears and phobias more clearly. I have included an exercise for those who are interested.

Exercise

1. Begin by using the centering technique and the "I AM" prayer from the end of chapter I.

   a. Remind yourself that you are always surrounded by the light. Picture your guides and angels surrounding you and with you wherever you go.

   b. Recognize that every situation comes into your life for a reason. Its manifestation is important. Ask yourself, "How does this serve me?

2. Visualize the patterns of your phobias.

    a. Under what circumstances do they occur?

    b. What is accomplished when the phobia forces you to avoid situations?

3. How do your phobias serve you?

    a. Gain an awareness that your phobia may help you in your current life without your conscious awareness; for example, it helps you to avoid confrontation or emotional discomfort.

    b. Understand that once the problem disappears, it may mean you have to learn how to take care of yourself in different ways. Sometimes, this occurs when you assert yourself or say no in certain situations.

4. Have you ever had a current life experience that would explain your current fears?

    a. Use all of your answers or intuitions that come to your awareness during this exercise. It may help you to gain a greater understanding of your fears and anxieties.

    b. Develop your goals and begin to accomplish what's important to you.

    c. Remember to spend time thinking about the situations, and write down all information that presents itself.

Write all of your experiences in a journal. The journal can be a wonderful way to help you become more aware of the process and your progress with specific issues.

4

A Past Life Regression Therapy Session Integrated Into a Current Life

"You must be the change you want the world to be."

~MAHATMA GANDHI

People often ask for the details about how PLRT works, what other people experience, and whether they believed they enacted a "true" past life regression. My answers to their inquiries were as varied as the people who reenacted their past lives.

During my extensive PLRT work, many people reported to me their beliefs that the regressions were real. They told me the regressions affirmed for them the belief in a progression of the soul after death, with the soul continuing to return each lifetime in human form for further spiritual growth. A few people were concerned and shocked about their regressions, especially when they saw themselves as a member of another sex, race, religion, or in a less favorable situation.

Some described their past life regressions as so overwhelming that they couldn't take them all in. After their experiences, others told me they thought they would have had different past life regressions from the ones they experienced, that their regressions were far from what they had expected. A few described their previous deja vu experiences or vivid dreams, which they thought were past life experiences.

Most people who said they were on their spiritual paths told me they believed they had received information that was for their highest good. They said that it was important for them to work on that information during this lifetime.

Claire is a young woman I had worked with using traditional psychotherapy. As a graduate of a prestigious university, she possessed an extensive knowledge of literature and history. She was shocked by the nature of some of her past life regressions. Of the multiple regressions she had experienced, Claire believed that only 2-3 of these were "real" past life regression experiences. Her criterion for this view was based on the idea that these regressions were so totally out of the realm of any story she believed she could have made up. The remaining regressions, she believed, could be the stories of a fertile, imaginative mind that had been influenced by her extensive reading.

I've included two of her regressions so you can see how the past life regression flows and the individual questions that I asked Claire in order to clarify her experiences. Through this process, she was able to move to the next important event and describe her interpretations.

Claire was influential in the development of an animal shelter program in a large city. She worked with other active, caring, committed members, and her passion for animals kept her deeply involved. The program was rapidly growing, demanding increased political activism. The work had become quite tedious and very labor intensive.

At the time she came for PLRT, she felt "burnt out" and had decided to explore other work possibilities and a new life direction. As her following experience unfolded, I don't know who was more shocked, me or Claire. Claire began the regression by saying that she felt sick, nauseous, and trapped, which she didn't feel at the end of the regression. I asked her where she was trapped; she said it was like being underground or in a cave, and she couldn't see anything. She said that she used to have fainting spells as a child and would always feel this way before she fainted. This had usually happened to her when she was between the ages of eight and ten, early in the morning in school when she had to stand in the chapel.

C: I felt fine until just now. It's like something's trying to tell me something.

B: Tell me about this trapped feeling. What that means.

C: It's connected with the fear in the arms. Feeling tied up. I feel nauseous, tied up, powerless. I can't breathe properly. I feel sick. And it feels a lot like what it felt like when I would faint when I was a kid. There was never any—I could never understand why it would happen. Some days it would happen, and some days it wouldn't.

B: So what's this feeling of tied up mean to you? What do you mean by "tied up"?

C: I feel like I'm being punished. I've always had that feeling like I've done something really awful. And I can try and say okay, you feel like you did something awful 'cause your mom left, but I think it's deeper than that. I'm trying really hard to make amends in this lifetime. I can feel that. But I can't quite get a grip on what I did. It was something really bad.

B: Let's talk about this feeling that you've been tied up.

C: I feel like I've been trussed, you know? Tied up with rope and my wrists are tied together. My body is constricted in rope, old rope, and maybe I'm feeling nauseous 'cause there's something pushed down my mouth and taped over it. I've been shoved in a cave or a hole somewhere and left to die. And I deserve it. That's the worst of it. Whatever I've done, I feel like I'm lying here figuring OK, you know, they caught me.

B: What did you do?

C: Something bad.

B: Let's hear what you did. Let's see what happened. What happened before they tied you up? Do you remember?

C: Could have something to do with fire. I'm not sure though.

B: What do you mean fire?

C: I could have set fire to something, but I don't know what. Just crippling fear, like this, like being tied up so you can't breathe. There's something about, maybe it's setting fire to something, and being killed for it. But wanting to blow something up. To really destroy something.

B: See if you can get an image of what it is that you set fire to.

C: I see a barn and I see horses. I feel like I killed the horses, but it's all so disjointed. I don't know where I am, or why I'm doing it, or why I would want to kill the horses or set fire to the barn. (She began to sound panicky.)

B: Remember, this is just an image; some thoughts. So you're going back to see some things. See if you can just keep yourself separate from that, and just to see the image and see what there is to learn about it. Take some breaths and let's see what happens.

I tried to help Claire relax by telling her that she could see herself as being on the outside, watching this event unfold. I kept talking to her in order to help her breathe more deeply and to become more relaxed so that she could see what was important for her to see. I used this technique to help her to defuse any panic that began to arise.

C: The image I see; I feel I'm a young man, about 18 or so. I'm angry at something. Something isn't running the way I think it should. I'm getting back at people by setting fire to this barn, which is a pretty serious offense back wherever I am. I mean, if it's somewhere in the West. It's like those horses are valuable. And I don't even care if they die, but I'm realizing that I've done this terrible thing and they catch me, and they kill me. But they don't want to get caught killing me, cause then they'd commit manslaughter, which is a lot more serious than burning down a barn or killing a couple of horses. But I feel this really horrifying thing of being trussed up and gagged and feeling that I've deserved it, and it's a really horrible, slow death.

B: So be outside your body looking at this, because you don't have to re-experience it. See what happens at the time of your death instead of allowing yourself to go through it. See what happens at the time of your death.

C: I feel like I have to go through it 'cause I don't understand it. I can't get a grip on this. I can't understand why I would have such a desire to kill and hurt, and such an anger, such a rage.

B: Where do you think this anger and rage came from for this young man?

C: Not feeling he's getting what he deserves or credit he's due. Not feeling people are paying enough attention to him. Not feeling he's getting what he should get. Wanting to blow things up, burn things down.

B: So he doesn't know how to handle his feelings or his rage. So what happens to him at the time of his death? What happens when he dies?

C: I almost feel like it's kind of like hey, you want recognition? I'll give you recognition. You want to be famous? You can be famous, but you're going to have to learn to cope with your rage and your desire to destroy things. And I still haven't figured that out. I haven't learned how to cope with my anger and my desire to destroy things, including myself. I want to kill myself too.

B: Why is that?

C: Don't know. I guess 'cause if nobody loves you, you might as well be dead. I don't know. It's that feeling of not being loved and not being able to accept love, or recognize it, or enjoy it or appreciate it. Feeling like it's a nuisance. People offer you love, and you wonder what they want in return.

B: So what is there for you to learn from that life?

C: Not to make assumptions about how others see you.
Not to expect too much. Not to give physical vent to your anger. Not to suffer, not to cause suffering, not to punish others.

B: Anything else before we come back? Anything else that you think you ought to see here?

C: I want to stay here a little bit longer 'cause I hate to think that all this stuff with feeling for animals and wanting to save them in this lifetime is simply cause I feel guilty about something I did in a previous life. I hate to think that it's that cut-and-dried or that connected.

B: Maybe in some lives we do things that we're not so proud of, and in other lives we do things where we want to repay and take care of something. He was young and didn't know how to handle things. He took lives without being responsible about it. Do you have to be punished the rest of your life for doing something like that? Can you give yourself credit for doing what you did, for whatever reason? That's an admirable mission.

C: There's nothing admirable about this guy.

B: But I'm talking about in the here and now. You, in the here and now. There are a lot of people who've done things like that in the past, Claire, and they don't come back into another lifetime and do what you've done in this lifetime.

C: I feel so sick. I would just like to try to get this feeling of sickness out of me.

B: What is the feeling of sickness? That you're supposed to be punished for what you did?

C: I'm just getting kicked in the stomach or something. And I've always had this real fear of horses, too in this life. I'm really terrified of them. I see an angry, sullen, hot-tempered, ruthless, cruel, but basically a wimp. I mean when they finally get him, he just gives up and they just tie him up like a stuck pig. I feel like a stuck pig. And I hate myself. I can't justify what I've done and I can't get over it. I don't feel any kind of release from death. The death is just like you know, being squished like a beetle kind of—*ouch*. You know, there's a lot of people who go through their whole lives really hating themselves. And they never get out of that. Then they hate themselves and they hate everybody else. There's no release and there's no relief and it doesn't get any better. And you can't feed that hunger, you can't feed that hatred. A lot of me stuffing myself is trying to get over that feeling of self-hatred. 'Cause there's no way to stop it.

B: So when do we break the karmic cycle? How many lives do we have to go through to suffer? To learn our lessons?

C: I don't think this is just from being a horse thief. Maybe I stole the horses and I was trying to kill them, so they wouldn't get caught or something like that. But I don't think the horse thief is where it starts. Before that I've just done a lot of really awful things.

B: To improve in a karmic way is to keep coming back because we want to transform our actions from the past. We've all done things that are not so enlightened and so loving. The key is to know that we can change our lives and begin to do something that is very loving and is very creative.

C: But why do we do bad things?

B: I think it's learning about "spirituality" and learning the law of karma. Sometimes, we do things because we don't know better and because of ignorance. Sometimes, we're very angry or hurt and we don't know how to handle things the correct way. Sometimes, we're not even shown the way. We all have the potential to do what this guy did. We all have it in us. There's no human being who's never had that experience or the potential for that experience. What's more important is whether people can transform themselves, which is why we keep on coming back into body form, to work on our soul and to evolve our soul over time.

B: What is remarkable is the kind of work that you've done in this life with animals. I believe you've more than repaid your karmic debt. I think you should step back and take a look at that. In a spiritual way, you could have been nice to one animal and said okay, I repaid my debt. Take a look at what you've done. You've affected the lives of so many animals and people. That's a wonderful thing. And you've been very self-less in it, and I think you have to stop punishing yourself. The time for punishment is over. You don't have to keep on coming back and keep on punishing yourself in every lifetime for this. You have to learn that. 'Cause you're the one, now who has to forgive yourself. In a spiritual way, you've been forgiven. You have to learn how to let go of it and to learn how to love yourself more. Accept yourself and know somehow that guy back there wasn't loved. That's why he's walking around with so much anger and rage that he didn't know how to handle things. Right now, you have certainly much more than made up for lifetimes of that. So I'd like you to think about it that way.

C: I guess I don't know. If God is love, if there is this force, this spiritual energy force for love out there, why is it that we can still be so wicked and suffer and cause suffering?

B: Maybe it's a lesson to learn about what's life with love, and what's life without love. A lot of people have not been here having love in their life, and maybe it's part of their spiritual lesson, too. To understand that you can finally transform, come to peace, and do loving things. If you can come from that background and do what you've done, I think that's amazing. That shows an amazing transformation of the soul. Part of the lesson is about the soul's coming back to learn lessons and to change the behavior. You've certainly done it. The point is, you still haven't forgiven yourself, and that's the one piece that you have to work on. I don't think that's right; I really don't think that's right.

C: Well it's an ongoing thing. I'm not satisfied.

B: OK, you don't have to be. Know that you're going to continue to search for answers for this, but not in a self-punitive way. I want you to feel the energy coming back up your legs, to your knees, to your heart, to your throat, to the top of your head. As you continue to breathe in and out, I want you to feel all of your energy come back. Feel yourself very centered and very focused, and to remember this is a past life memory of an event. It is something that you have to work on, and to heal from, and not to treat yourself as you literally did this and punish yourself. So remember that. This is something that you have to continue to work on. Feel all the energy come back, allowing your body to become very alert, very focused, feeling very energized and relaxed. When you're ready, open your eyes, and we will talk about what you just saw.

When Claire came out of her altered state of consciousness, she said that she still felt nauseous.

C: Well, that wasn't so bad I guess. I mean, it's nice to get some kind of grip on why you hate yourself.

B: Did you hear what I was saying, in the sense of karma, and why we have to come back to work on stuff? Because everybody's done things that are not so nice. But the soul lesson is that we come back and keep working on our stuff so that we begin to transform things in the world. We don't keep on repeating, because it's easier to repeat bad lessons—to not change our patterns of behavior. So you took the hate and internalized it, and it's time to change that pattern now. 'Cause you've repaid your debt to mankind, to society, but you haven't repaid the debt to yourself, yet. You've got to learn to take care of yourself better.

C: Yeah, I guess I still don't really want to. There's still a part of me that really wants to like, just beat myself up. Oh God. I just feel, I wish I could have a good cry, but it's not coming out. Okey doke. (Sits up and laughs.)

As a result of this barn-burning experience, Claire gained a broader perspective into her feelings of incredible responsibility. This may have been translated into her need to help all the stray cats and dogs in the world. She said the guilt from that lifetime still feels very real. Being a male in that lifetime did not concern her.

C: I feel that I did my bit in this lifetime, and then moved on. Interestingly, I've always had this real fear of horses with their huge bodies and big teeth.

Claire said that her past life regression helped her enormously. As the regression progressed, she found that her current lifetime feelings of nonverbalized rage became more obvious. Perhaps her severe depressions in this lifetime were a result of that unexpressed anger. Her current lifetime lack of feelings of love and security were probably an outgrowth of the lack of attention she received as an infant due to parental illness. She experienced poor parental communication, felt unloved, and did not know how to take care of herself. Claire couldn't believe people loved her because she saw herself as an unlovable person. Perhaps this theme was part of her unfinished business from that past lifetime. As she was killed in that past life, her energy was probably stuck with a lot of unexpressed anger and rage. She was unable to process these feelings by working through them and making changes in that lifetime, and these feelings continued into this life. However, she could make changes in her current lifetime beliefs.

During our further discussions, Claire told me that she does believe that she came into this lifetime to work on dealing with her feelings of rage, guilt, and love. This happened as she learned how to develop intimate relationships. She recognizes the importance of self-acceptance and self-love. Perhaps she chose to reincarnate into her current family in order to reenact the issues in order to become more whole and facilitate her healing. Through her regression experiences, Claire was able to highlight the important factors in her life that needed to be addressed.

Most recently, she decided to break through and work more directly on her fears. During her follow-up, she told me she had decided to begin horseback-riding lessons. This was a big step forward for her to conquer her fear of horses as well as to overcome her multiple fears. Through these regression experiences, Claire was able to highlight the important factors she needed to address during this lifetime. She is now able to deal with her anger and rage more directly.

The reenactment of this past life regression affirmed for Claire the ongoing evolution of the soul. Life purpose exploration is one of her goals. As she said, "I know this is real, because I couldn't have made up a story like that!" Perhaps her passion and commitment to serve abandoned animals in this lifetime are a connection to this past lifetime when she was responsible for the death of a "couple of horses." This is contradictory to her current lifetime passion of caring for animals. In this lifetime, she would have never made a statement like that. She is devoted to and has a passion for the animals she takes care of.

This regression is similar to the hundreds of regressions that I helped to facilitate. The experience of the regression gives an individual the opportunity to view an experience from within as well as from the outside looking in from a safer distance. The gestalt of that experience is so much more powerful than simply thinking about it. As a therapist, I was able to say things or make suggestions to clients in a way that most therapists would not in traditional psychotherapy. I found most people will accept recommendations while they are at a deeper level of consciousness. This often results in a long-lasting attitude change.

During her untiring work within the animal shelter, which included political organizing, Claire served as a role model for others she worked with. As Gandhi said, she was the change that she wanted to be.

5

We Are All One

"Injustice anywhere is a threat to justice everywhere."

~MARTIN LUTHER KING

During my initial PLRT work, I had constantly questioned the work of mediums and psychics as well as my own and others' spiritual experiences. Initially, these experiences were hard for me to understand because my educational background followed the medical model paradigm. I held the common view from the 1980s that people who described these experiences were a little strange.

However, what was revealed to me throughout PLRT work with people's reenactments of multidimensional experiences demonstrated experiences along a continuum. They described reports of past life regressions, out-of-body experiences, in-between lifetime episodes, future lifetimes, parallel lives, and the channeling of information that predicted future events. These reported events became more of the norm. They continued to unfold while I was documenting the truth of peoples' journeys.

As a result, my vision broadened considerably. The scope of people's experiences led me to become more open to receiving this information, which was unusual for me. However, it was reassuring for many people who felt for the first time that their lifetime experiences were being validated by a health-care professional. At the present time, there is infinitely more published work describing these events.

Many health-care professionals have traditionally expressed difficulty acknowledging the spiritual experiences described by many world-renowned professionals including those of psychiatrists Drs. Carl Jung and Elizabeth Kubler-Ross. While reading Jung's work, I was encouraged by his detailed descriptions of his personal and professional spiritual experiences. He reported a very powerful incident surrounding an unusual circumstance of his friend's death.

One night, Jung felt as if the friend was at the foot of his bed asking Jung to "go with him," and Jung said he did "in his mind." He visually saw the friend go into his study, climb up on a stool, and show him some books. The vision then broke off. Jung went to his friend's widow and asked whether he could look up some books. He went into the deceased friend's study, saw the stool, and found the title of the book that his friend had shown him. It was entitled, *The Legacy of the Dead.*

Jung recalled other dreams about his father; his father appeared to him in one dream as if he had traveled from a long journey. The dreams occurred several times before Jung's mother's death in 1922. Jung felt this was a significant dream since he hadn't thought of or dreamed about his father for a long time. Both Jung and his mother had severed their relationships with his father before his death in1896.

In another instance, he dreamt that his "wife's bed" was a deep pit with stone walls; it was a grave. At 3 a.m., he heard a deep sigh, and then a figure resembling his wife sat up in the pit and floated upward. In the morning, Jung and his wife found out that his wife's cousin had died at 3 a.m. In a subsequent dream, he saw his sister, who was currently living, and another friend who was deceased. He said that he immediately "knew" that his sister was going to die—and she did.

One can see that Jung's dreams helped him shape and confirm his views on spirituality and dream symbolism. He believed that one's psychic existence is affected by the relativity of space and time. Relativity appeared to increase in proportion to its distance from our consciousness.

The psychiatrist Dr. Elizabeth Kubler-Ross's 1970s' work with thousands of dying patients was reflected in her world-renowned book, *On Death and Dying*. This has been, and continues to be, a worldwide primer for both medical practitioners and lay people. She described the five stages of dealing with death and dying: denial and isolation, anger, paralysis, depression, and acceptance as she brought the subject out of the closet. She elaborated on how the process of death can affect patients, their families, and health-care professionals.

When her book first appeared, it was a godsend for nurses like me working at the bedside of dying patients. Up to that time, nurses and often doctors were forbidden to tell patients that they had cancer and other terminal illnesses, but the patients knew anyway. In fact, any talk about death and dying was not allowed, inhibiting our ability to help patients deal with their illnesses.

As a result of her work, workshops and seminars on Death and Dying rapidly flourished throughout the world. Lay people and health-care professionals alike were given the information they needed. The result was that people are now able to recognize the grieving process. After many discussions, Kubler-Ross's work dramatically changed the discussions health-care professionals had with their patients.

However, Kubler-Ross's subsequent work, *The Cocoon and the Butterfly* (2000), was very controversial at that time since it centered on her belief about what happens after death. She refers to reincarnation as an established fact, making a symbolic comparison between the death of the human body and the soul's release to the butterfly's emergence from its cocoon. According to Kubler-Ross, when the body dies, the soul is released. She described death as simply moving from one house into a more beautiful one.

Her very positive references to reincarnation were an outgrowth of her work with thousands of dying patients as well as the groundbreaking experiences of her own physical decline. She said that her goal was to let people know that there is no death; she was a forerunner of work with the "afterlife." People who practice Buddhism and others who also believe in reincarnation as a natural process of life, death, afterlife, and rebirth have no problem with this belief system. Once again, Kubler-Ross has proved to be a truth seeker, even though this topic continues to engender a lot of controversy.

According to Schopenhauer, "All truth passes through three stages. First, it is ridiculed. Second, it is violently opposed. Third, it is accepted as being self-evident." Many living in the Western hemisphere report that reincarnation is a very unnatural belief that people continue to derogate because it can't be "proved." For people who live in the Eastern Hemisphere, it is a much more natural belief system. The groundbreaking beliefs that Kubler-Ross describes are followed by many people, and over the past 25 years, the concept of reincarnation has become increasingly accepted.

Throughout my work with hundreds of seekers who chose to experience PLRT, I found that most people were able to describe at least one lifetime regression experience as members of the opposite sex. Both men and women who experienced regression lifetimes as members of the opposite sex were confident in their identity and more in touch with the masculine/ feminine and creative part of their psyche and thus were comfortable with their regression experiences. Many said that they did not feel influenced by traditional sex-role stereotypes and were often more androgynous in their lifestyle attitudes. People described a greater appreciation of their diversity and displayed a wonderful balance of both masculine and feminine attributes. Expanded consciousness and self-fulfillment were a result of their experiences.

Most felt comfortable with these regressions, and as a result, they displayed an increased openness to the idea of reincarnation. This included a broadened awareness of all peoples' interconnectedness. As a result of their opposite-gender experiences, many people were able to more fully understand opposite-sex traits. The small numbers of people who were upset when they found themselves as members of the opposite sex during another lifetime usually expressed current lifestyle views about traditional sex-role, stereotyped behaviors and that all men or women should act in "traditional ways."

My next leap of faith was not a surprise. It came about in relation to racial experiences. One of the first regressions began with Joan, who is Caucasian, and a healer who works with the homeless. Joan believes that she has been a healer through many lifetimes, all the way back to biblical times. She believes that she carries a sadness connected with those times. Joan also wanted to know if she had any past lifetime connection with her current lifetime ex-partner. Her regression starts as follows:

J: I'm talking to my husband. We're going to be sacrificed because he was sold to someone named Cook in Gettysburg, 1859. My name is Virginia and my husband is Hal. We have eight children. He is sold and I cry and feel a heaviness in my chest and torso. I'm confused and angry. Why someone else has the right to do that. He's killed. He's beaten by the son of the plantation owner. I felt devastated like a boulder sitting on top of me. My son takes over. He keeps an eye on things. He's 17. His name is Hannibal.

B: Go to the next important event in that lifetime.

J: I learned how to read and write. It's wonderful. By the son of the plantation owner. I'm a cook and I cook for the Cooks. I get access to more education books and I preach to my neighbors working on the plantation. I just work to 92 years. I didn't do much by that time. I was there and not working. I laid in a room with white sheets. The family. Scott Cook was the son.

B: When you die, what happens to your soul?

J: That we had a good life in spite of it. My kids were good. The year was 1887.

After Joan awakened from that regression, she spontaneously said that her current ex-partner was a "witness in Gettysburg." She felt good knowing that they were connected in another lifetime. Joan experienced intense emotions during this regression.

Upon returning home, Joan walked into an antique store and saw sheet music on a piano entitled, "Old Black Joe." It depicted a young girl, 10-12 years of age, sitting and looking into the distance with a book in her hand as she was teaching a black man how to read. When the owner asked Joan if she was interested in items "like that, Blacks in the 19th century," she quickly said yes. The woman then brought out a poster that was a listing for slaves, and the first position was for a cook! Joan felt a little spooked. The owner gave her these items that had been in her store for four years, refusing any payment.

Joan told me that she had a photo of a Black woman, circa 19th century, hanging in her home. When she originally found the picture some time ago, she felt the need to purchase it as she thought it was a picture of herself!

Joan has absolutely no problem recognizing herself as a Black woman. In fact, she told me that she currently works with a lot of black people and she has always felt in "sync" with them. Her regression experience as one of her past lifetime experiences confirmed this. Her spiritual beliefs led her to recognize the interconnectedness among all people. Joan was one of the many people who described their past lifetimes as members of another race.

Alison is a Reiki practitioner, very spiritual, and open to a range of life experiences. She decided to explore her current lifetime relationship with her boyfriend and his ex-girlfriend. The following experience was revealed to her at the end of another regression session. She and her current partner are Caucasian.

A: We lived in the South on a plantation and "she" was one of the slaves.

She said this in relation to her current partner's ex-girlfriend who happens to be black.

A: He had an affair with her in the 1760s and "got her pregnant." I was cool with it, because there was nothing I could do. I was very angry at him because of her situation. She lived in her quarters.

Alison described plantation life during her next regression as follows:

A: I see myself in a black dress. One of those dresses with a large skirt. We live in this big white house, with pillars in front. Very rich, but not that happy a life. Dull, because something inside of my heart isn't happy and I think the reason I wear all black is because I lost a child and there is nothing much he can do to make me happy. Bad luck. The child was sick. He's trying to make my life comfortable, and he's frustrated, at not making my life happy. I keep people at a distance. I have a staff. It's every day in and out and nothing gives me joy. I sit in the garden. I'm not really here. He takes care of the estate. But he really can't reach me, and it makes me sad he can't reach me. A glass wall between us. I don't know how to help him get through. He's trying to be understanding and buying things. But I don't enjoy anything because he's sad, too. He's losing me, the self I was. But I lost the child. And I don't know when I found out about her. And I don't even blame him. She's a very pretty, very young, Black woman. She works on the estate. I kind of like her. I can understand it.

She takes a deep breath.

A: I'm so tired and I'm not really afraid of losing my position. He'll never divorce me. It wasn't done then. A no-no. It's late 18th century. Before the war. I don't want to know all the details. The most important thing I don't want to know is whether he fell in love with her. He's so attracted to her. She's very young. He's too much of a businessman, don't rock the boat. He's a man. He would never do anything stupid.

B: What state are you living in?

A: Southern Georgia or Louisiana. It's a beautiful estate, 1760ish.

B: Bring yourself to the next important event and see what you see.

A: I know she's pregnant or she's had a baby. Something's happening to her. I see people running. She's not making it. A lot of people. Something's wrong. People go nuts and I'm so calm. Something's happening in the quarters of the help. Something spills over and starts a fire, and it feels as if I've been released from prison and I can be free. And realize how much I love him and he loves me. He was helpless. Needed some affection and I feel it was sobering. And the affection I had shut off from him and this tragedy, almost gave me the ability like someone turned the light switch on in my heart.

He's on a recliner in the study with a cover on his lap. Napping. I go over to him and I take his hand, and I haven't touched him in years. His hands—like the first time, the spark back between him and me, and I hold his hands, and squeeze him and he wakes groggily. And he looks at me and doesn't say anything, but all of a sudden I see this tear run down his face, and we sit there in silence. And so much love and so much truth between the two of us. I had the courage to come back to life. I said, let's take the baby and bring it into the house. So we have the baby come into the house. It's not my baby, but it doesn't matter. It's out of wedlock. Rest of our life we never talk about it. This child has brought us back together. This child is growing up to be a very handsome man. And I'm so proud to be his mom. He's the future and so smart and elegant. He's just awesome. The child that died was my brother, who died in this lifetime. My name was Caroline. It's always in the eyes, and when I see Alan's eyes (current boyfriend), I see a hundred million stars.

Alison's depression was a consequence of the death of her baby in that lifetime. She had pulled away from her husband. Today, she probably would have been diagnosed as having postpartum depression. Her husband ultimately had an affair with a young female slave on the plantation, and her male child was born as she died. So Alison and her husband raised this baby as their own son and their "love child." This was unusual for the social mores of the times, since he was half-Black and half-White and born out of wedlock. Through the process of raising their son, she was able to heal her pain. She learned through this regression, *"I'm not afraid to be a mother anymore"* in this lifetime.

Alison was not surprised at this regression. She said that the most important thing was their love together as they watched their son grow to manhood. The reliving of this past life regression experience allowed her to work through her current lifetime issues with her partner, who is white, and his ex-girlfriend, who is African American. She was also able to explore her feelings about becoming a mother in the future.

A few people reenacted past life regressions as Native Americans while talking about their experiences in relation to the natural environment. Paul described his preparation for a buffalo hunt. He detailed the wearing of the buffalo skin and how the Native Americans prayed to the spirit for the hunting of the animal. Animal spirits were an integral part of the Indians' living experiences. Paul explained the importance of asking the spirits for their food sources to be available for them to eat.

> How to kill the buffalo. We have the skin from the old buffalo with the head which we wear in a dance the night before the beginning of the hunt. Happy and serious because we have to get the faith of the gods. YAKU. We wake up early and travel to the prairie. As a young boy we did this. Learn how to sneak up to the fields where they are and we run very fast. Looking for the young and old that are weaker. Corner them off from the rest. Big spears and with sharp rocks, attached by a leather thong. As a tribe there are many people. We skin

it there, and break it up into pieces, to bring back to the tribe. And we say prayers for the spirits. Because, as we have been blessed we have been provided for. It was good. It gave us faith. That we know we don't have to worry. We will be provided for.

Through this experience, Paul was able to affirm his gentleness and his spiritual way of being in the world. These descriptions simply portray the spiritual connection of the Native Americans to Mother Earth and their thankfulness for their food. This belief has been described by many people who reenacted Native American lifetimes.

Sophia is a tall, energetic, vibrant, spiritual soul who envisioned herself as a Native American living in Arizona with wind running through her long hair. She began her regression:

S: I am a man; very powerful and had a "gift of the spirit." I was able to "tell things." I was very free and lost my freedom when White men came and took the spirit away. We had to move, but the White men were afraid of us, and wouldn't let us leave. So, we went back to the mountains and became the mountains. The "whispering pines." We would never give the spirit up to the White man but gave it to the mountains. *Never give up the spirit. Protect the spirit. Keep the spirit alive.* Show other people how to protect the spirit. Don't do dishonest things, because it helps the spirit. Look up but not down. It helps the spirit.

To this day, Sophia embodies these beliefs and transmits that powerful spirit energy to all of the students she works with as well as her family and friends. In fact, when you meet her, you can instantly feel her powerful, spiritual energy.

As a young African American performer in the arts, Josepha had a horrific reaction when she saw pictures of a magnified view of germs in the newspaper. She became hysterical, and no one could understand why she reacted that way.

B: One, two, three... *Be there now and see what you see...*

J: First thing I saw was a Dutch cap. The kind you wear with wooden shoes. And a lot of sun and like Amsterdam. But long time ago. I feel like I'm happy, because it's very sunny and a lighter feeling then the other place I was. I said to myself, sick children and I'm taking care of them in a dutiful way. Pour water into a bowl and doing dutiful tasks.

B: Are you related?

J: No. I just care about them. I guess it's possible to get images stuck together. I wonder if it was a nurse's cap instead of a Dutch cap. I think it doesn't matter.

B: What does matter?

J: That I'm devout. And I feel like a nun-type of a person and someone, not a passionate, it's very...and studied, and a feeling of purpose and I don't know if it came from feeling religious, or I'm that kind of person.

B: One, two, three...

J: Well, I feel like almost like a missionary, to get help for the children. I just know, some supplies. Food or medicine. I have a vision of leprosy, and makes me feel, so hard to say. In this life I've had so many disturbing images, in relation to skin.

B: Do you see their skin?

J: Like a lot of sores all over them, and like it's something that's getting worse each day. I see myself tending to them like, with a damp cloth on forehead, but I don't ever see myself embracing them, or touching them...I don't know if I'm afraid to for myself, but the feeling is that, people around me don't understand the magnitude of the problems. Because they don't care like I do.

B: One, two, three...

J: Saw myself alone in a chapel and not even a chapel—more like a room. A small room where you could sit or kneel, and I'm older. And I feel those children are long gone. Long since gone. I'd like to know if there's something about this, that can help me.

B: Bring yourself to the time of your death.

J: I feel like it's—like I'd be sick through the night and early morning and I can almost see myself. Can't see what's wrong with me. Old. I don't feel, I feel like there is a death. When I know it's coming, doesn't take me by surprise, and that I was afraid, and then by the time I died, I wasn't afraid. And I see an open window at the foot of a bed, and I can see out the window.

B: Where does your soul go?

J: Like I can imagine a feeling of sleeping. Feels like...I... just like, straight out the window and up. But, I don't, I never considered that question before. To get a greater understanding of your purpose now. I always had faith. And I needed it. And I really need it now. I've just got to be happy in my work, and I just know that I had a lot of strength, and my soul has been through a lot of challenges. The lesson is that I'm not drawing on the knowledge and strength I have. If I had a business, the more I used the things I know I benefit from the things. I try to squeeze myself into—the more doesn't work.

Josepha had described herself as a Caucasian female missionary who was working in a leper colony. Unfortunately, she was unable to save people from this deteriorating disease. The helpless experience resulted in her acknowledging similar feelings in her current lifetime. Even more importantly was that it explained her childhood reaction when she saw germs on the front page of her newspaper and "freaked out." At that time, her parents thought she was having an emotional panic attack. Through this regression experience, she now believes in reincarnation and continues to work on her spiritual path and her professional life.

In addition to these experiences, I found that some Asian people saw that they had been African Americans in their own past lifetimes, and vice versa. I believe that these experiences demonstrate the universality of the soul experience. I began to see the uniqueness of every regression experience for each individual; it varied with an individual's personal perceptions of a world view.

Some people's regressions unfolded as a projection onto a movie screen, revealing the story of an event. Others described one scene or thought that captured the quintessential knowledge of a lifetime experience they described as a "knowing" but was not visualized.

People experienced the world either as a visualizer or one with more cognitive experiences. Their regression experiences were a reflection of their styles as their regressions unfolded.

They would ask themselves, "Where is this coming from?" or say to me, "I have no idea about what I am telling you, because the thoughts are spontaneously flowing out of my mouth. I am not visualizing it, so how can it be true? This doesn't make sense!" And you could see their astonishment at the different experiences they described that had no connection with their current lifetime experiences.

As I continued using PLRT, I began to see how the snippets of information people described were similar to an understanding of the crux of their current lifetime problems. For example, people who experienced a psychologically abusive early childhood remembered a past lifetime of being abused or murdered. As their vivid descriptions of those events occurred, people often cried as they talked about those regressions in a cathartic way.

I believe the discussions about these early lifetime experiences furthered their healing experiences in a freer way. This often resulted in feelings of relief from their current lifetime memories. Some people have told me they believed this current lifetime experience occurred in order for them to explore their spirituality and to search for their life purpose. Most important, judgment cannot be made that if you had an abusive experience in the past, you will have one again. Each person's experience is unique, as it highlights the issues that need to be currently explored.

As an Adlerian psychotherapist, I use early recollections from this lifetime as a tool to gain a snapshot of a person's perceptions as well as how those recollections may be organized into a coherent lifestyle. I ask people to describe their earliest childhood memory of any event that would be important at this time to work on. These are usually vivid memories that we all carry with us throughout our lives. They are used in psychotherapy to help people to gain a greater awareness of their lifestyle. I found that for some, these experiences are often descriptions from another lifetime. In a very dramatic way, people would talk about their discoveries across gender, race, and nationality. They expressed their amazement at their regressions and their diversity across the ages. This highlights the importance of ensuring the eradication of injustice anywhere. This should be a personal goal.

Most of those who described horrific past life experiences transformed their lives to ones that are increasingly more accepting while working toward equal justice. They are living their lives in a way that accepts the notion that we are all one.

6

Spiritual and Religious Universality

"I have yet many things to say unto you, but ye cannot hear them now."

~JOHN 16:12 (NEW TESTAMENT)

Many people in the United States say that they do not believe in reincarnation since it is not accepted or addressed within their religion. The 2005 US Gallup poll documented that 20% of people reported a belief in reincarnation as the rebirth of a soul in a new body after death. A 2007 European study found that 20-25% of European people believe in reincarnation. A 2009 US Harris poll of 2201 adults reported that 71% stated that they believed in the survival of the soul after death. In this group, 63% think that they would be in heaven. Of the total group, only 27% stated that they believed in "reincarnation—that you were once another person." A 2009 Pew Forum on Religion and Public Life reported that 1 out of 4 believed in reincarnation. A 2014 Harris poll of US adults aged 18 years and older found that 24% believed in reincarnation. Within this group, 40% were people aged 25 to 29, and 14% were aged 65 and older. The question was specifically worded to ask whether people believed that they were reincarnated from other people.

These polls show the importance of distinguishing between a belief in the survival of the soul after death or a belief in reincarnation—the rebirth of a soul into a new body.

Along similar lines, 34,000 people responded to an after-death questionnaire on psychic John Edward's *WE* Internet survey. When asked, "Do you believe the soul lives on?", 97.95% said yes. They were then asked, "Do you believe in life after death?" To this question, 98.59% replied yes. On further questioning, only 11,000 responded to the following question: If you answered yes to the question above, through what concept? They responded through heaven/hell: 38.17%; reincarnation: 17%; and energy: 44.77%.

This group is a devoted audience of people who follow the work of John Edward who purports to communicate with the deceased and transmit messages from people's departed relatives. These findings may be attributed to people's increased search for spirituality and meaning in their lives even when their religion doesn't accept beliefs in reincarnation. Many find that these beliefs can be used as a "spiritual underpinning" that can provide a structure to illuminate their current life experiences. This may help them to understand the broader dimensions of race and religion. People who came to me to experience a past life regression were self-selecting this work, so it is difficult for me to determine the percentage of the population that believe in the concept of reincarnation.

As I continued to work with PLRT, pieces of the puzzle were coming together, especially those pieces that were related to religion and spirituality. Obviously, religion is a very complex issue for many people. It is important to recognize that many religions believe in the everlasting soul.

I found that most people who sought PLRT had already accepted a belief in reincarnation. As a result, they were open to their regression experiences. Research has shown that people's use of alternative therapies (PLRT is considered an alternative therapy) has increased from 33.8% in 1990 to 53% in 2014. This includes a broad spectrum of diverse race/ethnic differences as well as sex, age, and income variables. Researchers found that the use of these therapies by many individuals reflects their beliefs that these therapies "embrace a holistic, spiritual orientation to life."

This was emphasized to me when Aaron, a middle-aged, professional man, decided to try PLRT for further exploration of his spirituality. In one of his first regressions, he begins:

A: See two hands. They're like touching in prayer. It's not clear. I think it's an olden landscape.

B: What are you experiencing now?

A: It's kind of, a kind of devotion.

A: Like praying to the sun or some kind of light or being.

B: And what's the praying in relation to?

A: It's like the hands are over my head. It's like I'm feeling the hands.

B: Whose hands are over your head?

A: Some kind of a teacher or maybe God.

B: And where is this happening?

A: It is an indistinct landscape—nothing is recognizable.

B: What are you doing there?

A: Like I've been called.

B: Called for what?

A: Like for a mission. *They said to ascend.* A sense of ascent. Like to illuminate darkness.

B: And how would you do that?

A: I would find them?

B: In what way would you illuminate the darkness?

A: It would appear just as a journey as an ascent. I would be told, and like it would come into focus. The illumination is always there. You can only see it when you get to a certain point.

B: And what point is that?

A: Like I've gotten partly up the mountain. It's still black, and at the top is the light. At the bottom of it, it's lit up. That's the progress I've made. And I have more to go.

B: What's important to bring into your life at this time for your questions about your own spirituality?

A: Someone is watching over me.

B: And who is that someone?

A: God.

B: What else is there to understand about this experience?

A: I could make the climb to the top of the mountain. It won't give me illumination. It won't illuminate me. Maybe a little bit. I think it comes very slowly. First, you have to get to the top; but that's not the end, and slowly it will come to you. But very, very slowly. It's like the mystery, and I've become part of the mystery. And only afterwards does the illumination come over me on the mountain, very slowly, and then it gets bright and I see myself. I go into the…air, becoming part of the sky. Then I just lost corporeality. Like my heart opens wide and I meet God. My body feels wonderful. God is.

Aaron's experience brought him great joy as he recognized his levels of spirituality and gradual illumination. He said that the past life regression was very helpful because it allowed him to access this spiritual experience, and he believes that this is his spiritual direction. During his next regression, he once again speaks about his religious journey.

A: I see Chinese pictograms. Like a preparing thing; food, a kettle, a woman churning butter, she's in white. Thick clothes.

B: What is she doing?

A: She might be in a convent.

B: What's her purpose?

A: Seems to be preparing food.

B: Is she a nun?

A: Dressed like one. Wearing light colors not dark.

B: What is the significance of that being in light colors not dark?

A: A sign of goodness.

B: See what happens to this image.

A: Surrounded by pots and pans and she's twirling around in a happy way.

B: What's her name?

A: *Angelique* comes to mind.

B: What else is important about this image for you to see and understand about yourself?

A: She's happy to serve people by preparing the food. Other people. I think it is a convent. Kind of a large, dark structure, but there's light in her window.

B: Where is this convent located?

A: France comes to mind. 1400s. Southern. Montpelier comes to mind.

B: See what happens in life to Angelique.

A: See her older and she's staring out the window. She's dressed now in black front and white hat. She's staring out into the night.

B: What is she thinking about?

A: Her whole life. What she had decided to do versus what she could have done, and she's not married.

B: How could it have been different?

A: She could have been married and had a family.

B: How come she didn't choose that?

A: She felt a calling. To do this and lead a spiritually fulfilling lifetime.

B: Bring her to the time of her death in this lifetime.

A: I see her all laid out with candles all around and nuns all leading in prayer round her. They have a lot of respect for her. I don't know whether the black outfit she wore meant she became one of the leaders. I think it's the black outfit—she may have even become the leader, the Mother Superior. But I think it's the kind of place where even if she was the lowliest servant they would have still appreciated her and that they would stand around her in prayer. It seems like a place which is not hierarchical in that sense. Everyone is united in their common and separate purposes, and everyone does what they're most suited to do.

B: So what happens to her when she dies?

A: She goes up and looks like a saint.

B: How does that look? What do you mean?

A: Like there's a golden halo around her; just like in the picture. Like pictures of medieval paintings.

B: What did she think about as she was up there?

A: She's kind of hovering in prayer.

B: And what messages does she have for you today that can help you in relation to your life today, and how you live your life?

A: She's saying, *I should follow my calling.*

B: And what's that?

A: Same as hers.

B: And how would you do that?

A: I see writing; It's like an old sagely man is writing, with some kind of instrument. He's writing like instructions to show and to teach. It's like writing on stone tablets, and he's showing, he's facing me and showing them basically to me.

B: And what did it say? Can you see the message? Can you see what he wrote for you to see?

A: It seems to be like ancient writing, like ancient Hebrew, and I get the sense that he is showing me in the name of God and he's sort of pointing up.

B: What do you mean by that?

A: He's giving me the tablet and the implement he's handing it to me. He's sort of wrapping me up in it like a cloth.

B: How do you interpret that?

A: He's become part of me.

B: Did you get the message that's important for you to get from this experience?

A: He's sort of pointing me in a direction to go. Like it's a lit-up road toward the rising sun.

B: Before we come back, is there any other message for you to get from that experience?

A: The road goes into the world and the world is a complicated place. It goes into the forests and on the side of the road, but I still have the tablet and so sometimes it's appropriate to just sit down and take out the tablets. Write and read, and then when I'm ready, get up and there's the road again. And I'm taller—a little more confident and have a sense of accomplishment. And I emerge from the woods. Bright sunshine, and there the one problem is that the road is obscured by everything...is so bright and it's like I'm on the edge of the cliff and everything is white. So I don't know where it goes.

B: What's important for you to think about the white light surrounding you and your life purpose?

Prepare yourself to come back and think about all of the things you've seen and ways of implementing them into your life. When I count to three, open your eyes and remember all you saw and heard.

A: It was very emotional. (He was crying as he spoke about the experience.)

B: What feels emotional about it?

A: Well—it's what the woman said to me. She seemed beautiful. Like she fulfilled herself in the right way and she sort of turned to me and said, *"That's your job.. That's what you have to do."*

B: What do you think about that?

A: I feel that it's true and she was a saint and you know, at the end of the day, she may have been doing the cooking and maybe that was her job. And by the end, she became a saint.

B: She was serving.

A: Yeah, she was serving, and in the best way she was capable of, and that gave her nobility. She was happy in what she was doing. Like, those are my instructions, and kind of I was sent off on the road.

B: Back on the path?

A: Yeah. I got the sense where I am now is the place that I stopped in the woods, and the road becomes obscured, and so I stopped by a tree and took out the tablets, and read in them, and write in them. Like I said, it's very emotional. It's like I have the feelings, you know, that I told you I get the feelings.

B: Do you feel that it's a sense of what you're doing? What you're supposed to be doing now? Involved in your spiritual pursuits?

A: Well, you know I feel that I'm making spiritual progress. Being in my profession is like being in the woods. It's one of those complications about the world.

B: How does this experience permeate your mind? When you talked about your writing, you said, "Am I doing the right thing?"

A: I support my family. And in the world in a highly spiritual way and joy and sense of purpose. It may be there are times for pause and learning, and it might be where I am right now. I work in my profession. It's like the path takes me through this. You know, not to do what I'm doing. It's part of what I have to go through. Like I have these tablets. I have my instructions and I know that. There's a further goal; an ultimate purpose which I have to think about, contemplate, study, and work through. I'm supposed to gain the knowledge that will allow me to continue.

B: That was very powerful. Was it shocking for you to see yourself as a nun?

A: No, because I always felt I was very close to them.

I also found this to be a very emotional and spiritual experience. However, I was shocked at Aaron's experience as a nun. Since Aaron was a religious Jewish man, I was sure he would be upset. How wrong I was! He felt differently. Aaron said he was a religious and spiritual person. His spiritual beliefs are the universal language in his acceptance of God. So for him, the universal truths of religion preclude a belief in only one God. That was quite a lesson for me as well as for him.

These experiences only serve to emphasize the universality of religion, giving us all something to reflect upon as we seek individual understanding of the meaning of religion. Is it the traditional trappings and rituals of traditional religions that are important, or the underlying, universal message of unconditional love, peace, and service?

Through Aaron's descriptions of the multiple dimensions of his spiritual journey, I am reminded of the teachings of Sai Baba, the Avatar whose works are known internationally. *Avatars* have been described as the manifestation of God in mankind. Sai Baba talks about an individual's struggle upward from the mud on an evolved, spiritual path. An individual's ascent continues when the ultimate goal of merging with God is acknowledged. Along the path, higher light descends into the person. When the spiritual journey is finished, and there is no longer a desire to return, one decides to reincarnate only because of a love for mankind and a desire to help in their spiritual struggles. It is said that if an individual does reincarnate, this is like God reincarnating, as the person is one with God.

Iris returned for work to help her heal her past life and current life issues around sexual freedom. She said, by the time I had counted down to take her into a deeper trance, she immediately saw the cut-off, lower part of her body become bright.

I: I see a path in the jungle, and I'm barefoot, and I have dark, Indian skin. I'm walking through the path—it's pretty small. But people from the village use it. South America. Monkeys in the trees are loud. Trees are really tall—it's very beautiful, green, and moist. All kinds of creatures in the forest, and I'm not afraid. Might be a hunter. I'm not wearing much. Think I'm a man. Wearing a loincloth. Have a blowgun with some arrows strapped around me. Small—dark hair and smooth skin. Some ceremonial paintings on my face. Think I'm alone. End of clearing. A little green mound of grasses. Alone, and I sit up there and there's sun. Feel like I'm on a vision quest. Like I sit there for awhile. Like North American. You sit in one place and wait for visions. Like fasting—like a rite.

A deer comes to me. It's so sweet and nuzzles me, with its mouth and nose, and I pet it and it disappears. A female deer—no horns, and then a fox comes up. Real pretty. I just watch the day-night-day-night and felt I was ready to take that challenge.

A woman appears to me. A spirit guide. Tells me I'll be a woman one day. Oh no! But felt I was ready to take that challenge. It's like a mystical journey. Maybe I was a healer in the village, and different spirit guides would come. Like steady flames. Somehow, you're ready to take in the most difficult things. To be a woman again—as if I took a breath from time for that. I can use some crystals to help myself heal.

B: What kind and what colors?

I: Like ruby—but also just clear crystals because it holds all the colors. Fragrant hot baths. I was one of the only village shaman. This was a vision quest because he was near death. In that lifetime, I'd be able to decide the next lifetime. And next time, would be fraught with…deer represents very feminine, sweet, and gentle energy.

This was a very powerful experience for Iris, as she recognized this shamanic experience provided a spiritual underpinning for her life and her soul evolvement. The fact that she was being prepared for a lifetime as a woman after having had many lifetimes as a man felt very empowering. The role of spirituality was affirmed for her as she was able to acknowledge increased emotional strength, knowing that she is spiritually guided. Iris's subsequent regressions are included in Chapter 7, and was an extremely violent rape experience, which is described in chapter 9. It was so traumatic that she is still suffering the aftereffects in this lifetime.

Randy is a young man from a Roman Catholic background who suffers with chronic life issues. He decided to explore the genesis of his problems and thought that past life regression work would help him on his journey.

R: A building. Like a tenement. Lower East Side. Jewish. I feel poor—dirty clothes, wearing a hat. Brick buildings with fire escapes. It's blank again. Old-looking clothes, black hat, like a fedora—crushed. Just looking and staring and desperate, desperate and sad—poverty. The white light is there. 1927. His name is Fyodor from Eastern Europe—pretty old. In his 60s or 70s. He's alone and he was very sad. He lost his family in the war. WWI—Eastern Europe. He's in the US. In New York. He doesn't have a home. The building was home. I think he lives on the street. Does he die outside?

B: What was his purpose?

R: To protect his family. He didn't do it. I'm getting dizzy. Before you said white light, as I was going back, I saw this. I felt he was really sad. I'm very into that time period. Somerset Maugham. Dostoevsky. I saw the tenement and the man, and all of those thoughts came rushing out. Not visual.

Since he is of the Catholic faith, Randy was shocked at his experience as a Jewish man. What was unusual about his experience compared to other people whom I had worked with was that he would get a visual image (in this case, an image of an old man), and then all of the words would come tumbling out about the man and his life—the images rapidly unfolded for him. This was quite different from other people's regressions in that they would describe a scene unfolding like a movie on a screen.

In his current lifetime, Randy knows and strongly feels that he is hurting his family through his personal actions, and he is striving to understand his current behavior more clearly. Randy was dumbfounded because he couldn't relate to the information presented in his regression. His experience as a person of a totally different faith led him to an increased belief in the possibility of reincarnation since he now knew that he could not possibly be "making this up," especially this complex reenactment. I have found that experiences that are so contradictory to a person's lifestyle and beliefs often highlighted for them the possibility of the soul's continual evolution through many lifetimes.

In the next instance, I told Courtney to imagine a path, and the following scenario unfolded.

B: I'd like you to imagine a path, a path of any kind, a path that will take you back to any time, any place, to any experience of any event that would be important for you to look at right now for your highest good. So when any thoughts or images come up, just begin by talking out loud with your eyes closed.

C: I see a beach. It's kind of misty out.

B: Where is this?

C: I can't tell if it's the Northeast or Northwest. There's a bunch of us collecting shells. We're clamming or digging in the sand for clams.

B: Who are you there with?

C: Two other people. We have darker skin, not White. The shells are going to be used for some ritual/ceremony. Look like conch shells, you know, you hold the seashell up to your ear and hear, and then the smaller shells—we're gonna make beads, jewelry.

B: And what are you going to do with the beads and jewelry?

C: Some are used for sacred rites, and then others are made for trade.

B: Who do you trade with?

C: We trade with other Indians or with the French.

B: Are you an Indian?

C: Mmm-hmmm...Seneca.

B: So where do you live?

C: Seneca or Mohawk.

B: If I asked you what year this is, what year comes to mind?

C: 1600-something. Everything is pretty pristine right now.

B: So what happens next?

C: We're in our village. I have long black hair. I'm pretty sure I'm a boy.

B: What's happening in the village?

C: We're getting ready for whatever, the next carnival day. The next ceremonial day. I think it has to do with the solstice. We're collecting honeycombs and honey. Pine cones. The animals have been very generous to us 'cause they've let us have their skins.

B: What kind of animals?

C: I wanna say beaver, fox,

B: What do you do with the skins?

C: Some of them we use for ourselves, but a lot of time we use them to trade. We get food and we get metal. Buttons, and I think we also get muskets, but we don't hunt with the muskets. We keep them just in case—we don't trust the people coming into our land. We might use the muskets against our enemies that are other hostile tribes.

B: Who are the hostile tribes?

C: The Shawnee come up, and they are very hostile to us.

B: What happens next?

C: I'm with the hunting party. We're tracking. I think we're tracking a large bear through the woods.

B: And what are you using as weapons?

C: Bow and arrow and spears, and there's a certain way we kill the animals that it's sacred. There's just a certain way that we kill the animal that it pays reverence to the animal's spirit. That's why we don't shoot it with a gun.

B: You said in reference to the animal's spirit, what does that mean?

C: There's a certain way to kill the animal so that the animal feels gratitude from us. And will continue to bless us with its body. When that animal's spirit, when they get angry, they're not happy with us, and then they—we don't see much of that animal anymore in order to catch them or kill them. We have to make sure the animal spirits are happy and treated well.

B: So do you aim for any part of the body?

C: I think once it's down it's almost sorta like a kosher killing. We're with older men like grown men who perform it. It's so the animal doesn't suffer and it's very quick. They cut its heart out.

B: Why?

C: In reverence.

B: What do they do with it?

C: It's the power center of the animal so—like the most sacred part of the animal universe.

B: What are they going to do with it?

C: We each take a piece—we each ingest a bit of it. So that animal spirit is now inside of us, and I think that whatever is left over is buried in the ground. And the rest of the animal is used. We use the skin, eat the meat, use the bones, everything.

B: So as you continue to breathe in and out, bring yourself to the *next important place* there and see what you see.

C: I'm in the woods alone…and I'm lost.

B: How did that happen?

C: It's part of a rite, an initiation rite. And they didn't leave me any food or water. So I have to find all of that stuff.

B: How old are you?

C: Like 14. I look very Asian—high cheek bones—my eyes look Asian, almost. But my skin is dark. I'm out there for days. I mean they're not going to come and get me. I have to find my way back. I know I'm crying at some point.

B: So what do you do?

C: There's a bird, there's like a hawk or something that's—he's around me.

B: What does that mean?

C: I dunno. Feels like one of my ancestors is watching me through this animal. And he follows me. I think the hawk follows me and then I follow the hawk. And then I'm led to a place where I can actually find food.

B: What happens next?

C: We're dancing around the fire. And they give me some sort of drink. Very potent. It feels like an aphrodisiac almost.

B: What happens next?

C: They basically tell me I can have sex with any unmarried woman I want in the tribe. It's like it's condoned.

B: So what do you do?

C: I have sex! (laughs)

B: How many women?

C: I think two.

B: What happens next?

C: I've married one of the women.

B: At 14?

C: No. I think I'm a little older; couple of years older. Maybe 16 or 17.

B: And what's her name?

C: Something like a tree or a branch is in it.

B: What's your name?

C: It has to do with a hawk. With that hawk.

B: Bring yourself to the *next important time* there and see what happens.

C: There's more White men coming in. And they just take things. Like they just squat on the land and they just pace it out and say this is mine.

B: What do you do?

C: Well, we have to move our village. We had to move farther West.

B: How come you don't fight them?

C: 'Cause we're not—we're just a small band. We're a small tribe. But I know that the elders are trying to get the other tribes to unify to fight them. But the other tribes are being nitpicky—it's just dumb—it's just politics, politics. It just makes sense that we would all band together because we were all there first. But some of the other tribes say we can't, there might be something good for us, and there's nothing good for any of us. If you befriend them, they'll just take more. There is an actual confrontation, and guns are fired. I see some of my people dead. Not that they're part of my village. I think they may be part of the...I see people of another tribe—like the Delaware. Just had to keep going deeper and deeper into the woods.

B: Bring yourself to the *next important event* there and see what happens.

C: There's snow on the ground. I'm much older. I had children and grandchildren. People come to me for wise counsel. I am also some kind of an astrologer. Like I'm keenly aware of where the sun is in the sky in any given day, and how the light changes. And what it means.

B: How old are you?

C: I want to say I'm in my 60s or something.

B: Are there any people around you who you know in this lifetime in 2004?

C: I feel like Ellen's there. She's my wife, or she's one of the women I had sex with. It's kind of fuzzy. Everyone else is sort of in an *Astral plane.*

B: What does that mean?

C: Like I know them, but I don't know them from this life. Not from this life. They're still, I guess, in the *Bardo.*

B: Bring yourself to the time of your death in that lifetime and see how it happens.

C: I'm in a long house, and the chief is there, and people are there. I foretold my own death. They knew when it was gonna come. And I'm not sick or anything. I just know that I'm going to leave. I don't know if they give me some sort of elixir; something to drink. Which is sort of hallucinogenic. But I can see all the ancestors around me. The people who have already passed on are there with the living. I don't even feel whatever that death thing is. I just, I just walk over. Move very like on a clear placid pond.

B: And what would be important information for you to bring back to the here and now about that lifetime? What would be important for you?

C: That even being still and active has just as much potential for growth than being productive. That you can be, you can just be. And that's fine and expected and not feel like you have to do. Observe all the subtleties of the day. They say you can fly in the void. It's okay. It's part of the journey.

It was interesting to listen to an account of the Native Americans' dance ritual in reverence of the animal's spirit. Courtney described a religious service. I asked her what information would be important for her to bring back to the here and now, which I ask all people who reenacted regressions. She replied that food is taken only when necessary. Great care is taken so that the animals don't suffer, with the prevailing awareness that all creatures in nature must live with each other in harmony and respect. The recanting of this young boy's initiation depicts the interconnectedness of the tribe members with their ancestors and their belief in the continuity of life. His interaction with the hawk was a very beautiful and spiritual experience. I almost felt as if I had been part of it and felt honored that I was allowed to bear witness.

The influx of the White man who squatted on the Indians' ground and forced them to go farther out into the woods was a story told to me by other people who had experienced Native American lifetimes. There has to be an acknowledgment of how we have infringed on people's rights in the past and gain a greater respect and understanding of the interconnectedness among peoples within the universe. The measure of a culture's greatness is its ability to become aware when it has harmed or infringed upon the rights of others and to make restitution and right those wrongs.

Lara is a very spiritual woman who has been able to predict future events in people's lives. She doesn't like the word "psychic," but she does have the ability to foretell things that will happen. This was a rough period of time in her life after her husband's death. Lara has been involved in a variety of healing modalities and really liked PLRT. It helped her deal with the depression that she felt was holding her down. These "stuck" issues were what she decided to address in her regression.

Lara verbalized that one of her big fears is not having freedom. "I'm afraid of being all too powerful, and I have to live life more fully. I must claim my power and write this. It is important that I stay and inhabit more of my soul in my body. I cannot leave the path."

Lara had the following regression.

L: I see a breaking of light—by the village.

B: Where is this place?

L: It's in spirit but I want to see; I feel like I'm halfway.

B: See if you can find a path.

L: There was no path. Was the column of light...I went out [to] the column, and it all opened up. I am before a huge being. I don't know why I'm here. Why I'm in this. So I'm just going to wait for a moment to see what happens. In front of me. Another aspect of me. Another layer, and standing in front of me. I'm being enveloped by this aspect, and I'm in the center of bits of consciousness. I feel frustration. I heard Egypt. I can see the landscape of the larger place, religion, dogs, and red-colored housing. The coloring of the housing changes more like sand.

I am in a temple. I am a healer. I am also (begins deep breathing) the energy, more energy in my system. I am an *oracle*. My body craves more energy. *I need to be larger.* I'm too small.

She's breathing deeply and moving her arms, as if she is trying to accommodate more energy, which appears to be stuck from her back and waist down.

L: My system is not used to parts pulling. I have to be big. I'm too small in this lifetime. My system needs to open up. I bring lots of energy into the temple.

B: What does energy do?

L: It heals people, it is energy. It's a burst of energy. I don't know, it's not me. I'm a conduit for the energy. It's a belief; it's a pattern to physically break through. I need to be bigger in this lifetime.

Breathing in is so confining. So much trouble. I need to help. I need to help in the lower part. Waist down must relax. I think it's only resistance. I don't know how to break through and be fully connected. Stuck back and waist to midthigh. What is it that doesn't allow? And I don't know what's happened to me in that area.

B: Bring yourself to the time of you death.

L: Crowd in front of me. I am standing in front of the temple. I am an oracle. My name means "one who speaks." This one in front is very angry—they don't like each other. I have told them, but it's Jim in the front. He's very angry and they're very angry. I think I'm going to die. I'm in Upper Egypt.

B: What year?

L: 1042. but I don't think...I have a spear through here in the abdomen. I'm not afraid of my death. I am afraid of that rage and that anger. Jim is like a village elder but not an elder village. I'm trying to understand what I could have said to bring such anger and rage. I see there is a part of my essence; a purple vortex is leaving before the spirit. That energy spirit is leaving.

I had many lifetimes...it's a violent place. It's violent; it's dangerous to stay. I am home in spirit. In spirit a belief that my body has enough energy that I am too small to hold. I am small in that lifetime. Separated my body in half. I didn't know my energy. I am only a conduit.

Lara is petite in size in this lifetime and a powerhouse of energy, healing, and light. Because of her height, her current lifetime, irrational belief is that the vast amount of power she has can't "fit" into her body—as if spiritual energy "fits" into a physical space.

Her deceased husband had a violent temper, which frightened her a bit. How he treated her in the past lifetime is an indicator of how he emotionally battered her in this lifetime. Apparently, his soul didn't evolve very far. Seeing his violent actions in the past allowed her to see his behavioral patterns much more clearly. It allowed her to recognize his karmic patterns and realize that there was nothing she could have done to make their relationship different. His being out of her life is good. In her next regression:

L: I have a cloth white—off-white—wearing dress. I'm a woman. I have a cloth bag that holds my things wrapped and tied around my shoulders sits on my back, and I have a stick, a walking stick. I think I have an animal with me.

B: What kind of animal?

L: Like a donkey, but I don't use my herbs or unguents on my animal, because something might happen to me, the bandits might take them.

B: Bring yourself to the *next important event.*

L: I'm working with the unloved, the lepers.

B: What are you doing?

L: I'm helping them with salves—healing.

B: How do you feel about the work?

L: I do good work but I'm alone, though.

B: Why is that?

L: I am so sad. *The one who walks in the light is dead.*

B: Who is that person?

L: You know him as Jesus.

B: Did you know him?

L: There were many women who followed him, but could not walk with the men. They're foolish. They're so jealous of the women. The women could heal. They understood the healing. It was more difficult sometimes for the men. There was a schism.

Why do I have to suffer or have a belief that I have to suffer? Why do I believe that I have to suffer? But what I was taught. There was suffering all around. The men and women and children. There was always death and dying and suffering and death all around.

B: Did it give you comfort to be a healer?

L: I was a good healer. I'm having problems with the brutality. When you walk in that light, you're so filled, it extends for miles. All of that. I don't understand why...what has happened. Something I have to... to.... There is a split between the teaching and everything I understand. All I saw was violence after and dissension and greed and arrogance and ego. Where is the teaching I understood? Part of me has become better. I have taken on that mantle. It was not necessary. The guilt was so enormous; huge. I was lonely, and I was looking at my life, but it did not stop. I taught, and I have students healing. I looked forward to my death. I died an old woman.

Lara was working on her spiritual issues, and this was her third regression over a period of time.

L: Looking lovingly at this body. This woman who helped. Mankind was violent and did not feel the split. Ah, I was feeling the energy in my body, and it was whoosh, just like that, and it wasn't safe to hold so much energy. Why? You could lose your life for the healing, but the people had nothing else. I remember the rage of the God. Such rage, and the split and at the same time, I have so much. The wailing and the split in relation to the killing of Jesus. It's all so distorted. There was nothing harmful in the teachings. There was nothing harmful in the healing. I can feel the energy in my body. Even though I knew such a split, as if I am...as if I'm two people split off. I was looking at rage. I think that's in this lifetime. The body was not safe. The rage.

B: Were you hurt?

L: Yes and no. What were they rageful about? It was fear—their own fear—that I have more power in my body. I have a strong field. I'm making a strong field. Now, it is a distinct energy pattern, when I feel it, but there's another lifetime? So much violence in that life, such a sense of peace and connectedness. Always this split between the men and the women. Such jealousy. They walked right with him, and women were...if you walked with him, you had complete access to all this spirit. More receptive—women. Between male and female unhuman. You keep healing work on yourself and become more. The split. I think he came to heal the split because there's no sense. It was to heal the whole. Healing and having all that knowledge. Like being in the work, and the system energetically shocked, and mobs of violence, rage, and sorrow.

B: What happened when he was resurrected?

L: I had the rage. It was so great. Energetically, it was so large and such a shock. A huge split—where there wasn't a split energetically was set in motion. The energy pattern in the planet changed and set in motion for a new shift. It's like walking in peace and an energy pattern. Take your power back. You don't have to be sick. *Be who you are in your body.*

Lara was not surprised at her experience because of her Christian background. However, she is not observant of traditional religious practices. As a healer, she is very sensitive to all things loving and spiritual. When she talked and cried, some of the negative experiences of that lifetime were accentuated, and she was able to let go of a lot of rage, hurt, and sadness. After the regression, she felt so much lighter.

In her regression, she had described a time that was often chaotic and dangerous, and it was very different from what she would have imagined. Lara expressed her feelings of deep despair at the death of this healer and religious person, Jesus, who brought forth so much love and peace. There was an incredible aura that radiated from him. This was such an incredible loss for her. The experiences within the regression allowed her to cry and let go of a lot of pain that has surrounded her through many lifetimes.

I was able to be more articulate about my belief that I, too had lived during that time period. This awareness came to me when I was working with other people's past life regressions. I saw myself as a man and one of many followers of Jesus Christ. Even though I happen to be Jewish in this lifetime, I still use the teachings of Jesus Christ as a model of behavior and action that I and others should follow.

I find it hard to believe that some people can call themselves "religious" while they preach hate and the ostracism of people of different faiths, races, and sexual orientations. We were all created by God, and as Jesus, the son of God said, "Judge not, lest you be judged."

Over time, I have worked with many people from dramatically different walks of life. I realized that our discussions surrounding their regressions highlighted the importance of their occurrences for them. They helped people to transform their current life problems, and at the same time, our discussions of those events helped them to discern their life purpose.

As we are born, each soul comes into this lifetime with a goal of service to humanity. However, when the experiences come along, we are usually not consciously aware of that purpose. The ultimate goal for our individual soul development is to the highest level of "godlikeness." We keep coming back until we reach perfection, which is called "enlightenment." And as Jesus said, we cannot "hear" all of his messages, but we have to engage in life experiences and learn the lessons through our own involvement.

7

Weight Issues

"The creatures that inhabit the earth—be they human beings or animals—are here to contribute, each in its own particular way, to the beauty and prosperity of the world."

~DALAI LAMA

Many people tend to flow from diet to diet in their frenetic search for the right one. Unfortunately, most usually tire of these short-term fixes and their inability to maintain their own comfortable weight. Some obsessively "work out," trying to eat as little as possible; others often gain a distorted body view of how they "should" look. As a result, they lose all sense of how much food is necessary to maintain a healthy body and an appropriate weight for their body structure. Most people deny the psychological reasons for their weight issues. I have found that for some, PLRT uncovered their own psychological issues or residuals of past-life issues that needed work.

Melanie believes that her long-standing, day-to-day difficulty with weight management was influenced by "something" that had occurred in another lifetime. Her regression began, and she saw herself living in Germany, part of a Christian-German underground group. The Nazis were rounding up Jewish people who were then put into concentration camps. Melanie and a group of people were helping people in the camps.

M: It took a lot of planning. We all knew that one day we just had to leave our apartments, to walk out and never come back. If anyone found out about our underground activities we would have been killed. So one day we went to work as usual and just disappeared. We snuck food to people in concentration camps and our existence was spent trying to help people. Food was hard for us as we gave whatever we had to the people. We never knew whether there would be food for us to eat.

Melanie is Christian and instantly recognized that this past life regression reflected her current feelings about habitual eating as if there were never enough food. Her spontaneity and honesty dramatically changed her attitude toward food. When she described this very powerful regression, she thought this could be an explanation for her food problems. She retold the way people simply walked out of their homes leaving everything behind so as to cause no suspicion. This regression was very intense for her. Apparently these people went through a lot in order to avoid being detected, and they just "disappeared." Melanie said that this was not a lifetime that she would have predicted. In fact, she found this experience so unnerving and shocking that she never returned for a follow-up session.

After I listened to her regression descriptions that she had found so surprising, I began to believe more and more in the legitimacy of people's experiences and that they were not made-up stories. Her experience highlighted the contributions that so many people made for others in horrific circumstances throughout the ages.

Years later, as I was writing about Melanie's experiences for inclusion in this book, I had an interesting synchronistic conversation with a person I worked with. She spontaneously told me a story—apropos of nothing—about a Jewish family who had been living in Baghdad in the 1970s. The Saddam Hussein regime in Iraq was rounding up and killing all of the Jewish people. Since they had family members living in the United States, they obtained visas to visit them, allegedly for a big, family event. She described how they left their home without taking any possessions or money lest they look suspicious as if they were fleeing Iraq. They fled their homeland in order to pursue their religious freedom. I got a chill as she described this event and then remembered Melanie's descriptions that seem so vivid to me to this day.

The magnitude of people leaving their homes and all of their possessions behind is hard to imagine. However, this was a matter of life or death. The fragility of humankind's treatment of one another begs all of us to become more involved in making the world a more hospitable place to live for all of its inhabitants.

Ironically, the simultaneous timing of this conversation with my writing of Melanie's past life regression experience was very important for me. I view this as the spirit's way of showing me the importance of writing this book to document others' experiences and to continue to work toward awakening myself and others to make changes in the world.

Iris came to experience PLRT because she wanted to explore her difficulties with chronic bronchitis and food binging.

I: I went through a period of time when I couldn't expand my lungs fully to get a deep breath. I have suffered from recurring bronchitis and used a variety of treatments, remedies, and acupuncture, which didn't work. There's been a real theme in my life, of not being able to breathe, especially the past few months. My ability to breathe increased around my fear of being alone.   When I broke up my relationship, I suffered from pneumonia.

Iris's breathing (what she meant above was her difficulty in breathing increased) and food binging has always been an area of vulnerability for her. During a past life regression, she described the following:

I: I see a sandy, gravelly path. I feel like I'm wearing a black shroud like Muslim women and that's why it's difficult to see the path. A sandy location and the darkness of the shroud. I feel like I'm in a village. I see other women in black shrouds completely covered around the eyes like nomadic. I'm walking toward something sandy, like in a desert. A couple of tents. It's all I sense. I'm trying to move forward and see. Hill-like sandy dunes. Windy. So sand blows off the dunes. I'm in my young 30s with a child holding my hand and walking with me. Stumbling, child pretty small, 3 years old. Seems to be getting windier. I have to [be] brave myself, and walk towards the wind. Maybe it's developing into a sandstorm. It's getting really bad, like we're trying to get away from the sand, but it is very windy. I think it's so hard. The boy is holding my hand and keeps calling mommy. I keep going but I don't know where I can possibly go. No shelter no trees. Seems endless. Seems to keep trudging forward. I think at times I feel tempted to stop because of the shroud, at least I'm not breathing in sand....Yet I feel that was it. Is all over-consuming. No sense of direction. Not enough oxygen. I start to get more and more scared. I feel that it's inevitable, that I have to stop and be buried in a sand dune. I see no other option. I feel sorry that my son will die so soon. I have a feeling; I have a tall dark handsome husband. I'm kind of having him stand by my right side. Dark blue indigo outfit and white turban. He seemed to be kind. I'm sorry he's not with me. He is somewhere safe. My legs are feeling very tired. Don't know what to do.

B: What happens next?

I: *Two conflicting images:* 1.the storm continues; 2.the storm stops and there's blue sky.

B: 1-2-3, be there now and see what you see.

I: I see I'm buried.

B: Bring yourself to the time of your death.

I: I feel like I must be buried. I think I gathered up my son. I hold him real tight. I think he went first. I don't think it was too long, the suffering. Not so uncommon for nomads to die in this manner.

B: What's important to bring back in this life? Where does the soul go?

I: I'm seeing blue sky. I see the sand everywhere way off in the distance. I'm watching, so alone in a way. I was very independent. I acted like I didn't need anybody. I guess to let people know I need them. I don't know.

B: Is your son anyone you know today?

I: He seems familiar. I can't tell. He's very cute. Somehow I see John's face plastered on him. Like I know my husband is upset. I went out on my own. Middle-Eastern Iraq. Desert is a very close-knit community. A lot of farm work. Like a big community. Mothers help raise each other's children.

B: When I count to three, bring yourself back to the here and now.

I: I didn't expect that. Before you counted down, I saw sand. The past few months my ability to breathe has lessened, as has my fear of being alone has increased. When I hovered above the village it did not seem that far away. I don't want to burden people with my stuff.

When she returned after that regression, she reported:

I: My obsessive food behavior and the feeling to eat compulsively went away after a few days. After the past life regression where I suffocated in a sandstorm, I have found that I can expand my lungs more fully and don't have a chronic feeling of lung discomfort. The past life regression therapy has helped me get over my breathing issues.

Iris described more of her reactions to the regression. Before we began the regression, she had decided to focus on her food issues. She told me that her expectations were of a spontaneous remembrance of an experience where she starved to death. However, during the regression, her focus was on her feelings of sorrow that she had to leave her husband whom she clearly loved very much. Their relationship was extremely intimate and profound and much more egalitarian than she would have expected in that culture.

Iris said her dying was calm. She attributed this to the nomadic tribes' view of death as a natural course of events since they were "in tune" with nature. These experiences were prior to the most recent war experiences with Iraq.

She believes that her child during that lifetime is an old boyfriend because of the mustache and dark eyebrows she saw superimposed on his face. Iris interprets this as an affirmation that it was her old boyfriend. She didn't recognize the husband as anyone she knows right now. However, she believes he will be the man she will most probably meet and marry in this lifetime.

Iris believes a lesson for her from that lifetime is that she needs to rely on others. She said that if she weren't so prideful, she could have asked for help and avoided death. Being very independent in her community, she chose to be more alone, perhaps even more extremely so than in this lifetime. Iris recognizes that it is important for her to build a community so that she has more people to rely on.

Iris stated that her breathing difficulties come from her being completely independent and out on her own for the past six months with no support. So for her, breathing and independence/aloneness are intertwined. She recognized that her food issues are a result of her "stuffing her face" when she feels out of control. Perhaps when she feels alone, feelings of hopelessness and being out of control arise, which often results in her food binging.

When Iris returned two months later for another regression, she reported that her coughing had stopped. She feels some sort of integration occurred that helped her, and she currently has no bronchial problems.

Through the reenactment of a lifetime in which she literally suffocated to death, this young woman learned the lesson of not being afraid to share her feelings with her friends because of her fears that she might be a burden to them. In this experience, her food eating was the trigger that led her to remember the past life experience in order for her to find the lesson that she was here to learn. This was an important lesson.

Another woman also wished to address her eating habits. During her regression, she promptly experienced a lifetime as a "tribal woman" in an uncivilized place who was left by her mate to find food. He never returned. She waited and waited. He never returned, and she was left to starve to death. She believes this experience explains her food cravings and eating volumes of food when she is upset. Living through this regression experience helped her to address her food issues in another context.

Louise is a tall, handsome woman who expressed an interest in PLRT. She is happily married with a supportive husband. This PLRT facilitated her ability to explore her chronic issues surrounding food and eating. Conscious of the importance of a healthy body, she works out at the gym to keep her body well toned.

Louise wants to work on many repressed feelings that she believes affect her issues surrounding weight loss. She had spontaneous thoughts that if she lost weight, she would be raped, and she became fearful. She thought that if she had less body weight, she would feel less safe. The origins of these fears were totally confusing for her. Even after she lost weight, the fear of being raped continued to haunt her. Louise was never raped in this lifetime, so this fear was so totally out of the blue for her.

L: I'm in a forest or something. There's grass. I think there's a tent or something like that and I see a woman with brown hair. Seems like it's Medieval times. I feel sad. I don't know who I am yet. I think I have to leave. I have to go to war. She's my love. We're not married. I'd like to marry her. Her name is Maranta.

B: What's your name?

L: Rolf.

B: Who do you have to fight?

L: The English.

B: Where are you from?

L: Germany. I'm here to say I guess that I'm worried about her. That something will happen to her. I think she doesn't have any family. I think she's alone. Her brothers are fighting too. I'm fighting with a sword—it's heavy. I don't like it. I'm a good fighter but I don't like it.

B: What happens next?

L: It's all over. The battle or the war and I go back to find her and she's gone. Killed. She was raped. I don't know by whom.
(She's very teary and starts crying.)
I withdraw. I go deeper into the woods and I live in the woods alone.

B: What are you feeling right now?

L: Emptiness, anger. Like Rolf feels one thing and I feel another. Rolf is totally shut down and I think I feel sad for him.
(She begins crying again.)

B: What's important for you?

L: She was very beautiful.

B: Were you in love with her?

L: Yes. I think I curse her beauty. If she wasn't so beautiful men wouldn't have followed her. *It's not an act of war!* Not the English robbers or something. Nobody knew who did it.

B: Go to the *next important place* in that life.

L: Still in the forest. A few years have gone by. Not so many. Living in the forest.

B: And your life now?

L: Not much and I'm out hunting and I'm attacked by a bear. He kills me.

Her answers to the questions about where the soul goes and messages that she was instructed to bring back into this lifetime from this regression are in chapter 11. The past life regression of a young man's loss of his love through wartime by rape and murder echoed through "her" soul. The regression and her crying were very cathartic experiences.

When Louise returned the following week, she said that her feelings of being unsafe had changed a lot since the past life regression. She has an important purpose in life, feels a lot safer, is dealing with her body differently, and is not so afraid of being seen. In fact, she now feels good about being seen, losing weight, and looking attractive, and is less worried about what other people think. Louise is no longer afraid of being raped as she understands why that fear from her past lifetime fed her weight obsession.

Paula's decision to explore PLRT was motivated by her desire to explore her binge-eating problems. An outgoing, attractive Christian woman, she doesn't look as if she has any problems with her weight. She knows how to eat in a healthy manner, knows all of the diets, can help other people lose weight, yet her own eating is totally out of control. Unfortunately, her food binging was a chronic problem that kept her obsessing about what she would eat all the time. Apparently, she is suffering from an emotionally based cause of her problems, which she has been unable to unearth.

P: I see different faces. The eyes are dark eyes. I was thinking about things about dieting. My hair is cut the way I just got it cut except a little shorter. I'm a girl—17 years old. I'm just standing in the dirt and my clothes are like potato sacks and I'm really thin.

B: Tell me a story about her life.

P: She's like nomadic. A tent. Like a burlap? I don't know what's burlap?

B: Are there other people there? *What is life like there?*

P: It's very dusty and dirty.

B: How do they support themselves?

P: Somebody with a hat—it's hard—gives us food. Bread, potato. We don't find food. We get it given to us. Soup. I really don't understand what's going on.

B: Where is this? What year?

P: Europe—1942.

B: Where are you?

P: Austria. Somewhere around there. I'm not from there. I'm from Poland. I just keep seeing a picture of a girl just standing there. He's wearing a hard hat. He looks angry but he's not really angry. It's an angry-looking face. A guy. He has a gun strapped around him. A sling.

B: What kind of uniform?

P: Like something official? From this country?

B: Where was he born?

P: He's from Germany. Somehow I see him with a hat that's hard with a strap and elastic-like and he's not so nice. I don't think he's going to kill anybody.

B: Are you running away from somebody?

P: I see my mom and she's crying. She has dark eyes. Most people look lost. We're reuniting. Her skin is all loose and we're near home but not home.

B: Any connections with food that you have today?

P: I still like those foods—ice cream.

B: What about the binging?

P: I think I binged a lot after that with my mom. Not a bad thing. My father never came back. Thin, but after awhile wasn't overweight.

B: Bring yourself to the time of your death in that life.

P: I died in bed with my husband in the room. I think I'm just tired. It was 1962.

Paula told me that her experience took place in some displaced-persons camp. She was surprised at the dark eyes, since she currently has light-colored hair and light eyes. When she and her mother returned home after being in that camp, they binged after that lifetime diet of bread, potatoes, and soup. Paula told me that now she has an awareness of where the binging could come from.

It was a shocking experience for her, since she had limited knowledge about European history during that period. She told me that she did not know anything about displaced-persons camps or concentration camps.

At her next session, she told me how she had searched on the Internet for information about that period and was still so shocked about what she had experienced. She abruptly stopped the work, which I believe was a result of her discomfort.

Rowena came from a South American country, and she proceeded to talk about her problems with weight management. She described her chocolate cravings, which would set her off on a binge. During her regression, she saw herself as a young woman starving to death in Ireland during the potato famine. This was so surprising to see herself living in a totally different part of the world. She believed this experience could change her eating patterns. I cannot say whether this helped with her long-term patterns since she was moving and didn't return for further work.

A woman named Lois sought PLRT to discover what she thought could be the genesis of her bout with Epstein Barr and her weight problems. In her regression, she saw herself as "twenty-something" with short, bobbed, blonde hair working in German intelligence in Munich. She sees herself mixing with the German soldiers, "the higher-up ones," at dances and describes them as very needy.

L: I have control of them. Working out of Freiburg, Germany area. There is a communications machine made of dark brown wood. A black telephone. I guess I'm communicating. I'm in a ball gown moving in a certain set of whatever's going on. Whatever I'm doing I must be in a certain crowd to be doing it. I'm wearing a tiara, a sequined gown and men in red soldier outfits and some in white cream-colored uniforms with medals, fancy. The dress is like at a dignitary level 1940s.

I'm helping people and saving people. Innocent people. Saving people in the country that were being rounded up because of the Nazis. *Anyone against what they want are getting out, and the high-up ones, they don't have a care.* They went to these balls wearing pristine outfits.

I guess I move in these circles and I'm in the counterintelligence. Obviously I'm on the Allied side. They trust me and tell me things and I go and transmit on the communication machines to the Allies. But I'm doing this. I see myself yelling, *"no! no! no! no! no!"*

In the session, she is violently shaking her head back and forth while in a trance.

L: I guess I've been found out. Maybe people I know have been killed. I can feel my body tensing up. Why did I have to do this intelligence work? I think an oven. I'm emaciated.

I'm in a concentration camp. You don't get much, a piece of bread a wooden bowl. I'm dressed in rags. There for 2 years. 1941-43? Dachau? I think I may have died. They did away with me.

B: What's important for you to learn from this experience that you can bring back to your current life and help you with your concerns?

L: Inner strength. Truth and honesty. Love—a love of people. I think my dearest friend today did the counterintelligence work with me. Did I know Jennifer in the concentration camp?

After discussing this incident, I suggested to Lois that perhaps her emaciation as she starved to death could be the genesis of her eating problems. She seemed to agree. It was beginning to become more apparent for me as I witnessed so many past life regressions that many people had made a choice to fight the horrors occurring in Europe during the war in whatever way they could. I think it is important for us to remember that and know that people did what they were able to despite the unsafe environment. Many people literally put their lives on the line for others without question. That's the important message we should take away from all of the horrific descriptions of the Holocaust. Many people cared and became involved. That is what we should celebrate.

Within psychotherapeutic explorations, people are helped to interpret their dreams or experiences. Throughout all of the regressions, there was no simple correlation between a symptom and an individual's weight problem. I found that each individual interpreted similar situations in a way that was totally unique for that person. Perhaps life situations arise that set us on a spiritual journey. Our path along the way is full of powerful, meaningful, wonderful experiences.

8

And Some Gave All

*"Whoever destroys a single life is as guilty as though he
had destroyed the entire world; and whoever saves a
single life earns as much merit as though he had rescued
the entire world."*

~THE TALMUD

It has become increasingly more evident throughout my work that the
commonalities of people's experiences are reflected through their past life
regressions. As people discovered places and lifestyles that were totally unknown to them, the culmination was their belief in the continuity of the soul
over many lifetimes.

In the beginning, I was awestruck and shocked. It was hard to believe
some of the past life regression experiences they described to me. However,
I was impressed by the sincerity, honesty, and courage of their stories, many
you can read in this book. As I witnessed hundreds of people's experiences, I
found that my belief in reincarnation was affirmed. Obviously, this was also
my spiritual journey.

Eventually, the use of PLRT in my psychotherapy practice rose to more than 800 people exploring this work individually. Even though this therapy is not widely used, I believe it has the potential to become a more widespread treatment. The information presented in this book can help people become more aware of the use of PLRT, accelerate their search for problem resolution, and include discussions about spirituality and religion in their therapy. It can also help them to understand that they do have a life purpose. PLRT has been a beginning step on the path toward greater spiritual awareness for many people.

Alison decided that she wanted to experience a past life regression in order to gain a greater understanding of the estranged relationship she had with her husband and others. She is a Reiki healing practitioner in addition to other work and is politically active in whatever way she can be for causes relating to people's rights.

She was breathing deeply as she lay on the sofa in a trance, and this first regression opens with her standing at a wall.

A: I can't see anything but I feel betrayed—denounced. I don't see anything. I just have this feeling I'm at a wall and crying and I'm so angry that I don't see anything. I see this wall in front of me and I can't see to the other side. Wearing brown stockings and brown lace-up walking shoes. They're worn, because I've walked in them so much. Some sort of brownish dress, with sort of tiny little squares.

I'm so angry he put me there. He's supposed to be the man in my life, and I feel he's betrayed me. He said something and they put me here. I think he did it to save his own political ass. I was in the underground. He feels like shit about it now, and I'm standing alone behind the wall. I want to say we have a child. Did he denounce me? How did they find me?

Berlin was a city. Some Gestapo guys came. I'm so disappointed he did that, and he was so careless with his worries, and not thinking what this means, and not how important my work was, this project. We will try to tell what's happening, and have them printed and pass to people so they can save themselves. It feels like the knowledge that I have of the times, is merging with what I'm talking about. I see actions. This has got to be a secret and I see I'm trying to do my job, and not give away what I'm doing.

Pretending to be a housewife, and try to find people who want to do the work and not spread the fears. I don't think I ever trusted him. I feel like, because I wanted to trust him and have this life, I took a chance to trust him and he broke my trust, and now I'm here and I cannot express in words how deeply betrayed and disappointed I feel. It's my fault I shouldn't have trusted him. I wanted it to be right, and work, and I see this little girl with me. I think he didn't want to leave. I think he's punishing me, for having her, and he's sorry. He's so sorry I can feel it. (*She starts crying.*)

Because I don't know what to do. She's about 7-8. She's very tall with thin brown hair and braids. She's looking at me. She wants to know why she's not at home. Why this is happening, and I don't know what to say to her. And it's not her fault. Because he was mad at me, for doing this political activity and now he's trying to pay me back for all of this stuff, and he's such an idiot. He can't take it back. I had to make people aware they had to get out. He's so stupid, and I didn't ever get a chance to talk to him about it. He gets me so crazy about it. I don't care if I die.

What about her? I feel so guilty, because I didn't want her to be involved. At least she could've stayed with him. I don't know where he is right now. It's just so pointless. I feel like it's a self-fulfilling prophecy. I knew when I went into this, there was a risk. I felt I had to help just do this. It is my calling. My responsibility to say all these things about the Nazis and not shut up. It isn't right. Don't feel so alone and I feel so selfish.

She begins crying again, saying, "Where is he?" and now she is hysterically crying.

B: Bring yourself to the time of death in that life.

She's breathing deeply and coughing, and then starts screaming.

A: Like dying. Don't breathe. I feel very dead. I'm dead. I feel like my soul is stuck in my head. I don't lift up. I feel I can't cope because of my daughter. She's dead too, but I feel I want her *forgiveness* and I want to say goodbye to Ethan. I want to see where Ethan is now.

B: Be there now and see what you see.

A: He's wandering the streets. In the bar drinking. He's so beating himself up. He feels guilty. I feel that he wants my forgiveness and like understands the consequences of what he did. He misses my daughter. He doesn't understand the work I did, and now he realizes I'm telling the truth, and he's overwhelmed. He feels like a murderer and I think he's still single. Never marries and never had another child. A suicide attempt? Eventually died an old lonely man. I want to ask my daughter to forgive me. She says I love you Mommy, and I think she doesn't mind because she's with me. I don't see him. Karin died in 1943 at age 26, as Karen Brand from Berlin. His name was Thomas.

Alison was born in Germany in 1957 where she attended school and does not have children. After the session she said, "The funny thing is when I feel threatened, I hyperventilate, and I never understood why I did that." She made the connection that her hyperventilation problem originated from being gassed to death during this past lifetime experience. Her husband during that past life regression is someone with whom she is currently involved. However, she didn't understand why it was such a conflicted relationship. As she saw how he betrayed her during that lifetime, she said that it is not surprising that she picked up on his negative energy. Perhaps this past lifetime experience is a reflection of that lifetime, and they came together in this life to heal a part of themselves. Alison agrees with this and spoke further about that lifetime when she was out of the regression.

A: What's interesting is that in my current life, I have always been reluctant to get involved politically. He didn't understand the encounter. We printed political flyers and got them printed someplace. Eventually, I was found charged with treason. They caught me with flyers and that was the evidence, during the demonstrations and politics in 1970s and 1980s in Germany. I know I'm doing the right thing.

We were both shocked as her description of herself innocently "standing at a wall" turned out to be inside a German concentration camp. She currently works in the United States and told me that while she was touring a German concentration camp, she had an eerie feeling, or deja vu experience, that she had been in that place as a prisoner. She immediately dismissed the thought as ridiculous.

Alison is currently on her spiritual path and is actively exploring her life purpose. She has an in-depth understanding about people who let their power be taken away.

Her partner in that lifetime is a current love interest. When they first met, she had been drawn to him, even though she didn't know him very well. She recalled the time that he told her that she sounded so "distant" when he called. Through the reliving of that past life regression experience, she recognized his betrayal; she can now understand why she felt so conflicted. Alison realizes that both of them have a need for further soul development. She believes they probably met in this lifetime for that reason, to help each other. I don't know who was more shocked at this regression, me or Alison.

As a result of this regression and analysis, Alison feels more focused and aware of the nature of this relationship. She believes that she can now move on without regret. Alison was pleased with her ability to step back into her current experience and resolve this relationship. I was surprised that as a direct result of that PLRT experience, she totally broke off the enormous emotional ties she had with him in this lifetime. Her rapid transition in her ability to sever that connection was contradictory to most people's tradi-tional psychotherapy experiences in dealing with and resolving problematic relationships.

Currently divorced, she believes her husband in this lifetime could have been her daughter in the past life regression. Upon further reflection, Alison realized that during the marriage, she took care of him in a very maternal way, choosing to overlook some glaring relationship problems. Perhaps it came from the guilt that continues to resonate from that lifetime.

Alison continued to experience multiple regressions from that specific lifetime regression that included details of her problematic marriage, her involvement in underground activities with other comrades, and life during the WW II Nazi reign in Germany.

Two weeks later, while she was attending a healing session with other Reiki practitioners, her Reiki Master—who had no knowledge of her regression experience— spontaneously suggested that she had a "Holocaust past in which an injustice occurred." Alison felt immediately relieved and told the Reiki Master about her PLRT session. Then the Reiki Master suggested that her current husband was her daughter in that lifetime, and Alison started sobbing. This affirmed for Alison that her interpretation of her past life experience had been right. The Reiki Master was obviously psychic as she was able to pick up this information about Alison's past life regression.

Alison said that during her regression experience, her current-day knowledge of those historical events was blurring with the actual experience. Many people had voiced this observation to me during their regression. They questioned, "Is this real, or is this information that I already know?" However, as their regression experiences continued, Alison and others came to believe that they were truly reenacting a past lifetime.

Sheila was a young, attractive, Jewish woman who stated that war was "unattractive." She heard her spirit guide tell her that she should trust me because I was going to help her. To our mutual surprise, in her regression experience, she described an image of herself as a young German soldier being hit in the head with a rifle butt by English soldiers. She described how they were laughing at the young German soldier and speaking in English, which "he" did not understand.

S: The soldier says he is doing the right thing by fighting for his country. "I'd die for my country." They throw a bucket of water at him. He speaks in German, and they proceed to break his wrist by putting his hand on a chair and break it with the butt of a gun. I tell them to kill me and get it over with. I don't know anything. I'd die for the Fuhrer because he's doing things he should, like getting rid of people like Jews and faggots. I am 33 years old and the year is 1942-43, and we're still winning the war. They stab me to death with a knife, and I laugh at the moment of my death and see a tunnel. I realize I was a bad person, and wrong for feeling the way I did. I still feel guilty and I am Jewish in this life. I took orders even when I realized it was important to respect other people's religion and to stand out and be myself.

Sheila's past life regression experience was graphically violent and painful. She could now understand how people have had lifetimes where their behavior was less than exemplary and then come back into this lifetime with the purpose of the growth and evolving of their souls to a higher level of consciousness. However, Sheila was quite shocked and stunned by her experience. I do not know what happened to Sheila since she did not return for a follow-up session, which was not surprising since her internal conflict must have been so overwhelming.

A similar experience occurred when another woman came for PLRT, revealing after a few regressions that she had been a Nazi soldier in her last life. It took a lot of courage for her to admit that. She chose to not experience any more regressions since she was afraid of what would emerge.

Soldiers usually believe that they are fighting for their country and doing the right thing. It is a universal feeling for soldiers to believe in their country, and in fact, die for their country. It is also amazing to realize that German soldiers were carrying out horrific acts upon other human beings while many people living in Germany and other Nazi-invaded countries saw what was going on and did nothing to intervene.

These Nazi soldier regression accounts shocked me. As the work continued to unfold, I thought to myself, "Why would someone 'make up' a story about being a nationalistic Nazi soldier, especially a person of the Jewish faith?" This last past life regression was one of the many that influenced my belief in reincarnation.

The intricate planning that led to the mass extermination of six million Jews and millions more, including Catholics, homosexuals, and gypsies involved more people than Adolph Hitler. Who were these accomplices who were complicit in these acts? As time has passed, we are finally becoming more aware of an increased number of underground groups who were feverishly working to get the word out about what was happening and save people. This was described to me by some people whose regressions revealed their participation. In February 2005, there was a movie at the Berlin movie festival about White Rose, the German underground movement of people who had worked toward undermining the German regime. More recently, there have been an increased number of books (see bibliography) depicting the underground resistance movement in Germany as well as in surrounding countries.

An important lesson to learn is that we all have the potential for good or bad. We must always question what we do and not steadfastly believe, "My country right or wrong." All of us must participate to ensure that all peoples' civil liberties are protected. As we continue to reincarnate and evolve, we can transform these experiences in the name of racial, religious, and ethnic consciousnesses. It is not for any of us to judge another person's experience.

Kenneth is Roman Catholic, and he recounted his very emotional experience that occurred after watching a movie about the Holocaust. He always questioned why there was so much pain in his life and why he had been chronically depressed since he was very young. He felt that a past life regression could perhaps help him to determine whether his depression was related to another lifetime.

K: I see an image of a young baby crying as it is being delivered. It is very bloody with an open mouth crying. The woman seems to be in pain as she looks off far away. This is taking place in a tent in Eastern Europe in the 1930s—Poland. It's a birth scene in a forest and soldiers are running by, wearing black uniform helmets—very smooth and very round and along fringes of the uniform is yellow. The mother in the tent is looking around very bewildered and the soldiers are outside. The mother is being dragged away by soldiers. The focus is on the mother. I think it was closest to the end of her life. I must not allow myself to be a victim. It is important for me to stand up for myself, and be more assertive.

After his regression experience, Kenneth described the woman as a war victim. He said the lesson for him during this lifetime is to be able to resolve conflict and not be a victim. After our discussions about this experience, which included ways that he could make changes in his life, Kenneth said he felt better and that his depression had lifted.

A young woman named Tanya came for PLRT work because she was afraid of having power. She believes if she is strong and powerful, no one will love her. Tanya said that she feels guilty about surviving the war and perhaps she shouldn't have. She has Bell's Palsy, which is a paralysis of her cheek muscle.

T: I feel that something happened with my face. Maybe they hit me with the butt of a gun. Soldiers. I'm a prisoner. I'm Jewish in this lifetime but I don't think I was then. I think I'm a gypsy. In the concentration camps. They killed a lot of gypsies because they were different. I feel a tightening of my body as I say this. Is it because I probably said something to them, like accused them? Is it fear from when I speak because I got hit with the butt of a gun? Getting paralyzed, from the fear of speaking out. I have a hard time saying what I wanted. I had to talk fast and get it out. I might have been a young boy who spoke out. Maybe Yugoslavia earlier in warlike 1938. Fifteen years old. I think, to not be afraid that people are going to hurt me anymore. I'm strong and what I have to say is worth something. Is it the message I bring, is not worth listening to?

After her regression experience, Tanya said it was important for her to learn how to speak with authority and courage, believe in the worthiness of what she is saying, and think before she speaks instead of "dumping it out." Perhaps her facial palsy is a reminder for her to speak out and appreciate what she has to say. She thinks her facial muscles are a "little better" after the regression. It is hard for me to evaluate her long-lasting effects since I worked with her for a short time. What is important is the effect of these experiences on the life of an individual.

Courtney decided to work more intensively with the PLRT work since she was suffering from panic attacks. She described her fearfulness and said that she already "knew" of lifetimes both in the Civil War and in the Holocaust. "I'm afraid of the Civil War and the Holocaust." (Her regression as a Native American is reported in chapter 6.) Prior to our work, she had a dream from another lifetime as a Jewish boy. However, her recurring high school dream was of herself as a young Jewish girl in France during the Holocaust who never survived. Courtney had no idea where this image came from, and her dream, as described below, was a continuation of that dream as a young Jewish girl in France.

C: Oh, I've been here before. Brick buildings and I'm hiding in a bathroom. My grandmother lives—was there a line drawn through France? She lived in a safety zone—Switzerland? There was a barbed-wire fence and we couldn't get away. And we marched and marched, and into the trenches and I was shot. I was 14 years old.

She said to me:

C: I think Lorraine was an aunt to me and she was Jewish.

This experience was so intense that she regressed to a totally different lifetime. Courtney said that she wasn't ready to experience either the Civil War or the Holocaust. When she returned the following week, she was ready for this next regression.

C: I see a stone building, and a cobblestone street, with smoke coming out of the chimney. Wagon on the road. Turn of the century or earlier. Looks like Europe or US. Looks like I'm wearing something long and black. I think I'm a woman. I'm running errands. Shops on that street where I can trade for stuff. Eggs and butter. I think I've done some sewing too.

As I direct her to go to the next important place, she replies:

C: I see a garden and there are grapes. Someone has a vineyard. I think there are women sitting out, and drinking tea. They're dressed in fine satin-like afternoon dresses, but they're very nice. I'm related to some of these women. I think it's my aunt's house and she has a lot of money. I'm a teenager. I want to say it's France. I'm on a street in a wagon. And we're being taken to my aunt's house, or back, and there's like tension. People are worried. Turn of the century. Someone set fire to a synagogue and people in our town. Everyone got upset. Northern France. It starts with an M. It borders on Germany. It just looks like I'm in a building grey building with children. It seems like I want to say it's an orphanage. I can vaguely see my mother. I think I lived with my aunt. My aunt left. She took all of her stuff and left the country to London. She just left the country. I think she was afraid all of her things were going to be taken by the town's people. They were going to loot because they were all on hard times.

Because of time constraints, I then directed her to the time of her death.

B: We can come back to this place later but bring yourself to the time of your death and see what happens.

C: I see barbed wire and it's dark and nighttime. It's out in the fields somewhere. I'm 13-14 years old. All of the children are with us. I want to say in the 20s 30s. We're so tired because they made us walk a long, long way. They shot us. They just shoot us.

B: What part of your body were you shot in?

C: I think it was my solar plexus.

Then I directed her in the following way:

B: So put your hands over that part of your body, both hands, and put pancake energy on that area of your body with energy from above to that area of the solar plexus. Just breathing in and out to bring energy to that part of your body. As you're breathing in and out, very relaxed, feel the energy come back up your legs, to your knees, to your heart, to the top of your head, and as you continue to breathe in and out, let all of your energy come back so that you are very relaxed, focused, and vibrant. So when I count to three, open your eyes: 1, 2, 3...

It was interesting that the wound was in the area of your stomach. Is that the area that bothers you when you have those feeling of throwing up?

C: Like right below my belly button. That chakra is all messed up.

B: So continue to bring energy from above into your hands, and it comes into your hand. Focus the energy and whatever color light comes to you. To see this as healing yourself. What is that chakra? Is it orange?

C: Yeah it's orange.
I was abandoned.

B: Who was your aunt?

C: My aunt was Laura. Wow. (As she mentioned a close friend).

She was surprised to see that her aunt was her current friend.

B: What happened to your mother in that lifetime?

C: I don't know. Mother is very hazy. I didn't see her at all.

B: And was this when they started burning the synagogues? Did you say it was along the German border?

C: Yeah.

B: Where do you think they took you?

C: I don't know where they took us. Across the border there was barbed wire. Maybe they marched us into Germany. Or maybe they marched us to Poland.

B: A large number of people?

C: Yeah. Hundreds of people.

B: Were there children, too?

C: There were adults. There were more adults than children. The kids I knew from the orphanage. We all left together.

B: If I ask you what year it was, what comes to mind?

C: 1930s? 1938. I don't know. It's amazing to survive and to be able to come back to teach.

B: (She meant that she has reincarnated into this lifetime and can serve as a teacher in her current life via her book and film writing.)

C: It's very weird. When I'm working on the film there is a fire in the story that always makes me anxious and makes me cry, like a big fire. When I started to edit the film there's a scene where they burn our house down. We went down South, built a house and then they set it on fire.

B: Does it have that same feeling?

C: Yeah. It started the anxiety as I was watching her house and I was watching her reaction to it, and it seemed so real. I had to leave the house. I thought maybe I was having an asthma attack. I had a problem trying to breathe. And then it got worse from there.

B: You described a feeling of the synagogue being burned and people rounded up and there must have been a lot of emotion around that.

C: Yeah. In fact I think I might need a drink—and I don't drink!!

The lessons her soul learned from that end-of-lifetime experience are described in chapter 11.

Courtney's initial past life regression was as an Englishman who accidently killed a woman during a drunken rage. She believes that she may have died in the Holocaust as described above, which was payback for killing someone else. She said it is important to understand the broader purpose of life. Perhaps this belief can be translated as follows: "If a life is taken, there is a burning up or repaying of karma from another lifetime." She thinks karmic retribution is a possibility that makes sense to her.

Originally, Courtney had come to explore PLRT because of her severe, lifelong gastrointestinal attacks, which resulted in her fear of leaving her house for any long periods of time. I thought it was interesting that her symptoms were in the same area where she was shot. That chakra is considered a lower-level chakra symbolized by the color orange, usually indicative of problems with digestion, especially the intestines. The psychological manifestation is the provocation of fear, control issues, sexual or emotional abuse, and the inability to assert oneself. These are all issues that revolve around what she is currently dealing with in her PLRT experiences. Courtney began to experience an increased number of panic attacks.

During the week in-between the regressions, she described a paper clip project she had seen on a television program that she thought was synchronistic with her prior regression. A paper clip was said to represent each person killed during WW II in the Holocaust. Courtney said that she felt that one of the paper clips symbolized her own past life.

Upon her return the following week, she continued this regression.

C: During the Revolution (Russian) I think my aunt seemed pretty well off. My parents weren't so well off. I think she's my mother's sister and my mother died after I was born. I can smell smoke. It's dark. I think I'm going home or I was home, and I just came out onto the street because I could smell the smoke. There's stone houses on the lane and people have their shutters closed.

It feels like France, a little village. I don't know if Mainz or I don't even know if I 'm saying it right. Manes. There are kids on the street with me. We're all kind of trying to figure out, what's going on. It seems like something's not right. Well, the smoke, at first it smelled like fireplace smoke but then it smells like something different. Like a bigger fire. Like other things are burning besides wood. The Northeast side of town. Closer to the border of Germany. It's still a distance, so we're not right on the border.

My aunt and whoever else is in the house wants me to stay inside. She's sort of, not hysterical but she's, it feels like she's overreacting to me. She's not crying or anything, but she's sort of running like in a manic state. Like she's agitated. She's not really crying but she's upset and she's pacing like out of sorts. There's another woman there and she's trying to calm her down. I don't know if she's a close friend. But it seems like she lives in the house as well. She might be a governess. I don't really know her that well. She's always with my aunt. She isn't with me. She's all in black with a little white collar. There's something that I don't have, papers, or something. It's sort of, I don't really exist, if I don't have papers. She wants to leave and she can't leave if I don't have papers.

B: Who do you have to show papers to?

C: Whoever. When you try to leave the country.

She wears very long dresses, so it feels like it could be the early 1930s or the late 20s or early 30s. They're packing a suitcase for me. The governess is trying to...my aunt is really upset, but the governess is trying to be the voice of reason. The plan is they're gonna leave me at a church, and they're going to come back for me. Because they can't cross the border with me, because I don't have papers. They wouldn't be going to Germany. That would be the wrong way to go? Is Prague nearby? Or Switzerland. But she's…I think she's of Russian stock. She's Jewish. I'm Jewish. They take me to a church, and they're kind to me but they just basically pass the buck, and they put me in an orphanage. I'm 12 or 13 years old. I'm there for a while. Know French though.

B: Bring yourself to the *next important time* there and see what happens.

C: It seems like they're teaching us. Like it doesn't seem like it's a Catholic orphanage. It seems like it's a state-run orphanage. Like there is no denomination. Like there aren't nuns there, but they're teaching us stuff. Christian stuff. But the kids are all different. Some of them are Catholics, some Jewish, some of them are Protestant.

I'm resistant to learn the stuff because I'm Jewish. There's a woman there. I think she's Polish. She tells me I have to learn it. Like the Beatitudes. I have to be able to spout the Beatitudes. She's explaining to me why I need to know and I understand it. She's explaining to me what's going on and she's saying that I have to pretend to not be Jewish or I'll be killed.

B: Bring yourself to the *next important time* there and see what happens.

C: Well the soldiers come and we have to pretend like it's not a big deal.

They're looking for Jews. Well, I'm dark, so I don't really fit the Aryan criteria. They don't really single me out, but they just liquidate the orphanage.

B: Where does everybody go?

C: They round up people from town and I'm not sure the orphanage is in the same town. They've rounded up a couple of hundred people, just like regular peasants (immigrants). Some Jewish, some Polish immigrants. Some are Catholic. It's a mixed bag. And they make us walk. Well they say they are taking us to the camp. I think it's in Poland, but it seems like it's way far to walk. All the kids in the orphanage are like misfits. There are a couple of kids who are Jewish but they're hiding one of them. Most of them are sort of immigrants' children. They're just sort of the outcasts. And we just walk for days and days and days.

They take the children, but they don't make the ladies from the orphanage go. I guess they have papers. None of the children really have papers. So what they're doing is they can just erase us and we didn't have papers in the first place, so it wasn't like we were ever there from the start. It's night and like we're camped out and I have this weird feeling that I can go back to heaven. I have this conscious thought, that I can go back to heaven. Like I can make myself go there, without experiencing death. There's an old couple that sort of looks after me. They just take us to a field and they, they tell us to stop and we just stay there. And I have this thought, like I know how the czar felt. It's weird. I'm standing there and I know, I mean they begin shooting at us. And I'm like okay. Well I'm going to go like the czar and his family. And I think about all the girls who were shot in that basement. Anastasia Romanov. We get shot. They just shoot us point blank.

B: As you continue to breathe in and out, I want you to prepare yourself to come back.

C: I'm still a little groggy. I think she knew what was going to happen. It was beyond her control. She didn't know what to do. French is not my first language. Maybe that's the only language I could read. Besides I was home-schooled. I think the woman that tried to teach me in the orphanage was Alice (her current friend). She's a teacher now. English as a second language. She said she went to Dachau to visit and she felt she might have been there during that time. My aunt was Esther (another current friend).

B: Why has everybody come back?

I asked this question in relation to their current lifetimes.

C: A lot of people in my age range have come back. Governess seems to be the reasonable person. Let's not get upset. I think they lived during the Russian Revolution. I think my aunt seemed pretty well off. My parents weren't so well off. I think she's my mother's sister and my mother died after I was born. My mother could've been my mother in this lifetime. Father I don't know.

I read a *New York Times* (2005) article after Courtney's experience describing how Jewish children were hidden during WW II. The people told the children that they were Catholic, hiding the fact from them that they were Jewish. When the Germans were defeated, these same people tried to ensure that the children continued to believe that they were Catholic, perhaps out of their own discrimination. Many of these children weren't aware of their religion since they were too young. (The former US Secretary of State Madeleine Albright found out at the age of 60 that her family was Jewish and that three of her grandparents were killed in German concentration camps.) So Courtney's fears were well-founded when she was asked to deny her heritage even though she realized that was a way to be protected. She was old enough to realize that she was Jewish.

It was necessary for Courtney and me to work using dream analysis, multiple regressions to this past lifetime, and to have long discussions throughout the ongoing sessions in order for her to eventually let go of the fear, tension, and anxiety surrounding this lifetime. The horrific intensity of that experience for a 13-year-old was very shocking for her soul.

While using PLRT with hundreds of people, I found that stuck energy during this lifetime is often the result of their being killed in a violent way in another lifetime. I observed these symptoms in many people who had experienced violent past lifetime deaths who had not experienced any current lifetime events to warrant these reactions. Often, this energy is manifested by symptoms of post-traumatic stress disorder, which needs to be worked out in the current lifetime. Symptoms include the repeated reexperiencing of flashback memories, frightening thoughts and nightmares, chronic panic attacks of unknown origins, or repeating dreams of being chased or tortured.

After Courtney's regression, I researched the area of France where she thought that she had lived. On the map, I saw a town labeled Mainz, which was the French occupation of the Rhineland from the end of WW I through the end of 1930. About seven weeks after Courtney's regression, while reading this regression again, I read a *New York Times* review of a book, *Suite Francaise*, written in 1942. It had been written by a Jewish woman living in German-occupied France before she died when she was taken to Auschwitz at the age of 16. Her wealthy parents escaped from the Soviet Union to France. Her manuscript, originally written in a notebook, was currently on the French bestsellers' list. It received the Renaudot literary prize and was published with wide acclaim. It depicted German-occupied France during that time.

It was striking to me that Courtney had described a similarly wealthy Russian background, had to learn French while living in a German-occupied area of France, and eventually was transported and killed. This shows the ongoing slaughter and relocation of many people within war-torn Europe.

When I cut the article out of the paper, it was not until I stapled it to another piece of paper that I noticed that the top of the page, in reference to the article above, stated, "The historical society expected the 'Jefferson' book to be a blockbuster." There was Courtney's current last name in juxtaposition to this literary article. I interpreted this as one of the many synchronistic events that have occurred while I was using PLRT.

I found it amazing to hear firsthand experiences revolving around the Holocaust depicted by both non-Jewish and Jewish people. Some of the individuals' experiences were so horrific and the screams so bloodcurdling that I felt frightened. In fact, one of the therapists in my office suite wondered what was going on in my office when she heard the screams. I sat through peoples' regressions literally holding my breath, and I felt fearful of some of these experiences.

How do you explain how a non-Jewish person who grew up without any knowledge of the Holocaust or the World War II era can describe experiences during the Holocaust in a simple yet vivid way? Why would anyone reenact such a painful and tortured experience?

The broader message I took from all of this work helped me to understand more clearly each person's path to his or her life purpose. All people have the potential for good as well as the ability to do evil things. Through our anger, we can lash out and say and do terrible things to people, especially when anger and hatred is allowed full rein. We might say that the result can be the "holocaust" of groups of people. This has been demonstrated in our treatment of African Americans, Native Americans, Jews, homosexuals, and other minorities throughout the world. Systematic physical and psychological holocausts remain.

The information that continues to emanate from the hundreds of past life regressions is that some souls choose to reincarnate in situations of atrocities and natural disorders during this lifetime in order to provide a lesson for broader humanity. One nurse stated that she had experienced a lifetime as a person with cerebral palsy in a mental institution in order to serve as a lesson for health-care professionals. While living during these situations, most people are not usually aware of the pact that they made prior to entering this lifetime.

If a Black man in Jasper, Texas is dragged to his death behind a pickup truck by three young White men, or a young man in Montana is killed because he is homosexual, or nine Black lives are lost in a senseless killing while praying in a South Carolina church by a young White man, something continues to be wrong within our current consciousness. Unfortunately, we have not learned enough from the millions of people who were systematically and brutally massacred during the Holocaust. What does demonstrate growth within our culture is the tremendous outrage by the broader culture and the immediate punishment of those involved. We cannot afford to continue our belief of "my country right or wrong" and must be part of a humanity that rights the wrongs. Inherent within the belief in reincarnation is the concept of the soul's evolution, which allows us to learn some lessons from these experiences.

The preeminent Nobel Peace Laureate, author, and Holocaust survivor Elie Wiesel gave an eloquent speech on 1/24/05 at the UN Assembly on the sixtieth anniversary of the Nazi camps' liberation.

He said, "I am convinced if the world had listened to those of us who tried to speak, we may have prevented Darfur, Cambodia, Bosnia, and naturally, Rwanda. The Jewish witness that I am speaks of my people's suffering as a warning."

The issue for UN member states is whether they have the will to stop further genocide, which is currently manifested by the genocide in Syria.

What was so powerful about this commemoration is that for many years, the Soviet Union blocked any efforts to condemn anti-Semitism. And, in fact, in 2003, a General Session resolution condemning anti-Semitism was withdrawn because of Muslim and Arab opposition.

Kofi Anan was the first Secretary General to recognize the Jewish people as the primary victim of the Holocaust.   He stated, "We must be on the watch for any revival of anti-Semitism and ready to act against the new forms of it that are appearing today; that obligation binds us to all others that have been, or may be, threatened with a similar fate."

Auschwitz survivors at a sixtieth anniversary ceremony commemorating the Auschwitz death camp liberation in a Berlin theater heard Chancellor Gerhard Schroeder express shame about the Nazi-era horrors. "I express my shame in the face of those who were murdered—and, above all, to you who survived the hell of the concentration camps."

Schroeder acknowledged that the regime of Adolph Hitler had wide support from Germans, but promised that his country would always try to keep the memory of the Holocaust alive. "The overwhelming majority of Germans living today bear no guilt for the Holocaust, but they do bear a special responsibility. We need to remember how individuals under threat of their own lives stood up and helped people in need. So when we talk about the Holocaust, we must also pay tribute to the thousands of people that saved others' lives."

As I read people's PLRT transcripts once again, it continues to amaze me. I can vividly hear each person's description and feel the poignancy of those lifetimes. They do not recount lifetimes as Cleopatra or a lifetime of frivolity. In fact, none of my clients remembered coming back as a former celebrity, for example, Napoleon, Mozart, or Plato. Every regression has not been a violent one, as they have ranged from mildly interesting to an extreme of emotion. However, all participants were able to integrate the findings into their current life situation and recognize that they have contributions to make in this lifetime in order to affect change.

The result for each individual has been purposeful and enhanced his or her own life. That they were individually able to make changes within their own psyches and lifestyles is an amazing fact on its own. In my own mind and psyche, these experiences that people entrusted to me have also benefitted me, too.

9

Healing Experiences

"There are two ways to spread the light. Be a candle or the light that reflects."

~ANONYMOUS

A young woman whom I had worked with many years ago using traditional psychotherapy had decided to return to explore some unresolved issues surrounding her mother's recent death. Debra knew that I was using PLRT and she was interested in using that modality for exploration. She told me that she had felt her mother's "presence" surrounding her even as she lay dead in her hospital bed. In fact, she said that she felt that her mother's presence continued to permeate the room where the funeral ceremony took place. Debra believes that her mother's energy surrounds her all of the time. As an only child, she had maintained a close and loving relationship with her mother even though they lived a great distance apart. Debra never had any prior spiritual experiences.

Throughout our discussions surrounding her mother's death, I shared with Debra some experiences described to me by the explorers of the hundreds of PLRT sessions I had facilitated. I told her about people's reports of time-of-death experiences during their regressions. They had talked about being "out of their body" as they had watched their deathbed scene surrounded by relatives and their subsequent funeral. Most people described to me their experiences of joy at being on "the other side" and happy to be out of their disabled bodies. One woman had described the human body as a suit of armor covering the soul. Debra told me that she had found these descriptions of other people's experiences to be very comforting as she recognized the universality of these occurrences. She now wanted to explore her own past life regression experience.

As she went into a trance, Debra saw herself as a little girl feeling the wonderful times that she had enjoyed with her mother. That brought a smile to her face. The following emerged:

D: I feel like I'm in my 20s, wearing a hat with horns on it. Wearing rags, furs, and a spear. I'm a guy. I think I got lost and left by myself and to fend by myself. It's very dark. I have to get out of the cave. I have to get food and water. But it's dark. I have a feeling I'm looking up at the stars, clouds.

B: When I count to three, come to the next important place. One, two, three. Be there now and see what you see.

D: Terrible waves, tides, big waves. There's a storm and it's black and everything is swirling around. It's a very bad storm—like a hurricane— swirling around. I think I get caught in it on a boat. I'm a man—a captain. Looking like Vikings. I have a Prince Charles haircut.

B: Bring yourself to the time of your death and see what you see.

D: There's more light and it's not so dark.

B: What are the messages from above for you?

D: Don't get so stressed out. It's all going to be okay.

B: When I count to three, come back to your current life, alert and focused and vibrant.

D: I was quite an adventurer. Another time back farther. Old reality world. I also saw my mom when I was young. She was happy and loved having a little girl. The cave had hieroglyphics. I'm a loner kind of person. I'm an only child.

This experience reminded Debra of her warm feelings and sense of adventure that she had shared with her mother. Debra talked through her experiences about feeling alone and lost after her mother's death. At the same time, she acknowledged that she is also an adventurer in this lifetime. She believes in the ongoing individual's soul experiences, feeling that she is surrounded by her mother's spirit. Debra was able to come to a healing place in relation to her mother's death. The healing occurred for her throughout our discussions and her past life regression, which lasted for a few sessions.

Was this a real past life regression or a metaphor for her current life experiences and memories, surrounding her life with memories of her mother while learning how to continue her own life without her? The important outcome was her ability to heal her feelings around her mother's death.

Theresa is a young woman who has a problem standing up for herself in all aspects of her life. As she went into a trance, she described a "Cleopatra-headed" lady. She talked about the phoenix bird with wide eyes that see things. She described this as gold with light coming from behind and an Egyptian eye with a symbol. Theresa saw different Egyptian symbols.

T: I see a guy—two people. It's an Egyptian slave master whipping a young pregnant woman. She's trying to explain. I think he is me. He's doing his job. He doesn't want to be whipping her but his job is to get them to work. His boss looks like Yul Brunner. She's supposed to cooperate. The boss is my mother. Wearing a headdress—beige and it fans out. A dress shirt thing with leather thongs—leather sandal thongs.

B: What is his name?

T: Ahmet—1639 or 1613 or 1669.

B: Where are you?

T: Egypt. I think the girl is my brother. Doesn't surprise me. If I don't listen he'll kill me.

B: How do they do that?

T: Put in places to starve or stab. I don't want to die or take a stand, and die anyway. I'm typically known as a nice slave master, but she has a big mouth. My wife is at the table. I hate this. It goes against everything I am. I think I'm trapped in the pyramids, for being bad. Am I rotting in cement? I'm 19 years old. Being in a block of cement. I don't see any struggle. I have this drowning fear.

B: Where does the soul go?

T: Spirit moves up in dark blue sky. I see someone holding a baby. People are in Wyoming—1940.

She then proceeds to describe another vision, which is a Wyoming reenactment.

B: What's the message to get from this?

T: That work doesn't have to be a bad thing. This life I farm wheat and get up early. I don't know who I am. The sun comes up early I feed the chickens. We eat breakfast together and I died in 1959. A rake went through my eye—an accident. Mother and father are Alice and Bob. I said I have to have some drama in my next life. The important message for me is, don't judge, love yourself, enjoy the joys, relax, know what you want to do, have a plan with a goal. Be a good man. Maybe I was crushed in a farm machine. Don't look for trouble—don't be an instigator. "I'm a closet instigator in this life."

Theresa listened intently to the messages, which she believes would be good for her to follow. She thinks this will help her to heal her current feelings about feeling unjustly treated and a fear of speaking up. It is important that she stand up for herself without fearing that it will result in her death. She felt so much better after that past life regression experience and said that she would try to implement a new way of handling her current life experiences.

When Leslie came to explore her feelings of, "I don't get what I deserve," she described feeling that she was being unfairly treated.

L: I'm looking down and I just seem to see I'm in a robe. I'm not really sure. It's like a monk's robe and/or covering. I think I'm barefoot with my head down, with other people dressed the same way. We're walking single file. I'm feeling that hopeless feeling. I don't know if we're being taken somewhere. I feel we're kind of. I'm going to start crying again. I think we're going to be taken somewhere. Think we're going to go into the pyramid, and we're going to go in there to die, because I think our king has died, and we're part of the people to be put in the tomb. It is an honor to be part of the people to be put in the tomb. It is an honor to one and that it's a mixed thing. An honor. People say this is an honor to be picked to do it and I don't want to die. I don't think I want to die. Also somebody has to go and most of us are peasants and poor people.

Not like anyone has a choice. People are just picked. Guards walking. It's pretty frightening. Getting closer and closer to the door. I'm trying to figure out. The vision. We're going in and when we get in, like people in the inside are very upset.

The rooms. People start crying and wailing and angry. All of us that are being put in there. Yeah a lot of us. Room—30 people surrounded in there, and a horrible feeling like we're buried alive, and we can't get out, and what to do. This is it. And there are still more people coming. Starting to get rebellious. Not enough space and they keep sending them in. People try to run out and guards say stay in, as something is at the door. More people trying to get in.

So they try to decide whether to close the doors. People are upset because they are inside. Guards are there. No one wants this. I don't know what to do. I want to get out too. Not sure if I'm a man or a woman. So they decide to close the door and now I'm really angry. And a lot of us are really angry and we can't do anything. Sitting there with people crying—getting angry. There's absolutely nothing I can do so I sit and it's almost like an acceptance of the situation and just let things happen in the way they're going to happen. Feel sad. The people outside sad.

I think I'm a man and there's a man with a wife and child. Doesn't make sense. A young man who could be helping the community. I shouldn't be in there. I'm looking around. There aren't a lot of young men in there; I think I was chosen because I was a problem. I spoke up, about how the things that were going on, were ridiculous. *To put people in.* So this was an opportunity for them to get rid of me.

The king was an older man. Died of old age and like a King Tut-type. Egypt/desert/pyramids but not people dressed in gold. Peasants. Raggedy clothes. I just sit there, and like I don't want to go any further because it's just death. People are deteriorating and dying. I'm going to wither away and watch everyone else wither away, and that is all for my standing up for myself. Got me into a bad situation. Couldn't do any better. Try just to be myself and not a bad person and wind up where I am. And people who play it safe are able to reap the benefits of society and stay with their family. *It upsets me because* (shouting) I couldn't be different. Upsets me it couldn't be safer. I think after days/ a week, think I'm going to die. I'm weak and died. I feel I feel *sad*. I should've done something very different. In the end everything was very nice. Enjoyed the family. *Would've been better to be quiet and stayed with the family. Accept that I did the best I could.*

Leslie's past life regression affirmed her current fears about speaking up or being negative as that lifetime resulted in a long, slow death. This experience piqued her interest since it was directly related to her concerns about speaking up and holding in her anger. She was able to get out her anger as she described this reenactment and was able to experience her feelings in a metaphorical way. As a result of this reenactment, and since she experienced herself standing up for what she believed, she feels that she will now be more assertive.

Theresa's and Leslie's experiences, which occurred in the late 1990s, seemed unusual to me. I had never heard of this practice of burying people alive either as a punishment or an honor when members of royalty had died. I was not able to find any information about this practice of people being placed within a tomb to be punished. Both of these experiences occurred with people who had no knowledge of Egyptian burial practices.

To my surprise, a March 2004 *New York Times* article reported new findings describing the practice of people being entombed when a member of royalty died. It was entitled, "With Escorts to the Afterlife, Pharaohs Proved Their Power." This revealed archeological excavations that recovered the remains of human sacrifices. According to Dr. David O' Connor of NYU Institute of Fine Arts, "The practice of human sacrificial burials in Egypt, presumably to coincide with the pharaoh's own funeral, had long been suspected but never substantiated." There was a shift in religious thinking, reflected by the power of the king, to force people to be present with him in the afterlife. These two past life reenactments took place 6 and 10 years prior to this new information on sacrificial burials by people who had no current lifetime knowledge of Egypt or past practices.

Iris is a pretty young woman who does not think she is attractive. She is spiritual, and her life revolves around healing practices. Returning after her experience with chronic bronchitis and food binging as described in chapter 7, she wanted to address her terrible habit of picking at her face. She described spending hours in front of the mirror, picking at her skin. Her next regression is as follows:

I: I don't see anything. It's very dark. I'm looking at a narrow passageway. Wearing a long cottony drapey (sic) thing with a shawl over my head, hooded, not covering my face.

B: What are you doing there?

I: Feel like I'm being chased by—a man. Being chased, like they're running up the hill after me. I think I have a beard and I think I'm trying to decide, whether going through this crack is more dangerous. I think they'd kill me. I think I decide to go in—a very narrow passageway. Opens up to a cave—bones of humans and animals. Shafts of light. Very murky to me now. I don't think there's a way out. I don't know what to do.

A sandy floor kind of a cave, with small opening at top lets light in. Skeletons all around sitting up like cuffs and chains around their necks, like some place to die for prisoners.

I think it's the Middle East. Iraq/Iran. I am dark skinned. But not Black. Suntanned. Arabic features. Thin nose. 649 AD. I think I hear people taunting me from outside. He can choose where you want to die. No way. I feel like I'm looking down at my hands. They have blood on them. Perhaps I hurt somebody. Think—a woman. A very beautiful woman with beautiful black hair, colorful shawl and a headband. Jewelry with pretty medallions hanging over her forehead. They're beautiful big eyes. That were like Larry (her current ex-boyfriend) caramel brown. I think she lied or did something to me. Because she's so beautiful and everyone wanted to be with her. I must've killed her. I loved her very much. Did she love me? I think so—she was my wife. I don't think we had any children. I think she slept with someone else.

I see a shadowy figure in a doorway. A guy she slept with? Perhaps she says she's going to leave me. I am too difficult and too demanding. I think what my options are. Either way I'm going to die. Go outside and be murdered. Somehow I think I stay in the cave. I die by a spear plunging into my chest by someone else. I try before I die to crawl out. I feel my fingernails and tips tearing around the ceiling. A weapon in that room, or I go outside and someone stabs me.

I think her name was Leila. She was so beautiful and young. My name is Iran. An Arabic place. The village is observable from top of the hill where the cave is. Everything is white. Sand dunes made into clay for buildings. Simple flat roof. One- or two-story buildings. It's the desert again. When I die, I see the area where the cave is on the top and a crowd of people outside and (where the) village was and light.

B: Where does the soul go?

I: I go up and see my beloved. This woman that I killed. She is being carried by her family. Lots of wailing. I feel so sorry. I should've let her go.

B: Time-of-death thoughts?

I: I had no right to take her life and mar her beauty. I've not been allowing myself to be beautiful. Especially her skin, is so beautiful. I feel that I don't have the right to…I took it from her. It's still difficult to let go of her. I think it's me, and my ex-boyfriend. It's his birthday today and I think we will be really bound. This is not the only life we have been close. In this lifetime, he was a profoundly jealous person. He was in that life. Maybe it served to remind me of jealous karma. We were mirrors in this life of each other's worst stuff.

B: What's the most important thing to bring back into this life?

I: In a way I feel I can heal her, by healing me. It's so risk loaded for me to heal my soul. To clean the blood off her face. To allow for my skin to take care of itself, and heal on its own magically across the ages and help heal her too. And I'm ready to do this because I don't have a right to have beauty, because I used a knife to mark her face. I think we've all killed others. To feel what it feels like.

After the regression, Iris affirmed her belief that no one has the right to take another person's life or her beauty. Because of this, she believes that she has no right to be beautiful herself. Her current lifetime punishment is that her face cannot be beautiful, especially her skin. Iris said that the blood on her hands came from scarring the woman's face, perhaps with a knife. So her current face picking is a self-inflicted retribution. She said that she cannot believe that she did that to another person.

I have to report that her intensity and vivid description of this event are very real and palpable. The many experiences that people had told me about confirm my belief in reincarnation. There was no motivation for people to describe such horrific experiences.

Iris is a Reiki practitioner. Reiki is an ancient Japanese hands-on healing technique and is an alternative healing modality. It is based on the belief of Universal Life Energy, or spiritual energy, which is channeled through the Reiki practitioner. This modality heals the client's spirit, which then heals the physical body. By using this practice on herself, Iris believes that she can heal her face and that it will make Leila's face beautiful again, too. This obviously is not a rational idea.

Iris subsequently decided to explore other issues, so she returned for further PLRT. She reported that she was no longer picking at her face. What drove her to seek this current past life regression experience were her feelings of being physically stuck from her waist to her midcalf. A result was her current sexual relations problems with her partner. She feels that she has invisible damage, and the words that spontaneously come up for her when she thinks about this issue are *"fear, anger, sex, intimacy, surrender, control, despair,* and *freedom."* This has caused problems within her marriage, and she is searching for the origins. Iris wants to be able to feel her lower body and equates sex with pain.

I: I wonder if my mind is playing tricks on me. I see dark, nighttime, a city, it feels like London. Wet streets. Walking down the street and don't know if I'm a man or a woman. Kind of a dark street with alleys to the right and left. Feels like cobblestone. An occasional street lamp casting a light. I feel like the me, now, does not want to see this.
(*She's taking a deep breath.*)

Ahhh. I have a feeling that I'm a woman wearing a coat, and long dress with layers of clothing, because it's cool out. I walk down the street and see in a distance a pub and men loitering. And I have to walk past them. Don't quite know how to do it without attracting attention. I shouldn't be out and about at night. Don't know why I'm out and I'm afraid, and I flash to them taunting me, and badgering me. I end up in the alley with all of those men. I see my white skin, my face and see my legs.

She was so distraught during the regression that I talked to her so that she could leave the situation. I said to her, "Go to the next important event in that lifetime, one, two, three…. Be there now and see what you see."

I: What I saw before. It was kind of a gang rape situation. I don't know how many men went inside of me. They were laughing and there was blood. At least a couple of them who wouldn't take part. I flashed to somebody picking me up in a dark suit. Maybe a policeman.
(*She begins crying.*)

They may be taking me to a hospital or something. Feels like there's blood on the sheets. I have dark hair. I think I'm pretty torn up and I don't know if anybody came to visit me. Is it because I'm alone? Or they're ashamed or I'm ashamed. I don't think I was a prostitute. I was pretty demure.

B: What is your name?

I: Sarah

B: What year is this?

I: 1900s or 1800s or turn of the century.

B: Do you have a family?

I: A grandmother.

B: Do you work?

I: I work in the bookstore.

B: How old are you?

I: I am 19 years old?

B: Bring yourself back to the time of your death in that lifetime.

I: I feel like I'm not allowed to go there. I don't know where I am right now. I wonder if I die in the hospital or live long. I go through many lifetimes of mistrust.

B: Anyone there that you know today?

I: Gerald was the policeman. (He is her current husband). It feels like a group of men. I'm easy to tear in this lifetime. I think I didn't die but I think I never had a relationship. I was shredded. I could never have children. I grew up around books and I get really hard and cold. I love reading books today. I get a lot of solace from them.

Iris visualized herself struggling and yelling and saying, "I can't get them to stop; how do I get back into my body?" She saw herself on the outside of her body, watching the inhumanity of the situation. The upper part of her body was being bathed in cooler colors. This regression was violent, graphic, and she was crying and thrashing. However, Iris reported that she felt 95% better the next day. She did not understand this experience since she had never been raped in this life. Iris questions how she can physically unblock herself and feel free without fear of pain and death. Since the core of the problem was based on a past lifetime experience, if she and her husband had gone for sex therapy, it still might not have helped the problem.

Then I helped her work with healing colors as follows:

B: What color can you visualize surrounding you in order for you to be healed?

I: Red, since all of the blood that spilled out of me had to be returned.

She began to feel feelings "opening up" in the lower part of her body, and her upper body was "seeing and hearing things" that happened during that time. Iris wrote to me after the session to let me know that all of her problems became unblocked after this past life regression experience. I found it astonishing that this reenactment allowed her body to awaken. This resulted in her being sexually spontaneous, highlighting the importance of the mind-body-spirit integration.

After Eric's past life regression experience in which he was shown that he could be a healer, he quietly scanned my body without telling me. The only thing he could find wrong was within my left wrist. He told me that there was too much calcium in the wrist. I told him that I had been taking calcium/magnesium supplements, but my muscles felt sore from a lot of writing. Perhaps I might have picked up something too heavy, which resulted in a strain.

Eric held out his hand and asked that I put my hand on his. Then he put his other hand on top of mine. He let the energy flow as he talked of breaking up the crystals. After a few minutes, the discomfort in my wrist disappeared. I was then able to write four straight pages of his regression material without any further problem. I believe he totally healed my wrist of all discomfort. I am typing this after two days of writing without any wrist discomfort. He does not believe me! Is the message from this experience for me to believe or for him to realize that he has more abilities that he is willing to recognize—or both?

Martha is a young woman who wanted to explore PLRT for her chronic inability to take care of herself. This was manifested in her lack of awareness of her own needs. She could take care of other people but had tremendous guilt and chronic sadness that something was wrong with her. She believes in spirituality and that things happen for a reason.

B: Picture a path of any kind, a path that can take you back.

M: Trees and grass and a band of men on chained horses. I guess they're going to battle. Metal breastplates, helmets and chain nail on big strong horses.

B: Are you part of this group?

M: I don't know. I watch from the road. I think they ride past me. I'm a little peasant. I'm torn whether to go with them or go back home. I go in the direction of the horses. Ripped pants—too short. Beaten old shoes. I'm small. I'm a boy 8 years old. Walking and climbing up in trees to see where they are. They're stopping and met another party. The knights from the castle. I gave them apples once in a while, and I love their metal.

(*She makes a grimacing face while in a trance.*)

B: What's wrong?

M: I don't know.

(*She is twisting and moving her hands.*)

M: I think there's a young woman with them. I don't know but she had a beautiful dress. I think she's a prisoner of them and she doesn't want to be there. I don't know if they're pulling at her. I think I'm shocked, because they're not supposed to be like that. I think they're raping her. I don't understand what's going on. I want to climb down the tree and run away and I want to help her too. And I'm just a boy, and I think they'll kill me if they know what I saw and she's crying.

(*Martha is crying and playing with her ring as she is describing this scene.*)

I sat behind the tree trying to figure out what to do.

B: What's happening?

M: Her cries are sort of a whisper now.

B: What's happening?

M: I go over the stone wall and run through the field. A man working in the field. I tell him what's happening, but he doesn't seem surprised. He tells me to be quiet and go home. It's the *law of the land*. It's just how it is. I start going home. I'm in shock. In town, a shop sign, bakery or shoe. And there's a knight out front with a flag (wearing the same clothes). I don't know if I can tell him. I thought they were all good. What if he knows and he doesn't care too? I don't say anything. He gives me a coin and pats me on the head. I feel bad because *I've chosen my safety over that girl twice!* I leave the soldier.

I think I'm in the shop and related to these people. Darkened wood and sit there and look at the coin and I feel really bad. The old guy who works there (Uncle) calls me Mikey. I can't tell him either, because he'll tell someone and get in trouble also. It feels terrible. You have to make a vow to tell no one. A boy, but you have to protect everyone from the truth. Do I stay and help Uncle work, or do I walk and think?

B: One, two, three. Go to the *next important* place. Be there now and see what you see.

M: I think there's a church but I'm 13 now. I always wanted to be a knight, and now I don't want to. I help Uncle deliver things from the store.

B: Go to the time of your death and see what happens.

M: Just that I'm defending someone. I think I die by the sword but I don't know how. (*In the left-upper quadrant under the rib cage*).

When I asked "him" what happens to the soul at the time of death, "he" said it goes up in front of the tribunal. (This is written about in depth in chapter 11.)

This was a horrific experience for a little boy whose innocence was shattered as he was disillusioned by seeing his heroes for whom they really were. He was tightly bound to keep the secret out of fear.

During this lifetime, Martha continues to carry this fear as she maintains her practice of standing up for other people sometimes to her own detriment. Through this very powerful experience, she could see her current dilemma very clearly and recognize the need to take care of herself in a healthier way. She recognized how her long-time need for caring for other people derives from this prior lifetime when she didn't speak up. This was a very cathartic and healing experience for Martha who gained a greater perspective of herself as she realized how she deals with stressful issues.

In a pre-Civil War life, Josepha revealed herself as a southern belle, attending a ball and wearing hoop skirts. She described how she was flicking her fan and dancing. She loved to dance!

J: I felt free when I was dancing. My father was a wealthy tobacco plantation owner who lost everything. My spirit was broken as the lifestyle was no longer there. *You need the spirit to be free...have to hold onto it and keep it precious.*

Josepha died in her 20s of a plague or swamp fever and said, "The spirits have to teach me in the spirit world how to hold the spirit." She described the spirit as charged-up, like a battery, so you can feel it and keep it. Josepha called it a training course, a seminar. It helps if you can feel it or remember. "You have to keep the radiance. It's hard because everyone wants to keep you down. It's good when you're around other light beings, like meeting spirit."

To date, she is a person who is very psychic. She wears the sense of spirit about her with everyone whom she is involved with. One of her usual sayings to this day is, *"Be radiant!"* This past life regression reminded her to keep the spirit and the light despite all odds in order to help herself through some very trying times.

A young man, Robert, who was exploring his spiritual path came to me looking for answers surrounding his sexual abuse at the hands of his stepfather. It had caused him tremendous grief. In fact, it was the impetus for him to seek a spiritual path. His fear of intimacy in his relationships is not surprising since he was violated by a paternal figure—someone he loved and trusted. He feels that in some way, it is his fault as he felt that "I must have done something wrong." These are typical feelings described by some childhood sufferers of sexual abuse whose lives include lifetime feelings of shame, often described with the words, "I must have done something wrong."

As an explorer of Buddhist beliefs, Robert was open to the idea of reincarnation. In fact, he thought that he had been killed by a woman he knows who was a prostitute in his past lifetime. He said he felt that he had been an abusive, cruel, mean man in the Old West and that he had abused prostitutes. He believed he had been stabbed to death while asleep in that life by a woman he had raped.

During the regression, he saw his relationship with this woman unfold during the 1800s. He saw that she had a 5-year-old daughter. She tells him that he was mean to this little child. He instantly realizes he sexually abused the child, which is why the mother wants him to leave. As he described his death during the regression, I could see his body physically twitching on the couch where he was lying.

When I asked him what there was to learn from that lifetime, he said, "I must be respectful. I mustn't use power to get what I want." He said he hit the child; he didn't realize how needy a child is. "I was afraid I'd have to take care of it. I need to learn to love and respect and love and protect others. *I may have abused her sexually, which is why she was upset with me!*"

The goal for Robert is to learn how to transform his power to positive actions and to respect the equality of all people. He was able to understand his lack of respect and abuse of power. Now, he felt elated and freed up because of this reenactment. This was a very healing experience for him since he understands the nature of burning up bad karma and healing from his wounds. He was able to look at this regression in a more productive way as his belief in Buddhist teachings allowed him to have so much more compassion and love for himself.

I want to stress that it is important for people not to interpret their own current sexual abuse as a punishment for sexual abuse that happened in another lifetime. This is only one person's experience and is individual to each person. People who have been sexually abused in this lifetime may be present during this lifetime to learn other lessons and should not attribute their sexual abuse to bad karma. This is not to validate anyone's sexual abuse or say that it was caused as a punishment for some past life experience.

When Bonnie came to see me, she was complaining that her apartment was very chaotic with magazines and papers strewn throughout. Was her apartment reflecting her internally disordered world? She believed that she had an underlying problem that perhaps could be explained by a past life-time experience.

As she entered the trance state, she describes the following:

BO: A cave—it's dark. I guess I'm hiding. I don't know. It's a very bare existence—like the edge of survival—just like the bare essentials. Not comfortable. I found things like…someone else's garbage…candles, paper. A fountain pen or a quill pen? Some skins—some animal skins—to lay on and lay under. It's very isolating—feet have sandals on. Leather-raggy (sic) things. Swatches of cloth wrapped around my head. I think I'm a man. I don't know if I'm in danger or if I want to live this way. In Europe somewhere—1856. It's about hoarding because you may need it. You never pass up anything. *Never.* Take it into the cave. You can use it for something…you may need it…even just for comfort and warmth…or something to look at or something to keep you from going crazy.

B: Bring yourself to the time of your death.

BO: This person was distorted physically. The body is deformed—not straight. Crooked in some way. He becomes a recluse. Because when he's alone he doesn't get stared at and humiliated and felt sorry for. There are no reactions to him if he is alone and there are no mirrors. This person tried to write thoughts and feelings to help him. To give him clarity and to help him keep his sanity. He wanted to leave something…he left it. At his time of death he died by a snake bite right at the foot of the cave. In the calf. He was crawling and gathering brush and he knew right away it was going to be bad. He is frightened and he wishes he could be with someone.

(*She screws up her face while in the trance and continues.*)

BO: The sadness. He tries to burn the air with a candle but he starts to feel funny. Starts to lose sensation and (she screws up her face again) he can't breathe—he suffocates. He goes out like the candle. He's dead. He can look at himself—this beautiful person.

After the regression, Bonnie said, "It seemed so poignant to me. I feel like I really went deep this time." She said it was hard for her to take care of herself because she lives alone. Four days after the session, she worked hard and cleaned up the whole apartment. She was able to do it in an efficient manner for hours and hours. She got enough done to feel satisfied with herself. All that had been covering the floor was gone. Bonnie threw out large amounts of magazines and newsletters. She believed that the need to hold onto information was a desperate attempt to have something to read when she wanted it. Bonnie feels that now she is able to take control and take care of herself.

PLRT is an intricate process. People learned how to identify a problem or concern, and they were then able to work through the feelings surrounding an event that had kept them stuck and fearful. It is important to weave and integrate the material gleaned from this process by coalescing it into people's current life experiences and beliefs. As a result, problems are healed, and people can become more aware of their spirituality and life purpose while opening their hearts. The mind-body-spirit integration is critical for the integrity of a healthy person.

10

Integration of Multiple Regression Experiences Into Current Life Experiences

"Everything on the earth has a purpose.
Every disease, an herb to cure it.
Every person, a mission.
This is the Indian theory of existence."

~Mourning Dove Salish, 1888-1936

My work continued with many people who had individually experienced multiple regressions. Some have relived over a dozen to more than 20 past lifetimes. In fact for some, it was their primary therapeutic modality. I believe that the depth of their inner experiences, which was a result of their reenactments, led them to resolve their chronic problems. They also achieved a deeper sense of relaxation.

During one of his many past life regressions, Eric narrated a very shocking event that was totally unlike any of his present-life experiences. He described how his "spirit guides" helped him endure an unpleasant lifetime.

E: I see pumpkin-colored houses. Frank is my brother. He's abnormally large and he has some sort of business. Like a blacksmith sign says "Frank's." I can't figure out who I am. I see a man. Is it me in a very Louis IV overcoat, pilgrim-type shoes, leotard, long white hair and thin-rimmed glasses like a Ben Franklin? My name is Aubrey Celeste. The store sign says, "Established 1789."

I'm stuck on the same block where the dentist is. I hear a clip-clop of horse-drawn carriages. Still see Frank's blacksmith shop—1763. I still see this person. A very evil feeling. He's overweight with long hair like Ben Franklin. A big nasty-looking smile, looks crooked. Wearing knickers with white stockings and Pilgrim-type shoes and a jacket. All done-up everyday clothing for that time. He tells Frank he's going to the office. He's very evil.

The "me," from the New Orleans plantation life (as described on p. 42) and a "healer" are with me. Are they spirit guides? Because they know. I don't want to deal with this. They each got me by one arm, and hold me up to see the office. It's dark and dank, with apothecary bottles and instruments. They cause people a lot of pain. He seems to enjoy it and while women are "out" uses ether and molests them. He's just mean and nasty. He molests a lot of them. He's a real degenerate.

They say that I can't be responsible for what "he" did to these people. He went out at night and hurt people. It's hard to say, he's always probing people. He knocks them out. He probes but looks like a doctor. Puts a finger in their orifices like a doctor and not enjoying it. They tell me mostly not to blame myself, for what he did to these people. I have been clenching my teeth at night. They tell me not to feel bad, but I do feel bad.

B: Eric, go to your time of death in that lifetime and see what happens.

E: I see the dentist in a jail cell; he's old. He says it's a mistake and was not him. He got found out and he's saying it was a mistake. A crowd of people outside the jail. I'm trying to see how he dies. I see him sitting in the jail cell. A feeling that he was mentally insane. He just followed his dark side. He could have fought it. He was too weak and lazy. You don't have to do the things your father does."

The guide who was a healer in another lifetime says to me, "You have the potential to be like me." They ask me if I can let go. I say better than before. I feel sorry for the guy. A part of me…I can forgive him. They say it's not my job to forgive him and then motions to me. He gets hanged. The soul is circling around where he is hanging.

Looks like the other soul from the Louisiana lifetime, mentioned now, is in an old gravesite, with a round headstone. Aubrey is trying to read the headstone, 42 or 52 years of age. It is a wasted life to hurt people. It's more like having the victims forgive me, and say it's OK. They gather in front of me. They're saying it's not your fault. We know what you do for the children. We don't have to forgive you. We all have bad thoughts. I wish I could heal to make up for what I did. I just want to heal. They say to me, "You will, you will." I say thank you, and walk through the crowd to try to pick my head up. They want to show me something. They tell me to look now. I'm on a different side. It's very dark. I'm looking down. I'm not afraid of the height. They're not going to throw me in. They laugh, and there's a cloud of smoke below, and something springs out and the clouds are separating, with a space in the middle. A woman is holding a baby and she is saying, "Christian, look at daddy," and a vision of me standing at the Academy at the podium, with a nice house with a garden.

They are showing me what will be for me in the future. Will I be able to love anybody? And they show me healing a little girl. They say there will be much more for you and then they take me back and say to me, now, this is your good side.

It is 1473. They show me as a healer walking down a winter roadside. People revere him. They run to him and touch his robe and hands. He has a cross on a vestment, white over red white bib-cross, red trimmed with gold, a clean-shaven head and bangs like a St. Anthony statue. But the nose is flatter, and rounder face. Thin build and as he walks people touch his robes and hands.

My spirit guide walks to someone and tells me to watch. A person with a crippled hand. He strokes it and moves it, turns it, strokes arm and guy is now moving his hand. And he bends down and kisses his feet. The healer says to me, "This is what you're capable of doing." He walks to me and says, "You can no longer inflict pain on yourself. I'm not going to baby you anymore. This has to stop." He is face-to-face with me and becomes part of me. That he and I are one. White light all around me. His hands outstretched. I see him in front of me. "I've given you part of me, to take care of you." To do this they say, "Go with love." It's time for me to come back.

They realized I was dwelling on the bad things that happened. With the insane person, the only way to get me back, was for me to be healed and be a healer. So I wouldn't have to feel guilty, through their giving me tough love. My father in this life has a lot of insanity in his family. Unless they gave me something extra, I was not going to recover. If I was able to heal people, it would make up for that lifetime. Like my purpose in life is to heal and have a desire to do it, because of what happened in a previous life, even if the people forgave me.

Eric was so shocked at this episode of being an *evil dentist!* However, I had been working with him for a period of time and I recognized that the experiences he described were totally unlike him. In fact, this was totally out of character as he is a very religious man and very accommodating to members of his abusive family. I could not understand this. Perhaps he was atoning for his past sins. His reference to the children describes his generous donations of money and toys to a children's hospital in this, his current lifetime. When he died in that lifetime, he told me that it was very healing for him to feel the energy pouring out from the people. As he reported this session, it made me believe in the overwhelming power of forgiveness.

Through people's reports of their past life regression sessions, I was able to more clearly understand the soul's journey through different lifetimes. It would have been easier for me to understand if the person reenacting these experiences had a degenerative lifestyle in the current lifetime. I told Eric that I had thought that perhaps he came into this lifetime to atone for these previous sins. He thinks that is a valid point. Throughout our in-depth discussions about this past life regression lifetime, which we compared to his current lifetime situations, Eric said that he now believes that to be a very good possibility. Maybe his abusive family situation in his current lifetime is also karmic payback that will allow him to feel what it is like to be on the receiving side of abuse. He finally said that he believes his current lifetime purpose is discerning between love and abuse. Most important is the message that he takes away from these experiences.

During Eric's next past life regression session, he was shown by his spirit guides, who appeared in all of his previous incarnations, how he could integrate the lessons to be learned from those lifetimes into his current life. All the people he had access to in his prior regressions came forward for him to see. They included: the plantation landowner who killed himself over the death of his wife and young daughters; the monk who was a healer; Red, an easy-going, well-liked guy living in the 1940s who was accidentally shot and killed in a restaurant; and the Samurai, who was killed on the path by a non-Samurai. The Samurai's spirit said to him: "You're a great warrior; remember your skills as a warrior." Eric told me that he had forgotten how to be that strong. The spirit suggested that he learn how to use the sword again.

E: They're there to show me the future. Just showing me a place I dreamed of before. It was a big apartment—bigger than I dreamed of before. I'm questioning whether I deserve a place like this. Because I don't think I deserve a place this beautiful. Other people have things—do they deserve it? My feeling when people have those things is they must deserve it. Everybody does. I realize you have to think in that frame of mind, to get to that place. They know I would appreciate it and I would do more for people if I was affluent. They're trying to open my mind, to not restrict myself. It's the same thing with a woman. You have to feel you deserve her. Nothing is beyond what you can get, if you can appreciate it. Instead of thinking that deserving means being like a Mother Theresa. They say I've suffered enough to think on these terms. They want me to start believing that's the way, I'm supposed to live. It's the next step up from getting these people out of my life. They say the place is reserved for me. It has been reserved for me. "Fit yourself into it. You belong in it."

They're all trying to help me in their area of expertise. The Samurai is talking the most, "Become the warrior; at least feel like the strong Samurai."

Red says he's been helping me with my personality, by making me more gregarious. He says, "See what I'm talking about?" Like he's been helping me all along.

The plantation owner says wait, and he'll help me when I'm in a position of authority.

The healer's there telling me not to forget the children of St. Jude and all the children that are poor. He says, "Concentrate on the children. Be your own person. We'll not try to control your life, but help you, and you can be very comfortable, affluent and generous."

They told me that by seeking them out, they can help me in all situations. They say, "Why you don't see the apartment is because you don't put an apartment in your head that is good enough." I dreamed about beautiful places, but not that I deserved to be there. The healing person says, "Just enjoy it, no arrogance, quiet reserve" is what he's telling me. They're just saying I can be more complete and more powerful. They say I have the wisdom. Now to do and to get the self to do it. They say be more in command. Everything they're showing me is a larger scale, like Versailles. They just want me to stand taller, act wiser. Like they want me to change my persona to be cooler and sharper. To carry myself like a king. There's a chair that looks like a throne. I sit on the step below. I'm not ready to sit in the chair yet. Eventually I'll sit on the chair. Like the chair is a position of authority. They say your wife should be your queen—able to serve as intelligently as you. In history no matter what the king looked like, he always has a beautiful wife. If you went out with lower-level people, there would always be trouble. He shows me a little girl and boy and me on a throne with my wife on my right, and the children playing in front of us.

They all tell me I should call on them separately. I should say to myself, "What do I need to learn this week, because they can't do it, if I'm not a willing subject." They tell me when I have the power of all of them more, I will fear nothing. Their concern is making me the person

I'm supposed to be. They tell me there's a position of extreme authority in the future and I need to be trained to do that. To have a strong good personality and compassion. All these people are combined in me, to bring me to where I am now. They tell me there's no kidding around now. The big thing is positive.

The plantation owner has a gun in his pant waist. Red, the guy from the 1940s, is wearing a suit, and the healer has a brown robe. I'm supposed to work on being a strong warrior, have a good personality, prepared to be a manager and make sure I continue to have compassion for children.

Eric's encounters of these past lifetimes resulted in an overall integration of these personalities. Each regression allowed him to explore another facet of his personality. He was helped tremendously in his everyday life. As a result, he carries himself in a stronger, more centered way while having become more social and self-confident. He knows that he needs to continue to call on his guides to help him. The powerful presence of all his spirit guides was enlightening for him.

When Claire described her feelings of being left alone, she had no idea that the following past life regression would unfold.

C: I don't know where this is coming from. I feel like I'm a gunslinger. I kill people. I'm in the West. It's like the Wild West of the movies kind of thing, and I kill people. And that's what I do. Basically I'm a gun for hire. And I don't care. I'm not concerned about going to hell for committing crimes like this. I just don't care. I make good money, I drink hard and I have a good time and I have people that I work with that can count on me. Basically what I do is work both sides. Sometimes I work for people who are robbing and sometimes I work for people who don't want to get robbed. I keep moving. Go around Texas, Nevada, kind of range across that cow country. Find basically people who want to get money, or protect money. And I'm fast with a gun and I take care of myself. I don't want anybody to get too close. It's not a happy life but it keeps me going.

I found this to be a shocking statement coming from this forty-something, college-educated woman.

B: What's important about this lifetime?

C: I like killing.

B: What is it that you like about killing?

C: Just like snuffing out the candle. People are so stupid, fat, lazy, ugly. Stupid people take stupid chances.

B: What kind of stupid chances?

C: I don't know; people are trying to save something, hide something, hold their money, their bags, keep them back, thinking that's worth dying over. They throw themselves in front of the safe or keep money in the bank. 'Cause I don't kill them right away. I give them a chance.

B: What kind of chance?

C: To hand it over, and if they don't I sniff them out. If they can't figure it out for themselves, then I kill them. Simple. 'Cause I feel like they deserve it.

B: Why do they deserve it?

C: I guess 'cause somewhere, there's gotta be some kind of contempt for money. Like, anyone who would give up their life for money, deserves to die. Twisted. It's like this twisted logic. I like… I like making people afraid. I don't mind doing it.

B: When I count to three, bring us to the *next important* place in that life and see what you see.

C: I'm too old. My fingers aren't quick anymore. I drink too much 'cause I like the buzz. I just like working on a buzz and hanging out on a porch somewhere. Looking out over the prairie, rifle by my side. I made it OK for myself. I didn't get killed. I got some kind of little shanty shack I put together. I lived alone with my dogs. And I can manage. I got a little money stashed away. And it's been a hard, rocky, lonely life. I haven't had much happiness, because I never let myself drop my guard. I don't care about anybody, and nobody cares about me.

B: So bring yourself to the time of your death in that life and see what happens. One, two, three. Be there now.

C: I feel like I'm still on the porch. I'm still all by myself. I can see the ghosts, of all the people I killed, coming for me. They're coming, reaching out to me and I hate that. (*She starts to cry.*)

And they forgive me, and that's what makes it so hard. If they wanted revenge, I would keep fighting, but they don't. They're welcoming me and I was such a fucking, insane bastard. (*She's crying harder.*) They always forgive the killers, 'cause they don't care.

B: What's the point for you to bring yourself back in this lifetime, in the here and now?

C: Can't kill.

B: And what's important for you to do in this lifetime for yourself?

C: I don't want them to forgive me. I cry because I'm so rotten and mean. The dead always forgive their killers. Just because you can kill, doesn't mean you have to. I still have the current of that person in my soul, and I can still kill people, and whack 'em good with my tongue. I can still hurt them. I'm still got that snake, that killer voice in my soul that just doesn't care about anything. Takes pleasure in killing. Feels completely alone. It's the forgiveness by the ones I killed. That really got me. 'Cause I guess I could've been valuable and loved maybe. Could have found people who cared, but they weren't there. I couldn't find them; I couldn't see them; I couldn't connect. And I still have trouble connecting. You know Jerry said to me the other day, "You're the only girl for me, you're the only girl I could love, I still love you so much." And I thought, "Oh, that's nice."

B: And you don't feel connected to that when he says that?

C: No, I didn't feel a surge coming back to him.

B: Did you feel a good feeling though when he said that?

C: Oh I feel like, oh, OK.

B: Are you afraid to open up that part of you?

Going back to that guy who said "I never let myself drop my guard," is there a part of you that feels that way, that you don't want to let yourself be open and vulnerable to other people?

C: I never liked being judged.

B: So now you're in this place, wherever you are right now, what message can you bring back for Claire to help her with her life, the joy and purpose in her life now? What can you bring for yourself from this experience, from this place?

C: I definitely don't like feeling vulnerable. I can also guess you could get away with it, but you can't get a feeling of doing good. You can have the thrill of looking cool and looking mean and I can see this guy was like a real glint-eyed motherfucker. And liked the power of making people afraid. Like you would really be scared of him and he knows it. And I know it, and I liked that. I liked that power of making people afraid. But I never lived. I never really enjoyed life. And then when I was confronted—even though I got away with it—nobody killed me. I was never touched, and I had my own farm in wherever the hell it was, in Montana or wherever. When I was confronted with all those souls with the sorrow in their eyes and the forgiveness, it just completely devastated me. I just felt like such a rotten mean snake. Really like a vicious snake, biting people just because I could.

B: What can you give yourself in this lifetime? What can you bring to heal yourself, to let go of that?

C: I don't know, I mean I do forgive myself, because I didn't go out of my way to hurt people anymore. I try to work against that, but I can't quite stamp out the feeling that nothing matters. It's like that Queen song: *"Nothing really matters, anyone can see, nothing really matters to me."* I think about that. I don't like that song much. I don't like that group that much, but it's such a problem. It's like people think there's stuff worth killing for, worth fighting for, worth dying for, but what's worth living for? You know? And like now in America, it's like you gotta live for your children, you gotta live for your family. Well, I don't have children, so am I living for my cats and dogs?

B: Maybe you're living for Claire. Maybe you've come back in this lifetime to be yourself and just to heal yourself this time.

C: I don't care enough about myself. I don't like myself. I don't know how to live for myself.

B: Before you come back, is there anything else you want to bring from this place that you want to bring to yourself in the here and now. Any thoughts come to you?

C: I think whatever forces surround me have a sense of humor. There's always that ability to laugh and cry at the same time. I think what

I'm hearing is, well, at least you were completely undefeated. It didn't solve everything. You know what it feels like to be a hard, mean killer and get away with it. You liked it; you got away with it. You recognized it doesn't answer anything; it doesn't solve anything; it doesn't take care of anything. All it does is, it takes away the desire to do it again. That's what I learned, is that it doesn't work. So when I see those shifty little attorneys going to kill each other basically, I think, okay fine, you think that will make you happy, it won't. 'Cause I know. So I got away with it; I did good; I got what I wanted; but it wasn't what I wanted (laughs).

B: I think the interesting thing, though is to see those souls forgive you. Maybe they were there for you to get some message.

B: So as you continue to breathe in and out, I want you to get prepared to come back and let the energy come back up your legs, to your knees, to your heart, to your throat, to the top of your head. As you're breathing in and out, all of your energy comes back, very alert, very focused. When I count to three, you will open your eyes. One, two, three...

C: That was fun. I liked that.

B: The last thing I would ever have expected to hear from you: you are a gunslinger from the Wild West. What was your name then?

C: I don't know. I don't even like Westerns!

B: Bring yourself to the time of your death in that lifetime.

C: Like he dies of a heart seizure. One of those creamy grey souls come up towards him. They forgive him because they come. Welcome. "We forgive him really." I could feel that because I had, like a tough name. Like a Jack Clancy name. Was the late 1890s, when the railroad just came in, or 1910. Bottles of whiskey—wooden stagecoach—shotguns—*Unforgiven* Clint Eastwood. Solitary—definitely like a motherfucker for how I felt.

B: What's important for you to bring back to this lifetime?

C: *Know what you want to live for. I haven't forgiven myself. Fear not.*

Claire's experience as a gunslinger for hire crystallized for her the nasty reactions she had as a young girl when she became upset at someone. She could turn around and call someone a "f---ing moron" without understanding the origins of that reaction. After experiencing her past life regression lifetime, she immediately understood where her earlier reactions had come from, which, in turn, allowed her to resolve certain feelings and understand herself more clearly.

She became overwhelmed at the forgiveness by the spirits. They told her that her lifetime was okay and she could move on at the time of her death. It was surprising to listen to her past life regression as a gunslinger, which was so totally different from the person that she is in this lifetime.

C: I don't feel guilty about feeling this way, because in this lifetime I cannot hurt a person or an animal. I feel that I have paid my dues. The gunslinger experience past life blew my mind so much, because I didn't know that was going to come out. It was a total surprise the way I felt. "Don't fuck with me or I'll kill you." Seeing all the people I killed, forgiving me, resulted in my feeling less evil. It scared me because it was too real and too weird, and I had a feeling I had to get back to reality.

What evolved from this experience was that Claire was able to be forgiven by the ghosts of those she had killed. She was allowed to become both more open and vulnerable. As a result of this lifetime, she was able to heal some of the negative facets of her personality. To this day, many years later, she still remembers this experience quite vividly, especially the forgiveness part.

In another past life regression lifetime as a male Viking, she felt so good and peaceful. Even though she killed in the Viking lifetime, she said that was an integral part of that culture, and she was part of a team.

C: I came from a good family, and was born into the right place at the right time. I have this feeling that I can be that again. For the first time, I'm not where I'm supposed to be.

Claire is changing her lifestyle patterns. Instead of taking drugs or medications to help herself feel good (like she did in her past lifetime as a gunslinger), she now takes herbs such as St. Johns Wort and practices yoga. This helps her address her problem with depression.

Claire's past life regression to deal with her feelings of chronic depression was described in detail in chapter 4. In that regression, she was a young man who burned down a barn, and she demonstrated the intense anger and rage that consumed her into the gunslinger lifetime. It was also manifested in her current lifetime by her internalized anger and rage, which resulted in her chronic depression. Her three experiences addressed some of the recurring parts of her everyday behavior that had been a puzzle for her. It allowed her to express these feelings in a safe way.

Claire has been able to transform herself to lead a more productive, meaningful life. As she said, "Let's hope Spirit will continue to guide me." Initially, her work focused on dealing with current severe and chronic bouts of depression. Through this process, she has healed certain aspects of her life and has moved on to accept the role of Spirit in her life.

Alison, whose regression is described in chapter 8, is a New York businesswoman with extensive work as an actress and a Reiki practitioner. She was able to integrate the information she received from more than 10 regression sessions into her current life experiences, which included most of her personal relationships. She does well in school and is knowledgeable about the world, is spiritual and a healer, and no one would ever believe she had problems with relationships.

Alison recognized how her soul confined itself by continuing to repeat certain patterns throughout many lifetimes. The overall integration of all of this information allowed her to transform her life patterns and goals. Some of her regressions included lifetimes as members of both sexes and different races throughout the world, none of which were "wonderful" experiences.

Alison reported that PLRT enabled her to highlight what was important, allowing her to work on her own problems. She was stuck in relationships that she knew were not good for her, resulting in panicky feelings that something bad was going to happen. She realized that her pattern was to pick men who were painful to be with, resulting in her not feeling well. Finally, she was able to tell her partner that their relationship was not working. Before she worked with PLRT, she couldn't leave these relationships, felt lost in her life, was depressed, and thought about suicide a lot. Through her acceptance of a belief in reincarnation, she can now acknowledge that she is here for the purpose of understanding herself better and transforming her life situation.

Through the uncovering of their regressions, subsequent discussions, and the integration of the information into their current lives, people began to gain a greater awareness of their life purpose. Many made the connection that they are here for the purpose of self-recognition. Each purpose is as unique as is the way each person chooses to live his or her life. Chronic problems led to their spiritual explorations, and they began to see the greater purpose of meaning in the universe. Their lives took on a meaning that was more global than a self-focus.

As I look at contemporary issues, wondering why there is so much chaos and disconnection in the world, I recognize that there is still a meaning that makes sense to me. We can understand why things happen as they do, if we can view these events as broader learning situations. Within these issues are some tragedies that can extend the meaning and life purpose of a person or groups of people in order to make beneficial change in the world.

One example is to perhaps view all events that have happened as a way for all of us to be awakened. Perhaps major historical events such as the World Trade Center bombing or Bandeh Aceh were the work of souls who came into this world for their life purpose to serve as a lesson for the greater good of humanity. I don't mean to demean those people, their families, or their lives and deaths. However, their participation—even though they may have been consciously unwilling—may be the result of their coming into this lifetime with a contract to make a difference for all humanity. That doesn't mean that they knew "how" they were going to accomplish that.

Or, perhaps these events occur to demonstrate the effects that hatred and disconnectedness can have on an entire world. The participation of all of these people led to an increased awareness for the greater good of all humanity throughout the world.

People have described their belief that souls, individually and in groups, come into the world with a predetermined contract to make a difference. This can be played out through whatever they might feel is an important piece of work for them, for the world's greater good. If we take this belief into account, we may view life events in a very different way.

One example that comes to mind is newscaster Katie Couric's campaign for early colon cancer detection. Obviously, it was a tragedy when her young husband died of that disease, and people questioned, why does a young man get cut down so early in his life? In the midst of her grieving, Katie was able to begin an educational campaign about early colon cancer detection on her national network television program, reaching millions of people. Her nationwide presence made people sit up, take notice, recognize the importance of preventive colon cancer screening, and hopefully follow through.

Perhaps her husband Jay came into this world with a life purpose of making a powerful change in the world. *I do not mean that he "chose" to have cancer.* However, one man's experience touched many people in the world in a very powerful way. This demonstrates so clearly for me the influence of two people's lives. I also think that Katie was his soul mate in helping him to fulfill his mission and perhaps hers as well. Some people might say they came into this world to make a difference. However, I am an outsider viewing their experience, and I'm sure they may have seen it in a different way. When I hear of an event like this, I choose to see a healing purpose.

The people I have described were able to make the public aware of their situations, which in some instances caused controversy; but other changes were made as well because of their individual plights. There are many other events that highlight for me the belief that a soul comes into this life with a purpose, which we will continue to explore in the remaining chapters.

11

Where Does the Soul Go?
What Happens at the Time of Death?
Spiritual Messages That Enrich Our Lives

"It is only with the heart that one can see rightly:
what is essential is invisible to the eye."

~ANTOINE DE SAINT-EXUPERY

His Holiness, the Dalai Lama, described his Buddhist belief of death as follows: "I view death as a normal process of life. Knowing that I cannot escape it, I see no point in worrying about it." This spiritually evolved belief has taken many incarnations to hone. Usually, most people do not begin to think about their own mortality and what happens at the time of death until a tragic and violent situation occurs. For example, I was shocked as I read the headlines on the newsstand, "Mowed Down by Punks." The paper's front page showed a picture of a 50ish, vibrant-looking woman in the prime of her life with her dog whose life was terminated by someone else's whim. It jolted me out of my everyday existence and relaxed state of mind. A common reaction by some was, Why was her life taken instead of the "punk's?" Where's the justice in that? Is there a God? What is the meaning of life?

I was surprised how casually people described their time-of-death experiences during their past life regressions. In the following reports, they talked about how the important messages that they were able to bring into this lifetime had helped them to understand themselves more clearly as they found their life purpose. A young woman told the story of her death as an imprisoned male soldier in the Middle Ages who was "stuck with a sword." His spirit stood up and said, "It's too bad; I could've done a lot more when I was young. What a waste of a way to die; it could've been worse. I could've done more." Her interpretation of the message was that she needs to live life more in the moment than her perpetual delaying and postponing. This demonstrates that her vision clearly encapsulated her life focus. What a powerful way to clear up a chronic problem. She was the one who interpreted this regression for herself.

In most past life regression sessions, I would recommend that a person go to the time of death in that lifetime in order to bring their past lifetime experiences to closure. The experiences that people reported were as varied as being burned, drowned, mutilated, or dying peacefully in bed surrounded by their family and loved ones.

During my early nursing career, as I worked on the surgical wards of a major medical center, I was often there when people died. They would often reach out and up with their arms as if they were reaching toward someone or something or murmur "Mama." Others peacefully slipped away. As I watched people reenact their past life regression death scenes, their reactions seemed so reminiscent of those days. To give the reader a sense of what they described, I have included some time-of-death experiences. This is Faith's experience.

F: It's quiet and I'm sitting, breathing deep, alone. I cry. I'm still alone. I don't talk much. Not much to talk about. When I die, I fall over from where I'm sitting. No one there. I feel my spirit come out of my forehead.

It goes up stretching out like the clouds. I feel like I'm swimming but in the air. Feels good to fly.

B: How does it feel to be out of the body?

F: Good.

B: What is important for you to bring back to this life?

F: It was a *long time* ago. Not to be scared even though I was alone, I still lived. During that life this woman died because she had a crippled leg..

B: Bring yourself to the time of your death.

F: *I couldn't walk anymore they left me there and I just died.*

B: What happened to you when you died?

F: The soul just goes up—becomes a part of everything. If I wasn't crippled, I could've kept going. There might not be a next time. Nothing made me happy or sad. I just lived. We were cave people and my future was like his. I'm so cold. I'm either a small male or a young woman. I didn't feel a romantic link to that man. I was 22 years old.

B: How did you know your age?

F: We counted time through rocks. Pebbles were the moons.

In another reenactment, after being brutally raped and murdered, one woman said: The soul has a hard time going up because of the sense of anger and such a sense of rage and anger. An image of loving. The soul left the body and is stuck in all of this rage. Almost as if it can't go away. It does it with help from angels who come and surround it with a healing light. And I just heal, ease it up. The wound just needs to be healed. Healing images—like holding a baby and put the arms of someone around. I'm held and I just have to be there.

This woman had never been raped during this lifetime, so she was surprised about her experience.

Another woman described a lifetime in which she was brutally murdered:

H: I'm sitting up, perched with these angels. They are all here. I need to go someplace and I slip back into a cloud. There's a scene—an open clear area in a marketplace. It feels terrible. Do we have to go through all of this again? I'm being burned to death. First I'm watching it and then, as if my soul has to escape quickly, not to burn. Such a violent act. The soul tries to escape with its life.

B: What do the angels want?

H: They give me a safe place to come back to and be. I just have a sense they are messengers with God. There are two with me. Their purpose is for me to have a place I can go to feel protected. These angels—what they do is a sense of comfort and security. I should never let something like this happen again and find a safe place to be. Important to find a correct place to be.

In another past life regression, a man answers:

B: Where does the soul go?

R: It's dark. See a light. See a door. I'm shaking.

B: Do you go through the door?

R: Yes.

B: What's on the other side?

R: White steps.

B: Where do they go?

R: To a garden. It's beautiful.

B: What's important to being back to the here and now?

R: Not to be lonely. To share—be happy with my children. Open up more.

One woman answers:

B: Where does the soul go?

S: It goes to a building with books. It looks at my book.

B: What does it say?

S: It sounds so weird to me. He lived an okay life except that he gave up after she died. That he killed a lot of people and all that stuff.

B: What message is important for you to bring back to the here and now?

S: That you can't plan for random acts of violence. That things just happen sometime and not for a reason. I guess I can't plan for that or you can't not cross the street because the bus will get you. Sort of comforting to think I killed people and did things I think wrong. But in this life it sort of worked out. A flash of him in that life. Some of his comrades wanted to have their way with women in the village and he said why do that and they listened to him. I was waiting to be raped or something and the bears in the forest in Germany got me. Her hair wrapped in curls and so striking. Rolf is with me and worries about me.

During one of her many PLRT sessions, I asked Courtney to go to the time of her death (TOD) during her Native American lifetime, and she reported the following.

C: I'm in a long house and the chief is there and people are there. I foretold my own death. They knew when it was gonna come. And I'm not sick or anything. I just know that I'm going to leave. I don't know if they give me some sort of elixir, something to drink which is sort of hallucinogenic. But I can see all of the ancestors around me. The people who have already passed on are there with the living. I don't feel whatever that thing is. I just walk over, move like on a placid pond.

B: And what would be important information for you to bring back to the here and now about that lifetime?

C: That even being still and active has as much potential for growth as being productive. That you can be—just be. And that's fine and expected and not feel like you have to do. Observe all of the subtleties of the day. They say you can fly in the void. It's part of the journey.

It is interesting to hear how a Native American viewed death as a natural process. It highlights the fact that just "being" is okay.

Courtney's end-of-lifetime experience for her during a past life regression about the Holocaust as described in chapter 8 is included here.

B: What happens to your soul?

C: I think I float up. It feels scary when I'm in there.

B: And how does it feel to be in Spirit?

C: I mean it feels scary when I'm there.

B: As you look down from up above, what would you say is important about that lifetime to bring back to yourself in this lifetime?

C: That we're all primarily spiritual. That it's just life.

B: And what do you think about that especially for this lifetime?

C: That we're all primarily spiritual. That it's just a body.

B: What did you come into this life to do?

C: To illuminate.

B: Know how?

C: I do. I just have to make sure I care for my body.

It is interesting that she has come into this lifetime to acknowledge the somatization of all her stress. She expresses this through her panic attacks and irritable bowel syndrome. Now, she is learning how to care for her body.

B: What happens to your soul?

C: Well it goes like it remembers the night before. The thought about being able to go to heaven without having to die.

B: You mean like going out of your body?

C: Yeah.

B: So where does your soul go when it happens?

C: It just goes back.

B: Where is back?

C: It feels like home.

B: And when you're there, how can you see what just happened? How do you understand it?

C: I dunno. I guess I feel I've just come back again.

B: And so when you're up in that space is there any understanding you have as to why things happen as they do? Like what happened to you?

C: I guess I just understand like we all have to die at some point.

B: But why does it happen now?

C: You mean why do I have to be murdered? I guess I feel like looking down that I came too soon. That if I had waited, I would've missed this really dark time.

B: And what was the purpose of this? What did you come in this time to do?

C: I guess to teach, to teach tolerance to the world.

B: And how would the world get that message?

C: I think that the people who were left behind whom actually survived would just get out and let it be known that the atrocities happened. It's cyclical and it seems like it's happened again and again. I want to say it was 1938–1939.

B: Is there anything else you want to say from this space or this experience?

C: The earth is small.

B: What can you bring back for yourself? Your life purpose at this time? What message do you want to bring back?

C: That I'm not a victim. That there's no end of time there.
That there's no end of time. That there's no end.

B: What did you come to do in this lifetime?

C: I think to be a messenger. To show people tolerance and patience and humanity.

B: Anything else?

C: I think I chose to come back. I probably didn't have to come back.

B: Do you have any idea how it will be manifested in this lifetime?

C: Through words and through the media. They show me the way. My guides—they come to me in my dreams and tell me what to do and how to do it.

Courtney's description of her time-of-death experience when she was killed during the Civil War follows.

C: 'Cause when you cross over you're fine. 'Cause everything seemed very peaceful and I was glad to see her and we were walking off into the rebel camp that I was gonna get some food and I was gonna get some. Right after the dream of the place in Manhattan I remember I went to a place that doesn't exist on this plane but it looked like Montana the prairie land. And my mom and my sister and Joan were there and I remember I took them with me and I said we were standing in front of this picturesque area and it was void of any animals and I knew that that's where the white buffaloes were. I said see they're pulling the blessings back. It's receding right now so we can learn a lesson. You couldn't see the white buffalo because they weren't there. It's not that they were all gone and doesn't exist. It was just that they're not visible or that they were hiding. That's the Native American lore; the greatest blessing is the white buffalo.

It seemed to make sense to me that the earth is pulling its blessings back 'til we wake up. You know you don't give a bad kid a reward 'til they start to shape up. The world has to wake up to the earth changes before the blessings will start to come back.

In this next regression, Courtney saw herself walking on the beach in Greece near the Aegean Sea. She is a man, a priest with a shaven head wearing small, thin sandals, and it is 1900 BC.

C: I have been schooled or I have been taught certain things that came from the Atlanteans. About how to travel between the realms. Prophecy. There's a tie to Egypt.

B: Have you used this knowledge in your current lifetime; in other lifetimes?

C: It's similar to the shamans from the Indian tribes. It almost feels like I'm relearning it to a certain extent now, or remembering it.

B: What's important for you to bring back to you—you, Courtney—in this lifetime? Are there any messages for you to bring back?

C: Well, the higher realms. The astral plane is very active and there is the Yin and the Yang, the dark and the light and so sometimes it feels chaotic. But if you rise just a little bit higher those realms are always quite peaceful.

B: What's important for you to bring back into your lifetime today?

C: That thoughts manifest very easily and so you have to be vigilant about your thinking and your thoughts and your desires. It seems I keep looking out to sea, like a portion of that island is still above water, like even just a small bit and it feels like there's a desire to go out there and find it, even though part of that land mass is under water (Atlantic Ocean).

B: And what is that?

C: Atlantis.

B: What keeps you from doing that?

C: Well, I have a whole—a large body of people that I counsel.

B: And why would you need to go there?

C: It seems like there's some sort of tangible information that I want to find or just being on one piece of rock that is still above water. Or if I'm able to touch it or that I will remember something.

B: Were you in Atlantis before it fell?

C: I am aware that I was an Atlantean in a prior life and this might have been the next life.

B: What year does this occur?

C: 25-24 BC?

B: So bring yourself to the *next important place* there and see where it is. One, two, three, be there now and see what you see.

C: There's a cave and there are several people sitting at a table like a wooden table and bench and they're writing down things…like…things.

B: And what's that?

C: It's like they're writing in Phoenician.

B: And are you there, too?

C: I'm there and sometimes I'm dictating. But other times—like this group of people. We all know that we were in Atlantis at one time, so we're all trying to remember information that was lost and we're trying to write it down.

B: Is anybody there that you know?

C: I think Kate is there.

B: Do you think Kate and you are together in this lifetime for a reason?

C: Yes. For spiritual awareness.

B: I know today we don't have a lot of time to go into an intensive (session) to fully flush this out, so with the thought that you can always come back here, alone or with me, is there anything else before you come back that would be important for you to talk about from this space? Or anything that's important for you to follow up on in this life? What would be important for you to bring back into this life from this space?

C: There is a whole bunch of people that I know and I will know that are from this Atlantean experience, to help ease the consciousness of the world.

B: Did you ever get the sense before that you were here?

C: This summer I did.

B: What came up for you?

C: Walking on the beach, like the way the light was hitting. It was weird the way the sunlight was hitting the streets and even though I was in Manhattan, it was something about the way the light fell reminded me of being in that place.

B: Have you ever been in Greece?

C: Never.

>   The light is so intense because the buildings are white. But I had a dream two nights ago that I had to go to the Olympics and it was weird. It would end up that I'd go to the mall and I would somehow take this corridor and then I would wind up in Greece, where the Olympics were. And it happened twice. Like the dream, I had to go to Greece for the Olympics. I found a corridor through buildings and rooms and hallways and then all of a sudden I was in Greece.

B.   Parallel universes; how do you get there?

C.   Yeah and then I remember shooting a project and (my friend who I currently know) I was there and we both wore a dress and I saw the crystal city. It was definitely futuristic. And I was aware of that in the dream. This is the crystal city. This is it—what about Alicia? Is she still seeing the crystal cities? (This is in reference to a regression she had with Alicia in chapter 12.)

The theme permeating all of these reenactment experiences is the understanding that there are lessons we are here to learn. Hopefully, we will avoid repeating the same mistakes and recognize that our life has a purpose. Often, our experiences can serve as a message to others when they begin to question their own lives. Only a few people out of the hundreds who had experienced their past life reenactments had trouble believing in reincarnation. For some, the idea of a life purpose was a new idea.

A young woman, Zelda, talked to me about the time of her death during the 18th century. She was involved in the French upper-class royal court, and everyone dressed in the pompous Louis XIV style.

B: Bring yourself to the time of your death.

Z: By guillotine. A huge crowd of people. In the crowd I see my sister. I don't know if my father is there. He doesn't want to watch. I am one of several brought in a cart to the podium stage. I'm wearing fancy clothes but they are more tattered. There's a big crowd with houses around the plaza. It was the 1780s. I was very young. I see my sister's face while I'm on the chopping block. I can see her with mixed emotions. Sadness and remorse. She can't do anything. My head gets chopped off. I don't think it's painful. I float above and see this big crowd. Thousands of people with dark hair and dingy clothes feeling angry and sad chanting "fouler"? (*Fouler* means *mistreat, trample, crush*). Mobs.

B: What happened to your soul?

Z: Family is important. My sister and I have to learn something about love and compassion. We're very different but have to learn to accept each other. I've always hated mobs. Or political rallies. My hair stands up. It is mostly about my sister. I've had a hard life this lifetime. I'm going there soon. I'm kind of in the sky reaching down to her. *The danger of the gifts of beauty.* To learn to use these gifts well. To use it for my highest good.

Zelda said to me afterward "When you were counting down at the beginning of the regression, I saw a flash of a fancy shoe and stocking and it looked like my sister's face. Like what I've seen now with hate."

During her past lifetime, Zelda was a beautiful girl who came from a poor peasant family and had been introduced into the royal court. She was able to see how she had been used and how her beauty had been paramount in people's attraction to her. Through this lifetime, Zelda has recognized the importance of family and the people who love her, especially her stepsister. Zelda knows she has to learn to communicate better with her stepsister.

Erica presented herself for PLRT to understand her problems surrounding her fears. When she is afraid, her throat starts swelling and she doesn't know what to do. She feels it has something to do with her work situation because she cannot speak up about things that are bothering her. Her prominent issues are a fear of public speaking and continual fears of dying by suffocating. This has also resulted in her fear of being in enclosed spaces, so she cannot ride the subway anymore. As her regression ensued, she saw herself as a man in an Italian palatial building.

E: I was taken to a man who had a lot of power, for a political reason. This was possibly around 417 AD. I took a position politically in front of a group that I had influence over and he asked why I did it, because it was against another person. I didn't want to say it in front of the people but someone said you better tell them. They freed me to tell what we were thinking. It is my opinion and if I tell them they will be influenced by me and a problem if this man found out. I was totally against the law about women. I was taking care of the army for him and the defense of the country and I think my guys wanted to see the women sometimes and they couldn't. I think I said I understood what they were saying. He said it in front of the guys and they came to me. I said I understand and I cannot do anything because of this man, and they were men. One man went to see him and said what I had told them and that the guys weren't disciplined anymore. And he said it first, so I didn't say anything. So he sent me to the arena to fight with this big guy. If I win at this I live, if not, I get killed. A game to death. The game can just be a fight, or a fight to death. We look (at the) guy and he puts thumbs down so we knew, live or die. Oh—go and broke it. I know he killed me and stepped on it everything in my throat. I cannot breathe and I'm shocked. He put his foot on me—did it. He put me in the ground many times. He—my throat and I don't dare move. And they all clap hands or look me in the eyes and he's stepping on it. He's huge. It's totally unfair but as soon as they picked me up and I am in front of him—but I knew it would happen. I was shocked the *way* he killed me. I didn't think he could do it that way.

And how I move up, up, up. Free. I'm going very fast. Like I'm waiting behind a door for people to let me in. A lot of friends and people. They're very nice and they run to me and tell me their stories and why they don't understand why I didn't say anything. They welcome me and they're happy to see me. They don't look like people. White stuff, unshaped. But when I look I see them, like they're in their body they were in before. I know how they looked on earth. Objectively white shape. When you go away for a while and they're happy, things we had together. A joy to find all of us together again. People I expected to see who are gone already. To another life or another stage. I'm not supposed to know about that yet.

After the regression, she talked a little bit more about it.

E: I know I didn't say something. It wasn't my fault. I didn't die right away. I was staring at him—I couldn't breathe. I was so shocked at the way he killed me. I couldn't believe it. I left my body very fast—like you're waiting behind a white screen. I left my body without looking behind and I was waiting and I don't know the way a screen opened and I recognized—we all talk together at the same time, and they said you should have talked.

Erica now realizes that she must speak up at work and not let the words get stuck in her throat. She won't be "killed" for speaking her piece about some of the work problems. Erica said that she felt immediate relief and would try to pay attention to what she had just learned and put it into practice. She was surprised at seeing the "spirits" of people whom she had known who were now dead.

Adrienne currently practices in the health-care field and is very committed to her profession She described her experience of a physical explosion in a past Atlantis lifetime. She brought forward a message for both herself and others of what she thinks brought down that culture.

A: Everything's destroyed. Something bad happens brought on within the culture, brought on by teaching ill will. The unenlightened way of interacting with each other and no common thread to pull the culture together. No way to understand or be interested with each other. Doesn't make sense? Something human missing from the culture and it can't survive. People in power are missing the critical elements. The advanced nature of the culture but it was out of control, very complex. We cannot be separate from the culture. A bunch of people who were political and missing a critical characteristic. There's no concern between people. No warmth or give-and-take between people. I feel trapped about that looming danger. The sense that there's disaster ahead! The knowledge that it could happen and that it did happen. Everybody's death was premature. There was an explosion. It's not just an explosion like an eruption and that was it and nothing after that.

B: What's important to bring back to this lifetime?

E: I can only tell you there's no point in living if you're not pursuing an individual path with nothing else. Only other thing that matters is doing that for good, as if you have to pursue an individual path regardless of who you are attached to. If you have a purpose, a courageousness to do something individual, no matter what's going to happen is going to happen anyway, and you don't want to be responding. Solely based on surroundings. Has to be something coming from inside. Something individual not complex and you see the whole thing. Keep your separateness and focus on your path. Build the structure first and the rest will follow.

Adrienne is a health-care professional who is primarily interested in healing the individual. She is also acutely aware of the political aspects of our culture and works toward ensuring that her professional practice is holistic. Obviously, this life has a profound meaning for her. Ironically, her descriptions of that time sound like a description of our contemporary culture. She believes that it is important to pursue an individual path. Maybe we haven't learned our lessons.

Leslie's regression in chapter 9 described her time-of-death experience in an Egyptian tomb. When I asked her to go to her time of death, she said the following.

L: I'm lying there and the light comes in. White light on me and I know that I'm going to die. Don't feel peaceful. I feel sad. (*She is crying.*) The light is trying to say OK. You did a good job and you're a good person. But I'm dying so early and the light says, "It seems that way but I'm a wonderful person lovely person. *It's not whether you live or die but the* *kind of person you are.* That is the thing that I have to work on. It's not about who you're in love with or what you do, it's about being yourself. To be true to yourself and just about love. How come I'm getting that message and other people do not? Everyone all in different places. I think I keep getting tragic endings and don't seem to be helping me. My soul has left in this life. I saw the ghost go into the light and ready to go right into another life.

B: What is the lesson you've come for this time?

L: Have to love myself.

B: How can you do that?

L: By accepting other people and not put the energy into it. And just come back to me. That feels lonely and they're really not there. If I can be loving and accepting of other people, I'll find it within myself.

Leslie heard the important spiritual message that what matters is the kind of person you are. The comforting aspect of the light was a theme throughout the regression.

When I asked Martha (whose regression is in chapter 9) what happens to the soul, here is what she said.

B: What happens to your soul when you die?

M: It goes up in front of a tribunal, a table with men. They're more compassionate than I am. They keep telling me I was just a boy. That I never hurt anybody. To forgive myself. (*She starts crying as she describes this.*) I feel conflicted. What I wanted to hear. It takes you by surprise. I go to heaven or the next level to review. Then I can meet the young lady who I saw that day. She forgives me too. (*She's crying again*). Like I go down on one knee and thank her. I'm led somewhere else. To big gold gates and I'm going into that mist or big cloud. I walk down this big hall with weird art work. Curator says you can look as long as you like, paintings change if you look long enough. A courtyard; there I see some of the souls of some of the knights I saw. I'm not afraid. I can now ask them, "*Why did you? How could you?*" They said, "*It was the law of the land. I feel like I held on so long I could have done something different in my life.*

B: What can you bring back from that experience into this life?

M: Our view is only a part of things. What we see is not always what is. Speak the truth with people and let everyone deal with their own things that happen. Speak the truth and stop protecting people. That young man that I was said, "M, we're here with you. Be strong, learn from our lessons. You're not alone."

This young woman's lifetime was as a boy in the 1640s in Celtic England/Ireland/Scotland or Wales. He witnessed a woman being raped by soldiers and realized that he couldn't get her help because it was "the law of the land." She talked about how her soul left and her ghost went to the light and said, "And now she's ready to go into another life."

Martha described how she picked her current lifetime and said:

M: I'm hovering around someone. I'm wanting to be born to this woman. This is the 1950s. The *Leave It to Beaver* type. It seems like this life is going to be more normal and more accepting. And the difference is, I'm gonna have support when it happens. I'm kind of hovering over this woman and waiting for her to get pregnant. She's gonna get pregnant in some months. Like the soul is empty and like none of my lives.

Have that power like a little angel hovering around this woman, in a Spirit kind of way. Getting to know her things in the past are just lessons. She's a nice person. I don't know why, but she's nice. I don't think I chose. It's chosen for you. Your next task here. This woman feels comfortable. I know her. We're going to go through this again. I'm kind of happy.

Then she described how she "picked" the person to whom she wanted to be reborn in this incarnation. It is her current birth mother. This was very interesting for me, since a few clients in my psychotherapy practice who were thinking about becoming pregnant had described to me their feeling that they had of a soul around them and ready to be born. In fact, one woman described the soul of her unborn child to me before she adopted the child.

After Leslie's lifetime in Egypt, she talked about the experience of her soul after she died.

L: I'm trying to see if I see anyone I know. I don't see anybody I know. People on the outside in Egypt, I know now are people I travel with. My daughter is there somewhere. Maybe my mother too. Maybe my daughter is my daughter and my mother my mother? The group travels together. Something that you travel together in one life and not the next. I look around for people I travel with during that lifetime.

B: How come they travel together?

L: Something about us that they've put together, and we keep traveling together. It is really comforting when you meet them again. It was real comforting to meet him again. Kind of like I miss these people because we're soul mates. Or lone encounter. Maybe I obsess because I really miss them and want them to stay around. Purpose of coming back is just love. What in this life to feel love again. I think there's more to it, but the people you travel with are love. And you're nurtured again and it feels real. They're part of your story and they *teach us lessons*. What you need to learn is on an unconscious level, and we push each other along and teach each other lessons. OK. I'm learning these lessons but why can't I have the loving feeling? If I'm a real loving person why do I have to get killed and get turned away? I guess the big question for me is, if I'm trying to be a good person why would these things happen to a good nice person?

Leslie's reports about soul travel have been described by many people. This understanding helped some people to recognize their connected feelings that they had experienced with certain people in their lives. These feelings they described were out of proportion to the short period of time they had known each other. Some have told me that they believed they have come into this lifetime together with certain people to help each other learn their lessons and the messages they should be receiving.

Another woman spoke about what happened to her at the time of her death in a past lifetime.

N: The soul just goes up and the soul needs to leave, because it was such a violent experience. The angels surround me and tries to heal her wounds. They give out a feeling of healing and the pain goes away. My open cuts just heal and they stay around me protecting. They form like a cup and they heal you. It is not finished yet! There is a different sense of time going by—going up—a sense going by—going up—a sense of needing to rest.

My being present with these time travelers during the time they regressed to the past, with all of the attendant joy, peace, or horror, allowed me to reframe these experiences for them. I believe there is a greater purpose to life that we are not always aware of. Perhaps we come into this life to serve others by pointing out a problem for others to see. One person's life or death can serve to bring international attention to a broader problem. The most consistent answer given by people was that they believe their life purpose is to serve humanity. Media coverage that catches people's interest can make one person's life or death an international example for change.

There are many events that highlight for me the idea of a soul coming into this life with a purpose. Some people who come to mind are Lisa Steinberg, Terri Schiavo, Mattie Stepanek, Christopher Reeve, among many others. In each of these instances, they took their tragic circumstances and brought them into the public spotlight as an example for millions of people. The magnificent, graceful, and courageous way they handled their afflictions and worked toward educating other people served as an inspiration to so many. Even people like Lisa Steinberg or Karin Ann Quinlan, who were not consciously aware of the way their tragedies impacted an entire world, had a life purpose, and their souls knew it.

Karin Ann Quinlan's long-term existence in a coma is one example. The controversy in this case revolved around her family's decision to take her off life support. A similar situation occurred in 2004-2005 surrounding Terri Schiavo. The issue here was whether her husband—who said that his wife would never have wanted to live in a vegetative state—or her parents—who did not want to remove her from life support—had the right to discontinue life support after many years. Terri had languished in a coma because she was severely brain-damaged. This worldwide controversy resulted in dramatic shifts in people's beliefs about a family's rights and options to remove a relative from life support.

When little Lisa Steinberg was killed as a result of long-term physical abuse in New York City, the recounting of the story and the resultant horror expressed by millions brought the magnitude of the problem of child abuse to the forefront of people's awareness. This increased awareness of child abuse and its high incidence within our culture were agents for change in the area of children's protection. People became more aware that other children could be saved by active intervention in ongoing child abuse situations.

This is an example of the way a person's life or death ultimately had much broader meaning for millions of people. The people I have described were able to make the public more aware of their situations. In some instances, they caused controversy, but changes were made as well as a result of their individual plights.

During my life, I have witnessed and experienced the personal loss of people in their 30s and 40s from breast cancer, ovarian cancer, and AIDS. For me, it was an eye- opening opportunity to see how people living with a terminal illness were able to achieve a state of grace during this process. They served as shining examples for their families, strangers, and the health-care practitioners caring for them.

I witnessed my sister-in-law's valiant struggle with breast cancer, my other sister-in-law's grace as she dealt with a degenerative cerebellar disease, and my cousin's wife's life and subsequent death from ovarian cancer. One sister-in-law's primary concern was her young children. She wanted to make sure that they would be raised with love and guidance during their childhood and hoped to live at least until they finished their schooling. My other sister-in-law struggled to hold on until her daughter gave birth to her first grandchild.

I was amazed at the way my cousin's wife counseled and cared for other cancer patients during her hospitalization—including her physicians—and *never* once complained. They all lived with grace and dignity that left their physicians and family in tears. Even and probably because of their transitions from this planet at young ages, they were seen as inspirations to many people. In this way, their examples—and their lives—continue to this day to affect us all.

According to the Tibetan Buddhist paradigm, our existence consists of four "continuously interrelated realities: life, dying and death, after death, and rebirth." This is a continuum of every soul's progression. Believers view death as a passage to a new life. During their PLRT experiences, many people reported time-of-death reenactments. Most were able to move forward in time from a few years to 60 years or more to their time of death. Some experienced the moment of their death and the subsequent events that continued to unfold. They described what happened to their spirit after death, and a smaller number recounted their experiences prior to a rebirth.

During most past life regressions, individuals described lessons for themselves that they could learn during this life. Those who weren't able to go to their deaths in a previous lifetime were still able to talk about their current life purpose. As you read these occurrences, you can see how they helped people deal with their problems from a different perspective. The vicissitudes of life were seen as a challenge, which they viewed as another life lesson.

12

Some Unusual Experiences

"Time present and time past are both perhaps present in time future. And time future is contained in time past. If all time is eternally present, all time is unredeemed.

~FOUR QUARTETS, ELIOT

Eliot's description of our life's dimensionality envisions the interrelationships between the past, present, and future occurring simultaneously. This demonstrates how our recovered past memories and reenactments can help to change the present, and through that, our future. The breadth of my understanding and corresponding spiritual growth have been broadly expanded by so many people who have entrusted their multidimensional experiences to me.

Life Purpose

Searching for meaning in life or our life purpose usually occurs during a stressful life event as people age and have many concerns about death. Many people are "frightened" that there is "nothing" after they die. These thoughts have spurred them into their own spiritual search to find meaning.

Often, religious beliefs assure us that if we belong to a certain religion we will get seats in heaven. Correspondingly, many think that people of other religious beliefs will be spending time in purgatory or hell. As we mature, we often realize that those answers are too simplistic and are tilted toward the supremacy of a particular religion. Thus, we are led to the realization that we can no longer say these events are not possible. For millions of people throughout the world, a belief in reincarnation is part of their religious or cultural belief.

Integral to this work is the realization that change is a universal concept. It is important to recognize that the very nature of change is an always oc-curring, ever-present part of all life. Change mandates the continual death of old ideas for new ideas. Nothing ever stays the same as we constantly change old patterns and the way we work in the world. The outcomes are the death of previous beliefs resulting in new beliefs. This process of transformation shows the concept of life and death as intertwined in a cycle of birth, death, and rebirth. In fact, this can be seen within our own bodies as cells are always dying and being replenished.

Through the past 30 years, people have described their incidents with psychic abilities, near-death experiences, out-of-body travel, channeling, and communications with their spirit guides, all while they traveled into the past and future, mediated in the "here and now." When people came to me for help with their concerns, they often talked about their spirit guides and other psychic phenomena in a quiet tone. Perhaps they thought that I would judge them. However, as I helped them to explore these events, they were grateful that I didn't think that they were crazy. Hopefully their views, multidimensional experiences, and explorations can now go into the world. Perhaps they may increase the knowledge and spiritual understanding of other seekers who wish to validate their own personal experiences.

People jokingly talked to me about the use of a time machine in relation to time travel, either back in time or into the future. Many were quite surprised to hear that during my PLRT work, I had helped many people to access an altered state of consciousness, facilitating their ability to travel backward, forward, and into parallel time frames while physically remaining in one spot. In fact, within five minutes or less, some people were able to access their past life experiences, an early significant current life experience, or another level of consciousness. A small percentage of people—me included—needed two or three attempts to have a regression experience. I believe that the large number of these events in a mixed population highlight the *absence* of the mind's dimensionality limits.

In addition to their regressions to current and past lifetime experiences, other situations were also described to me. Some participants talked about events as if they were in a parallel universe; they described themselves as being in two different planes simultaneously. They said they could "walk through" a wall and feel as if they were in a different dimension. Others talked about their astral projections during their sleep; they knew they were traveling throughout the world. They reported to me that they felt as if they were working in a different plane.

Initially, I was shocked at some individuals' reports of their out-of-body travels. Over time, after I had worked with many people who described similar experiences, it became easier for me to understand. All of these people were stable and functioning members of society. As a result of my work with individuals' past life regression experiences, nothing seems out of the realm of possibility.

However, these experiences are beyond the scope of this book and are material for another fascinating discussion, perhaps another book. For now,

I have limited our discussion to my clients' past life regression work and their explorations of their past lifetimes, but I wanted to acknowledge the other unusual experiences some people have had.

Physics

Currently, people accept the idea of the four dimensions of space-time, the three dimensions of space, and one dimension of time. One theoretical concept within physics is called string theory—the theory of everything. String theory is believed to be true by many within the physics community. However, the theory requires that space-time has ten dimensions and still has to be proved. Recently, the theoretical physicists Drs. Lisa Randall and Rama Sundrum described the strings within string theory as coiled, small, and out of sight. Their hypothesis is that string theory provides for a belief in extra dimensions. They are currently working on ways to test this new information. These newer interpretations may advance these beliefs to another level. Perhaps this information may allow us to keep an open mind to the possibilities of infinite dimensions and provide a scientific framework with which to explain people's ability to access other dimensions.

As an example, there may be parallel universes that are in juxtaposition to our universe. They may be accessed through altered states of consciousness. This could explain mediums' ability to "see" or "travel" into the future and/or past. It can be likened to Ruth's description in chapter 1 regarding the concept that the past, present, and future all happen simultaneously. We can understand four dimensions. However, just because the other dimensions are so small that we can't see them does not mean that they do not exist.

Interdimensional Experiences

What follows are the different types of experiences people described on their path to past life regression explorations. The work of these explorers and truth seekers with their own interdimensional experiences has inspired me to take the next leap of faith. By *interdimensional experiences* I mean those experiences that people described as happening between lifetimes or at their death, the "space" before they end their regression. I will present some regressions of interdimensional experience reenactments recounted by many travelers on their spiritual paths.

Mary was one of the original people in my earliest past life regression work. She described the following experience to make a point to me about PLRT, which she told me about in chapter 1.

M: I see an image of myself with my Sage Femme (the wise woman who she says is her spirit guide) in front, with my back to the stream. She stood up and took my body off me, like a body suit coming off my spirit. Floated it into the stream to clean in sparkling clean water and put it back on me, like a reverse out-of-body. When she put it back on it was clear and cool. When I asked my Sage Femme why she did this to me when she lifted my body off, she laughed. She said you didn't expect this did you, sitting there with your naked spirit, for your body clothes to come back?

Mary's spirit guide, who she called her Sage Femme, presented her with the visual imagery between the body and soul relationship. This is what happens when we die, and then we reincarnate back into human form. During this out-of-body description, she described past lives to me, explaining how people can use them. This is her message for the people who are searching for their past lives, which surprised both of us.

Betsy's ex-mother-in-law Kate was dying, and Betsy was unable to visit. She said to me:

BET: I knew she was very sick. One morning I had a dream that she was there, not as the older woman I knew, but a young girl of 17 who was so excited about life and her whole future ahead of her. I woke up in bed and dozed and later that day, I found out that Kate had died in the morning while I was asleep. Her soul was out of her body and celebrating. Though we were good friends for a while, when I became upset at her, I never forgave her. After my divorce we had no contact and eventually she sent me a card and we started to correspond. She had married at the young age of 17 and was furious at her husband because she felt trapped in her life.

Here she was, fired up again as that young 17-year- old who was excited about life. So at her time of death, Kate's soul seemed to reach out and contact Betsy to heal the animosity that had existed between the two and begin to heal the rift. Betsy took that as a spiritual sign for herself to heal a lot of her own anger and not ruin her life by holding onto past grievances.

While sharing this information with me, Betsy was afraid that I would think of her as odd for having that experience. She was relieved to know that other people have had visitations by their friends and relatives at the time of death. So, when I shared my experiences surrounding my own mother's death, and her unconscious knowing, and her "visitation" to me, I know that she was able to accept this experience for herself.

My Experience During a Patient's Regression

When Courtney returned for her regression, she had a severe problem with anxiety attacks and felt like a victim. She told me that in July 2001 just before the 9/11 incident at Ground Zero, "an older man sat at the foot of my bed. He was White Cloud. He said something was coming, and I was going to be getting a *Ki*, a breastplate and a head- band with a feather. I thought that this was a vision quest, and that I was being prepared for insight."

During her past life regression, she began to describe a campfire burning with foggy, smoky sky. Suddenly, I literally saw the head of a Native American over her left shoulder as she lay on the couch in a trance. He was wearing a headdress of all white feathers. I've never seen a spirit at any time in my life, and it totally caught me by surprise. I did not say anything—I was stunned.

Courtney continued in her lifetime to the past as a young male Native American Arapaho whose throat was slit. She had said something is coming. I then told her what I had seen during her regression. When she returned the following week, she told me that the spirit I had seen was the same Native American who appeared to her for two weeks in July 2001. She said that he told her of "something hopeful and transformative." Then he gave her a breastplate and headband with the number 81 written on them.

Originally, Courtney came to see me because she wanted to use PLRT to help her heal her panic attacks. These attacks had spontaneously arisen during a business trip to the Ground Zero area, almost three years after 9/11/01. Courtney had done volunteer work at the site in September 2001.

On the morning of 12/26/04, Courtney e-mailed me. She said that between the evening of 12/24/04 and the morning of 12/25/04, between 3 and 4 a.m., she woke up and there was a Native American standing by her bed. He said his name was Little Bear and he was Lakota. He had an electric white light around him, and then he said, *"Something was coming."*

She reported that on Sunday 12/26/04, she had a horrible feeling of despair and finality. It was just like 9/11 when she was at Ground Zero that summer, which she says precipitated her "meltdown." Courtney was feeling: "Oh my God, I'm going to die." She was nervous about this, and while she was processing the information, called her mother who was also experiencing the same feelings. She later heard about the devastating Indonesian tsunami and attributed her feelings to the coming of the tsunami. Courtney feels that she experiences precognitive feelings when something of great magnitude is about to happen. This is the second time it has happened to her.

On 12/26/04, a tsunami occurred in South Asia, Bande Aceh, accompanied by a 9.2 magnitude earthquake. The following week, there was an article in a local NY paper reporting that the animals "seemed to know" (since they can feel, sense, and hear the vibrations) that something was coming, because they all fled to higher ground and none were killed. Another article showed a boy from the Jarawa tribe—one of the five indigenous tribes living in India's Andaman and Nicobar Archipelago—who were also alerted by these natural changes. It was reported that the "ancient knowledge of the wind, sea, and birds, may have saved the five indigenous tribes from the tsunami." This was said to be the "great" quake, which consisted of an earthquake and tsunami that were unprecedented, and resulted in more than 300,000 people dead.

When the tsunami occurred, it was one of the first times that the world came together in such a magnanimous way. There was a tremendous outpouring of physical and financial relief. People felt that they had a contribution to make, and they could identify with the massive death and suffering from that part of the world. The tsunami occurred on 12/26/04, and there was a full moon during the weekend. That same weekend, there were terrible snowstorms in the midwestern portions of the United States, keeping people indoors over the Christmas holiday. At the same time, a computer meltdown at Com Air stranded people for days at the airports, as they were unable to travel during the Christmas holiday. Subsequently, there were terrible mud slides in California, resulting in the death of approximately 10 people. There was tremendous global upheaval during this short period of time. Do things happen in the world to jolt people out of their ennui? Could this be the way people are tested to allow them to grow to a higher level of consciousness?

The horror at the loss and devastation in South Asia brought the entire world out to help with money and aid for the survivors. There has never been such an international outpouring. It was as if we were "as one" and totally concerned about the welfare of other people and working together to help them without a political agenda. Aid continues to pour into that area of the world even today. This was the ultimate demonstration of love, peace, and compassion. So Mother Nature has been very busy with multiple earth changes as people begin to question why these events are happening.

This is Courtney's regression three days later, which was her third lifetime as a Native American.

C: Seems like I see these very very tall trees, a lot of evergreens. I can hear the ocean too; it seems like we're hiking up to an observatory of some kind. There's something significant about the evening star in the sky, which would be Venus. Seems like it's northwest of the US or Canada. We're *Blackfoot*. It seems like I've been apprenticed to study the stars. We fish a lot but we also hunt. The stars tell us when the fishing is going to be good. I think the man I am apprenticed to is my friend Rick. They call us dogmen.

B: Why is that?

C: It has to do with the constellations I think. We learned it. Seems we learned how to build the observatory from the Anasazi.

B: Where are they?

C: They're in the Southwest and down into Mexico.

B: So how did you get to meet them?

C: They, our ancestors met them; I guess they traded with them. There used to be long roads long like highways almost that they built and then we would follow. We would come out of the mountains and we could see the roads. And they were straight, and we would walk straight for hundreds of miles until they—like a spoke in a wheel—and we'd go into the center of their city.

B: Did you go there?

C: No. But you could still see the remnants of the old road.

B: How come it was no longer used?

C: I don't know if they moved on. I don't know if they moved back into the jungles of Mexico, but all of a sudden they disappeared. They were not there anymore.

B: What time frame is this you're talking about?

C: Way before the White men came. 500.

B: So continue on with your life.

C: There's another tribe that was along the coast and they built ships and we used to sit up on the cliffs overlooking the sea and watch the ships go out or come in.

B: What kind of ships?

C: Whoever they were they were like seamen but they were another tribe; they were not White men.

B: What were they called?

C: It starts with a Y.

B: What happens next?

C: I just see all of the people of my tribe sitting around the fire. Someone is dancing.

B: And who are you?

C: I'm not sure. I don't know yet. We put black on our faces but only on our upper half.

B: What does that symbolize?

C: We all look like raccoons in a way.

B: What does it mean?

C: I think it means we look into the black, we look into the night.

B: So what happens next?

C: There's initiation rites.

B: And what does that mean?

C: Something akin to a sweat lodge is going on. It's purification.

B: What's happening now?

C: I feel a sensation like there's something right over my heart. They're jamming a stick into my chest. I can feel it. It feels like there's something going through to my heart. Yellow dog or yellow something. I think that's what they call me.

B: What does that symbolize?

C: I dunno—might have had a yellow dog. Has to do with fire.

B: What happens?

C: I'm like in a cave sealed away or something, or an earthen house for many days.

B: What happens?

C: I go to the underworld.

B: How do you do that?

C: It's through meditation, and they gave me leaves to chew that are hallucinogenic. Women bring me water and food, but, they bring it at night
because I'm not allowed to see the sun. It's disorienting. When I come
out, I'm nursed by the women and the other medicine men in the tribe.
They refer to me as the prophet.

B: What does that mean?

C: I guess I have gone through all the rites to become the seer for the tribe.
Now I'm alone and then *I'm walking* down a path and it's snowy and I
see a huge moose. It's black. It almost feels like I can speak to the moose
with my mind. After awhile it moves away.

B: Bring yourself to the *next important event* there.

C: I'm laying on a funeral pyre.

B: How old are you?

C: I've already passed away. I must be 80-something.

B: What is important for you to bring back to yourself in this lifetime in
that place?

C: Black is not black.

B: What do you mean?

C: What you see isn't always what's there. All of the colors are in black.

B: What else is important for you to bring back to yourself right now in
that place?

C: *That you're always safe.* Even when it feels like you go to the underworld—you're safe.

B: What does the soul of this person have to say about what's going on in
the world today?

C: That it's cyclical. That the earth is being pulled gravitationally more
than it has in the past. And it has to do with our consciousness. Our
thought patterns are creating what's going on.

B: In what way?

C: I think that people are concerned with material and with consumption. With consuming and not recognizing cause and effect.

B: What is there for people to learn?

C: That even a thought has a cause and an effect on the Spirit Plane. There's a shift: *where a lot of souls will have agreed to leave all at once.* There will probably be a few more to come. Be a few more events.

B: Like what?

C: It could be a natural occurrence or it could be one of being aggressive man towards man.

B: Where could that be?

C: It could be anywhere.

B: Is there any way to stop these events?

C: The ones that happen as natural events like earthquakes and such. It would require people to know their mind. To know their thoughts. To be conscious. It would require a lot of meditation by a large number of people.

B: Is what's happening at one time what people used to call earth changes?

C: Yes. The earth isn't healthy and so it seeks balance.

B: What can we do to help people to understand this more clearly?

C: *Find leaders that have a conscience.* They have to be champions of the environment.

B: What else is important for us to do?

C: We're doing, the White man is saying, is doing to the third-world countries as they did to the Indians. It's not as blatant. It's under the guise of bringing wealth to the people. But if their people's spirit is robbed there is no wealth. It's wrong to Westernize people because then it makes them want things that are just material.

B: Before you come back, is there anything else you want to say?

C: *There are more changes to come.* More bad things that happen to the earth before people will wake up.

Courtney's session was on 12/29/04, after the tsunami in Southeast Asia. As she came out of this regression, she felt dizzy and it took her about fifteen minutes to get her bearings, which was unusual for her.

C: It's kind of scary what's going on out there. Causes the boundary—it seems like I'm just used to having boundaries like when I'm asleep I know I'm asleep and when I'm awake I'm awake and this is reality. But sometimes in those heavy meditational states it's blurred—it's very blurred.

B: Think about this—we probably live there in that space more than we realize. We think we have control and boundaries.

C: I think it's in my chart where in a past life I was mentally unstable.

B: Are you afraid that's going to happen?

C: Yeah. That's always my concern. I'm afraid that my friends might think that I'm daft or something.

B: What happens if you feel that they might feel that way?

C: I think that they may, so sometime I have to say I'm not feeling well.

Courtney's comments were about the disappearance of the Anasazi Indian tribe in Arizona, around 500 AD. She talked about how they walked south all the way to Mexico, and then they just disappeared. It has always been a mystery. Then she talked about her time-of-death experience as a tribal shaman. Her subsequent discussion describes the necessity for people to become aware of their individual responsibility as keepers of the planet. This is in relation to being good stewards of Mother Earth, as well as working toward evolving the entire world to a higher level of consciousness. I was reminded of Courtney's description of the Native Americans studying the stars, demonstrating their intimate interaction and attunement with their environment. This shows how at the present time people are disconnected from the environment.

Courtney said to me, "I'm not sure I'm supposed to be doing this." She said she recognizes all of the spirits. They come with tidings of hope. The transformation process, although rocky and uncomfortable, is ultimately for everyone to reach a level of joy and consciousness. After that session, she e-mailed her friend and told her, "I have to remind myself what's real and what isn't."

On 1/10/05, Carolos Barrios, a Mayan elder in Guatemala, delivered the following commentary: *Through the ancient techniques of divination and tools of prophecy, the Mayan elders are calling forth to humanity* **at this time** *to pay closer attention to the messages being sent forth by the Mother Earth and to immediately take the actions they have been calling for to unite in an effort to bring balance again upon our planet. The recent destruction that manifested in Indonesia is predicted to now occur rapidly upon five continents of the earth. This message is not meant to induce fear; to the contrary, it is a call for bravery and for action. The elders are concerned about what has been presented in their recent divinations and they call to warn their leaders and to work very hard at a spiritual level to prevent the impending destruction. This message, verified and brought forth by various Mayan elders in Guatemala, is for all of humanity. The hurricanes in the US and the earthquake and tsunami in Indonesia have been warnings, and we must now pay attention or the possibilities of floods in Europe, Los Angeles, earthquakes and other efforts of* *the Mother Earth to awaken us will manifest quickly. There is a specific call for people around the world to join in prayer, meditation, or whatever method of spirituality one engages in to unite on January 18th at the time of their local sunset (approximately 6:00 p.m.). This date is (9) Keme according to the sacred Mayan Cholq' ij calendar and has the potential for protecting humanity from disaster. There will be many major ceremonies in the Mayan communities for this purpose. An open invitation is extended to humanity that wish to join the Mayan people for the Waxa' qib B'atz' ceremonies on February 12th in Guatemala. Again, this is a strong message, not meant to drive us to react in fear, for this will only negatively impact the level of destruction and our own circumstance. This is the opportunity for humanity to rise to the occasion and come together along the strong lines that unite us and overcome the obstacles that divide us. Please distribute this message widely.*

Past Life Reincarnation Dreams

People seeking PLRT often reported having dreams before they began therapy that seemed like past life reenactments to them. Courtney fell into that category. She talked about a dream that she remembers as a teenager, more than 20 years ago.

C: I had a recurring dream of a young Jewish girl in France during the Holocaust who never survived it. I never saw the Eisenhower tapes of the liberation of the concentration camps. When I saw them later, my images matched some of the things I "saw" in my dreams. My mother now was my mother during that lifetime. When I was late for Passover dinner, I saw myself as a Hasidic boy wearing a fedora in the 1930s. What seemed familiar to me were the buildings and the railroad tracks. I remember being shot maybe 14–15 years old in a trench. The young boy was the life before. Also know I was a drunk/ womanizer at the turn of the century.

Courtney's dream depicted her two past life regression experiences. In one, she was a young Hasidic boy in the 1930s. Then, in a later lifetime, she was a young Jewish girl hidden in a convent during the Holocaust era (see chapter 8). In this lifetime, she is of the Christian faith; however, she has an amazing knowledge of Judaism and certain religious practices.

At birth, each soul comes into this lifetime with a pre-birth goal of service to humanity. However, as we live our lives, we are usually not consciously aware of that previously stated purpose. Remember, the soul continues to evolve lifetime after lifetime until nirvana is reached. So, the ultimate goal is for our individual soul development to reach the highest level of "godlikeness."

Some people described how their past life regressions helped them to see their life purpose. The numerous discussions that followed their regressions highlighted the importance of their help in transforming their current life problems. This was a major breakthrough. I found a common outcome of this work was that a simple, current lifetime problem often served as a trigger, propelling them to work on their current life purpose. This problem often was a remnant from another lifetime. The common belief is that we keep coming back until we reach perfection.

The next time that Courtney came in for her session, she told me about a very unusual dream she had the night before.

C: I had a very profound dream Sunday night, 1/16/05.

B: Is this dream in reaction to flying over Bande Aceh?

C: It has similarities to that but let's see. Okay this was on the 16th going into the 17th and waking up around 4 a.m. An island. But once you got up towards the top of the stairs, you kinda turned a little corner and then you could see all of Manhattan. Like right, almost as if you're on a helicopter flying really close to the building, and it was really super clean. And inside there was a spirit guide and he seemed to me to be Hindu or Buddhist in a way but he was ecumenical. And it was all of the common denominators of the religions of the world. And it was very spiritual. There were five of us who were incarnated souls that were there to learn. And above us were disincarnate spirits and they were all praying and meditating. All of the meditation went right to Ground Zero and they were saying that it's a portal, because the Trade Towers are down. Now it's more; it's open and an even wider portal and it's cyclical up and down and up and they were all in saffron color robes. And I remember we were learning something really spiritual and I remember I had to take my shoes off when I entered the temple. And there was a point where the instructor said to look out the windows. And we looked out the windows and he showed us what the skyline of Manhattan looked like or would look like in 25 years. There are a lot of buildings made of crystals or material that were like crystal and like wireless would become obsolete like the 8 track. Because people will be able to use that part of their brain more, so that there would be no more need for wireless. You just know that someone is speaking to you. Yeah just beam it in, you get it!

B: Who were these people who were there with you?

C: People that are on the earth. They're embodied. Now I didn't recognize anybody. But I'd be curious to know if I'd throw a fishnet out who'll know there (is) a point off the tip of Manhattan. That this place exists. You can't see it. I mean it's on a higher plane.

B: You know where Avalon is?

C: No, but it's like Avalon. They chant and meditate for the people of New York to be aware of the earth changes and to be progressively changing building practices.

I told Courtney that I had done regression work with Alicia who is also very psychic and currently works with a group of people who are very spiritually advanced. I thought perhaps she was one of the people who was there with Courtney, and I was going to lunch with Alicia the following day. I asked Courtney if she were open to my telling Alicia about her experience without revealing her identity. This might determine whether Alicia was one of the group Courtney had been dreaming about. Courtney agreed, and then followed up by talking about the place where this dream had occurred.

C: Yeah it's literally 10 yards where you would get to board the Staten Island ferry. And it's moved because all of that is landfill. 'Cause there are a lot of astral beings and souls that have crossed over and angelic beings that were up above us and everything was like this beautiful yellow orangey color. 'Cause they were wearing this type of robes and the chanting was really beautiful. It was like an OM.

It just went everywhere but they were focusing it on Ground Zero. The instruction was over but I knew I would be coming back, but I cannot find my shoes. So I had to walk back to Manhattan barefoot.

B: Have you ever been in this place before?

C: No.

B: And when you woke up, how did you feel?

C: I felt very calm and peaceful about it. Like I'd been up to a higher place. Like I wasn't afraid at all. Yeah that's right.

B: For you, what do your shoes represent?

C: They represent more of the material. In the astral plane you don't need shoes. They represent the material world and you don't need them. It's very vivid and sticks with me. He's a little pudgy and he's got a full head of hair and there's hair short with gray coming in, and he's dark. He's either Tibetan or Indian. He actually looks more Indian, because his eyes are big. I think he is disincarnate.

B: And what's his goal?

C: I think his goal—there's something about the Akashic records. That the living as well as the people who crossed over are learning to operate at a higher vibration. So some of the stuff I felt in August, that I'm being rewired. That's why the stuff is happening. Or that's what I'm perceiving. It's uncomfortable but I know that there's a purpose to it. Nancy was telling me that the first three chakras are being worked on by everybody.

Being (Re)Born Into the Current Lifetime

Two other unusual experiences were highlighted by the descriptions of the following encounters of Victor and Leila. They are reports of how they were born into this lifetime.

As Victor was awakened from a hypnotherapy trance, he described his birth.

V: As I was coming out I knew I was going to be cold. I was more aware of what my purpose was. I was being told as I came into this life that it was going to be all right and as I was pulled out from my right side

out, the guides were telling me on my shoulder, it's going to be okay—
eventually you'll be okay. I was coached while I was coming in.

And Victor said to me, "I don't feel alone anymore," and his face lit up. He
later called to let me know that this experience was healing because it allowed him to deal with his identity issues. As a result, he returned home,
terminated his long-term psychotherapy, and is now off on a new adventure
believing that he isn't alone. This was quite a powerful experience, and it still
leaves me feeling very humbled and excited at this man's transformation.

Leila discussed her choice to come into this life as follows.

L: I feel like I didn't want to be born, because it's not going to be a lot
of fun.

B: Then why are you choosing to be born?

L: I don't know. I feel really sad about it. The room—the green tiles—I just
don't like the physical that much—bodies—they're sort of complicated.

B: Any idea of what your purpose is?

L: I have to learn something.

B: What do you have to learn?

L: To be more comfortable in a body.

B: Why do you have to learn to be more comfortable?

L: Bodies are like rubber—smooth—rubbery and not natural for me.

B: Where did you come from before the body?

L: Some kind of spirit form.

B: And where does this spirit form come from?

L: From God. It just feels like I have to deal with the body. I have to learn
how to be in a body and be okay.

B: Is this the first time in a body?

L: Not sure—I don't like it and I don't want to do it. It feels like I wouldn't have been complete if I didn't do it. Something about completeness, having experienced it all.

B: Any other reason?

L: How to integrate it so I don't lose it. Blockage now. Not being able to balance the two—the spiritual and the physical. I have to learn how to blend and make peace with that. I have to be able to accept the things and I know that I knew coming in, with what I know now. I'm so caught up in the physical material now. I don't like it for such a long time. I'm mad about it and the anger was obsessing me.

"Walk-In" Reincarnation

A well-known psychic channeler, Kryon, during a live channeling session in New Zealand in March 2014, explained the following to his audience. (Kryon is a "messenger" who has channeled through Lee Carroll for many years.) Kryon said that after death, human beings often come back. However, some may skip over a seven to fifteen-year growing-up period. The purpose of these "walk-ins" is to *accomplish spiritual things quicker.* There is a soul agreement between the two souls, and another soul usually comes in at the ages of eight to thirteen. Thus, there are two souls in one body, which he says is really one soul—God. Kryon described walk-ins as very common, manifested by an old soul passing and then coming back quickly into a person who has already grown biologically. He called it a "system of benevolence" in which spiritual growth can take less time.

So, I leave it up to you, the reader, to ponder and try to understand where one person's experience stands in the realm of possibilities. A lesson to be learned is that you can't change a life, but you can certainly change your actions at any time. That's something that's within everyone's power.

A Past Life Regression With a Person I Had Never Met Before Describes a Past Lifetime With Me

This next experience totally surprised me, since only one other person had ever reported that I was present with them during a past lifetime. While in a trance, Alicia described herself as a young man hiding in an Egyptian wheat field near the Nile. Down by the river, she overheard men traveling in a *falucca* (boat with a sail) who were describing her people. They were full of violence.

She kept on saying, "I have to tell them, I have to tell them," but she knew it was futile. Alicia said that her people couldn't protect themselves because they didn't have weapons, nor did they know how to use them. She was "a member of a community of scholars that had something to do with Amon-Re, the pharaoh who is dead." Her people carried on the tradition of "*One*, the *One*." She said, "He is what you would call an ascended master who walks the path of power."

In this description, she was a male scribe transcribing secret writings on papyrus with the instrument that had to be dipped in ink and then etched into the papyrus.

A: We were in a domed room, with an ocularis, that allowed natural sunlight to stream through. I'm on a platform writing and when we were finished, we would take our writings, crawl on our belly and hide it. They found our dome and killed us, by throwing stones and dirt in through the ocularis and we were buried alive. I could feel it coming in on me and choking on the dust. I was writing the scribe's language. What we were writing about, came from all that is One. The priests hated us, because this threatens their power. People don't believe they can access the gods by themselves. It's direct, that's why it's not a temple. That's why it's round, because it's the circle. It's the illusion. It gathers, intensifies and focuses. I get my full powers from the heavens and it's all in metal. The pyramids are not like today. They're all metal and they gleam in the sunlight. We do not need such an elaborate structure, because the light comes down through the open center through that openness and the ocularis at the top of the dome. It symbolizes life. We are also so vulnerable.

And I know all of my people will die. Nothing I can do but lie here hopelessly. I wish I had some powers to fight, but I was so helpless and I wish I could summon some anger to make my father understand. I was a boy then. I can see that my father in this life, was the same as my father in the life I'm in now. I can be angry against my father for being so helpless. I just had to resign myself to my fate. It's a matter of faith, because I know that this is not the only life that I was identifying too much, with the outer form. I can see our own deaths, but I know and I'm afraid of the actual experience. They forced us and at the right time the scrolls will be found. It's as if when I write, I write with my own blood. Not the kind of death I had hoped for and in the right time the scrolls will be found.

And I'm not writing now but for the future. I want to write now. Feel it's selfish. And my father looks at me, because he knows too and he tells me we'll be together again (she starts quietly crying). And that I'll remember. Because I have the memory and he won't remember, but he will. I'm supposed to wake him up and I promise him that I'll wake him up. Even if he doesn't believe me. And I look around at all my friends and what we have is so precious, and we're all going to die, all by violence. Not the way we would have chosen. My brother and sister there, too. There's (*a friend's name*) and Barbara you are there too. You're writing the way you write now. And we're going to be very old and yet impelled. "We're all going to remember."

"We're all going to remember." She (*another friend*) speaks and sees. She's a fore-teller. Like an oracle. She looks into the water in the basin. There's a basin. She's my very good friend. She's older than I am. Like I was a boy and she was a boy. But she's my mother's friend. My mother is Joanne (*a friend*). She's like, in both worlds. There are those who work in the temple and some who write. Almost everyone in my group is there. But the one in power and the power was in the hands of the ones with the weapons.

It's about the heart. That's where the power is and it starts with it. It just isn't about the balance of the center. It's allowing the heart to inform other centers. There is a reason why if your heart stops so does your body. If your mind stops working through your brain, the body will continue to live if the heart is working. Remember this always. How significant the heart is to the system. It is involuntary muscle that continues to work. Even though sometimes you can turn the mind off through states of meditation the heart continues to beat. The heart can be slowed through intention, but the heart must continue to beat, is the key. And a blow to the heart means instant death.

B: So as you continue to breathe in and out, I want you to bring yourself to the time of your death in that lifetime and see what happens.

A: I'm older 18-19 but I'm considered an adult man. I'm sitting cross-legged and the sunlight is so beautiful. I am writing directly from the light, through my head and heart and through to my hands. It's effortless. It's all part of my training and my schooling which is classic and I worked hard to use my mind. Once it comes, it just flows. Each of us is here to write our joint experience, of what it means for us to be in the One, in the Oneness. And so now, not being a boy anymore, I feel much more accepting about my upcoming death. It's not being able to breathe and feeling the pain of having so much on top of me and having myself linger and feel the pain. Waiting to go—crushed—and I'm still holding onto my reed. My stylus—it's in my hands. I'm so attached to getting that down and preserving it. I fall on the floor. Death. Being buried and not being able to breathe and feeling pain. And I can't let my mind go of it and it's keeping me in my body and I didn't know. I was so attached to just a point of view. It's just part of you. Oh what a relief. I'm out of my body and my body is dead but I'm not dead. *Oh* I'm feeling relief and a feeling of peace. *Whew.* It will be all right. And here are my guides and it all comes back. And the happiness seeing all my friends and buddies, and they're moving up to the higher planes. Feeling the ecstasy. Ah, it's bliss and it brings back all the times in that life. Feel it—experience it—feels so delicious.

In this reenactment, Alicia's description of her time of death and subsequent out-of-body experiences sounded delightful. Her transition from life to death was just a momentary transition and painless.

B: So let me ask you while you're in this place, what is it that you chose to come into this lifetime for—your purpose? What are you here to do in this lifetime?

A: I came in to transmit. Transmit the ecstasy, joy. To not hold onto the anger and rage and not be able to hold onto it. And then the time passage. For I will live a long time. I have chosen a very long life and the genetic material that will allow me to do that. But more importantly, I will be open to, and I may write many books. It will just come, once I get over the fear, that it's not a matter of life or death. The opposite of death is birth. It's all opening up and it feels good. I want to have fun and to be serious. My occipitals are relaxing and my cranial sutures are relaxing. And I'm reactivating.

B: As you continue to breathe in and out, is there any other message you'd like to give to yourself in this lifetime, that you should be aware of from this central place?

A: It's about trust and faith. Just walk and leave the rest to divine order which is not controlled at all.

B: And while you're in this state, how do you feel you'll be able to do this? What is it you tell yourself—how can you transcend that fear? What messages do you give to yourself?

A: That it's not a matter of life. Well, the opposite of death is not life. It's about trust and faith. We were like a sect that kept the Amon-Re as the pharaoh. The Third Kingdom. I know of rumors of secret writings. I don't know if what is important is the physical artifact or that it's being remembered.

B: How did it feel for you going through that?

A: It's all a cycle. I think the fear I felt was more the fear of a boy.

B: How old was the boy?

A: I guess 7.

B: So it took a long time before they took over? Who were they who you overheard?

A: They were the ones with the temple power. And we were like a sect who kept on the teachings of Amon-Re, who was the pharaoh, who sort of—who had literally exterminated the hierarchy of gods and god-desses. And one god was the Sun King, Re is the sun and Amon-Re was the pharaoh.

B: What year comes to mind?

A: 3rd Kingdom.

B: Did they ever find those scrolls in this lifetime?

A: I don't know.

B: Because if they came in on you the scrolls were underground.

A: It was sideways like radiating chambers out of it. So it wasn't under-ground. No, I know that there have been rumors of secret writings and I don't know that it's so important. The physical artifact, as the fact that it's remembered.

Alicia is a very spiritual person who sometimes works as a medical intuitive and has transmitted messages from disincarnate souls. During that regres-sion lifetime, the scribes were secretively channeling spiritual energy from the heavens above into writings on papyrus. She described the light stream-ing through the center, which was the ocularis. These writings were then hidden because the belief system of this group was totally anathema to the ruling group.

As she lay in a trance and talked about the rocks that were being thrown through the dome of the ocularis and describing the way she died and that all of the scribes were buried alive, her hand that held the reed that she was writing with (in that lifetime) was clenched in a way as if it were still wrapped around that writing implement. Her hand was raised and literally quivering as she lay there. It was stunning to watch this regression unfold.

At the moment she described the rocks being thrown through the opening, I felt a fear arise in me. It reminded me of my own current lifetime experiences when I had felt an immediate panic-type fear about the thought of crawling into cave spaces. I had been petrified at the thought of being crushed to death while I was vacationing in a country with underground water caves. I was surprised at my spontaneous reaction at that time, since I had no prior experiences that would have warranted that type of response.

Alicia's description of being crushed to death brought that panicked feeling to the fore. It was then resolved for me as I realized that I probably died in a similar way. So when Alicia described me as being with her in that lifetime with another colleague of hers who I also knew, I felt that instantaneous *aha*. This is the second person who has ever described me as being part of their past lifetime, and I knew instantaneously that was true. What shocked me was that I had never met Alicia before this past life regression work.

After her regression, Alicia said that her reaction was very powerful, and she had felt it before. Her emotional reaction to the regression was as if it were happening in real time. Her feeling was one of experiencing the danger of holding radical views, which were not accepted by society. The emotion was still there. Is it fear? The past life regression experience was almost like it had just happened, and it condenses time. Alicia said that she can physiologically capture the peace and flow of life at that time.

The Third Kingdom, she said, was the Third Dynasty. Amon-Re was the most powerful sun sign and the One. The One refers to the one God that people looked to as they practiced *monotheism*. It was an outgrowth of *polytheism*, the following of many gods. "It was a blessed relief when I died." She said to me, "You were wearing a *balalaika*, like a gown-linen kind of thing, and you were a woman."

She was describing a spiritual practice. I realized that I had received my current lifetime spiritual training, including the use of past life regression techniques and other spiritual modalities, at a healing center in the Berkshires. Many people there channeled energy, and it was called The Center of the Light! This was similar to the channeling of energy that Alicia had described coming through the center of the ocularis. At that time in the 1980s, health-care practitioners did not openly discuss their spiritual and alternative thera-peutic practices. In fact, when Dr. Brian Weiss's first book, *Many Lives, Many Masters*, was published in 1988, it burst onto the world scene, bringing the practice of PLRT into the open.

In our discussions afterward, I told Alicia about my past lifetime as a Native American when my heart was cut out by members of another tribe; they were trying to understand the nature of our group. Alicia said she had the same image in Egypt where they made special containers for the heart, which they took out and mummified. She said that there are jars contain-ing these hearts at the Metropolitan Museum of Art. I thought of the many times I had been at the Museum, one block away. I had never seen the jars nor paid attention nor had any interest in the antiquities of that time period. I wonder why!

Alicia then talked about contrasts. If you knew that you were peace-ful and without weapons, those less evolved would eventually exterminate you—they just would! Of course, if you took up arms yourself, you were identifying with them. It's like Gandhi, who must have known he was going to be killed. The intensity of her descriptions felt as if she were "living in that moment," and I felt as if I were "there" with her. It was such a powerful expe-rience for me. The intensity of her descriptions typified most people's past lifetime regressions, with all the warts, passion, fears, and anxieties.

So, I asked Alicia about the people who were killing people in her coun-try during that lifetime:

B: Where did these people come from?

A: I get that they were the ones that were sleeping. But that was the majority and they also wanted temple power and over others and they used physical strength to do it and they were going to silence us. You knew eventually it would happen and that's been the fate of every peaceful nonviolent person. But in general that's what happens so of course we have fear around that. One of the reasons that we had to have that sunlight and be in that circle is that there is something literally about the shape of the dome which assisted us and the sunlight. It focused in and we could focus, and the sound, and something about the light. Just this shaft of light.

This was a very powerful conversation surrounding spirituality for both of us. It focused on the responsibility of the individual toward participating in peace throughout the planet. And of course, that evolves from a person's spiritual searching, growing, and treating others with respect and kindness. It then allows us to recognize that perhaps a tragedy such as 9/11 happens for a reason beyond our current lifetime understanding.

One way to view individuals' unconscious soul purpose for this lifetime is perhaps that they chose to come in and be of service to mankind. Those brave, conscious souls who were killed perhaps surrendered their lives to bring international attention to the horrors that continue to exist. And people throughout the world were brought to their knees at the horror of that event. They became more conscious and aware of their own interactions with each other. It forces all of us to pay attention as to how we can make a contribution during this lifetime. We must realize that our current lifetime contributions are what we came to do as *Bodhisattvas*—those who have attained enlightenment and are committed to the attainment of enlighten-ment for others

Kryon, whom I previously discussed in this chapter, channeled infor-mation that was presented before the United Nations many times. Some information was presented about issues involving the United States before 9/11/01. During a live channeling event in Vancouver BC, Canada, Kryon was asked how we were to have unity on earth. He specifically talked about the issues America had that needed to be resolved. These included internal gov-erning issues, for example, the need for elected officials of Congress to come together and work across the aisle and bridge their differences as well as to work together internationally. He said that the United States is currently in its greatest learning period and must transcend the concept of isolationism by joining the world. The United States cannot continue as separatists and must work cooperatively on global initiatives as partners of this planet. He believes that the resistance to changing our old ideas and ways of doing things is based on fear. And then he said that "the potential for the most profound creative changes come in the year of the three (2001)." He also said that we all have a role in making changes within ourselves, our families, and in our cultures that can reverberate throughout the world. The magnitude of this event was predicated on the belief that we all have to change our atti-tudes, to see ourselves as part of the greater whole, and see ourselves as *one*.

People's interest in becoming more involved in their own care while searching for purpose and meaning is reflected in their interest in PLRT. Increased public interest in spirituality and self-help is highlighted by the health-care paradigm shift to complementary and allopathic (alternative) medicine (CAM). Visits by adults to CAM practitioners grew from more than 25 million visits in 1997 to 354.2 million visits in 2007.

There continues to be increasing interest in the areas of spirituality, soul growth, and life purpose. People are searching for an understanding of life and death and what happens to them and their loved ones in the afterlife. The knowledge of our immortality can help dissolve the fears of death. That belief can also help us deal with the chronic life problems that most people experience.

Enough people must awaken, become fully conscious, and take responsibility for themselves, the planet, and all humanity. It is important to enhance each person's spirituality so that each person becomes more enlightened. There is a shift in this country and throughout the world as increased numbers of people strive toward peace. People are becoming more involved in organizations and peaceful protests for human rights while working toward the highest good for all. We have to bring everyone along.

A year and a half later, Alicia revealed to me that she was told that the domed structure she had previously described to me was called a *beehive*. They were abandoned structures made of mud and water and had been left behind as people moved on to build the pyramids in the Valley of the Kings. These scribes were using the abandoned structures for their spiritual activities. Perhaps those of us who were writing at that time were also channeling spiritual information from another plane that was out of the mainstream. I recognized my participation during her past lifetime, and as I write this book, this will be the third time (from various lifetimes) I've ventured forth by putting spiritual information out into the world. This time, I fully expect *not* to be crushed to death or have my heart cut out but to work toward having this work accepted by a much more enlightened universe.

As I further explored this period of time, I discovered that Amon-Re was highly regarded and believed to be King of the Gods. The Egyptian God was known as Amon (from 2008-1957 BCE). As the patron saint of Thebes, the city where pharaohs ruled, he became joined with the Sun God Re, thus the name Amon-Re. He represented wind, fertility, and souls.

Alicia returned for another regression months later and she easily went into a trance. I saw that her right hand was making movements as if she were pill rolling.

A: I'm feeling the strength of my bowstring, because I'm going to go out. There's two of us. I am a young man and my sister is with me and feeling the tautness and touching it. I get wounded in my right thigh by an arrow. I did it myself. A lot of blood. We live on the edge of the woods. She calls my mother and brings me into the house. The three sisters come and they take the arrow out and then they take a poultice and put it on my body. My sister watches and they put their hands on it and start chanting. Not in our language maybe in Latin. We are a middle-class family in what is now Germany. My father is a miller. I can see the stream. As their hands are on me, they give me something and I feel I am drifting asleep. And I wake up in the morning. And there's no wound. I take off the mud and it is completely healed, as if the arrow was never in it. Later in life, I saw they were both hung as witches. But it's too late for my sister, because she's already been made part of the group. But I arrange for her to get married, to get her out of this. Away. I say I have witnessed this. How can it be so awful? How can people not accept any healers in that time? I myself denounced their work as the work of the devil. I became so righteous. It's almost as if I couldn't stand to witness what happened. I had so much conflict and guilt that I turned it into hellfire and damnation and my sister continued to help others. She was buried alive. I tried to save her. It was such a horrible time to be alive and I was part of this 1490s 80s or 50s.

B: What caused you to talk against the healing?

A: I thought that if I talked against it, our family would be cleared and my sister would be saved and then I got caught up in it. It was true and it was the work of the devil. They were keeping to the old ways and the new ways were coming in. My sister became this healer, out of this love for me. I was very sad when I died in that life of ...TB of the lungs. It had to do with my heart. A very grey lifetime. Not to sell out because of fear. Not to try to protect. Where was my trust? Instead I chose to focus on the manifestation of evil. Tried to protect my sister becoming like those who were prosecuted. I'm so close, I loved her. Is she my sister in this lifetime?

The state of life he lives—a floating sensation—having no body but feeling so wonderful and so fluid. And when I come back into a body next time, I'm going to be one of those healers, that I have been many times.

Alicia was male in that lifetime and fulfilled her promise as she is a healer in this lifetime. She channeled the following information while continuing in a disembodied state in her trance.

A: Focus on the simplicity. All the great breakthroughs have been very simple. The universe, the cosmos, as complex as it might seem, are simple principles. The mind makes it complex. Know about the simplicity behind the complexity. There's one thing I want to say about this place, don't take it all so seriously. Everything if you allow it, will fall into place.

Keep your eyes and ears open. Just pay attention to telecommunication. Practice your telepathy; it's the wave of the future. Key is to listen. The key to telepathy, is that listening is so important, since human beings often can't wait to get the next word in. The way to tell who is devoted or committed to his or her spiritual path, is to look at the development of the chakra above the heart. The so-called aqua chakra-blue-dolphins one is present in almost all new newborns as a bird or a scent. My sister—I loved her, so much more than without anyone else. She's the one who didn't make it into this life.

In relation to the wound she suffered, she said:

A: There is an energetic template, on which energy is built. The body will flow into it. It helps to cover the wound so that you don't focus on the gash. The mind doesn't do anything, but to hide it from my own gaze and perpetuate my own existence healing of it. If you focus on it, it allows the illness to become real. It is very revolutionary and needs to be and is most important to remember. In even the belief, that there are good germs and bad germs, just opportunistic organism trying to do the best, that live within our bodies. In this day and age, there will always be an audience for new i-deas. Those meant to read and study, will come of their own. Is the center that allows you to speak with heart, green-blue. Touch the place and know if they're talking from the head or heart and you'll know you speak from there. Being a healer or a health practitioner of any sort, is a very noble enterprise. For you yourself will grow, through the intimate contact with others. I guess I should be born again. I'm going to decide what to work on nasty getting closer to the earth and I'm feeling so much heavier. This time I want to be a girl. This time I'm going to know what it is to trust and have faith and be patient. When you trust there is no need for patience. Patience is something that must be endured. Patience is in back of trust.

B: Is this your first lifetime as a girl?

A: No I skipped over a whole bunch.

B: I guess this is an important one, because you healed and yet you, for the sake of protecting, you had to go with the current feeling about the healers? At the time that was true.

A: Thirteen is the number that is sacred to women. They were all the healers 'til they were exterminated. I think there's something in this book (a book that she had been reading about healers) about the extermination of the midwives, the healers, and that's when the men took over. It's in the Middle Ages and thousands of women were killed.

During our conversation, Alicia told me that she was shown a book about women healers. For her, the synchronicity of the unfolding of these events was interesting. So, nothing is by coincidence. It is said that we often manifest ideas or objects at the time that it is important for us to receive the lessons that are necessary for our highest good.

We then talked about her regression and her description of how she was wounded by an arrow. She told me that she had been clearing brush on her property and was bruised by a tree branch. It was in the same area where she described being wounded by an arrow in her regression.

A: The other thing I couldn't laugh about was the tree got me right here (when she was clearing brush on her property).

B: Oh that's where you hit yourself yesterday. How did you get the arrow in your leg?

A: It was like this somehow and I showed I was going for a rabbit and the rabbit was on the ground and I pulled back on the bow and I hit myself through the thigh.

B: So, it's interesting what you said. There was a healing and it was covered, because if it was uncovered and you looked at it, you would be in the mind-set of, I'm hurt, I'm injured.

A: That was weird, isn't that weird?

B: It's a revolutionary thing. It's about what we're thinking about. If you keep on thinking about the negative, or that I'm sick, you'll be sick.

A: Right.

B: When my veterinarian said, "We can't find what we want, a lymphoma," I responded with, "Wait a minute, it's good that you're not finding a lymphoma just to prove that your diagnosis is correct." Because you're not supposed to find that! They say that if it's not a lymphoma, they really don't know what's wrong with my cat. So, what's wrong with not knowing?

A: You know the power!

B: You described how we think about illness. When we get an illness and keep thinking illness and keep thinking that way, instead of healing and health, we are in the illness mode and radiate that thought. That's a very revolutionary way of thinking and yet so simple. That's the complexity. What I was thinking about was one of the newer treatments for cancer is very simple—cut off the blood supply to the cancer cells so they can no longer be nourished. And how long did it take the researchers to realize that?

Two days later, Alicia sent me the following e-mail:

> So this morning when I woke up I looked down at my "wounded" right thigh (where the tree branch snapped back and zinged me). The bruise had completely changed shape fading from yesterday, and yes, was in the shape of an arrow, from the triangular tip/head through the thin shaft, with "feathers" and an entry wound near my hip where the tree did its worse damage. Not quite believing my eyes, I asked someone who had been seeing it for over a week, what my bruise looked like today. The reply was "it's much fainter today and looks just like an arrow!" I took a picture of my leg.

Alicia's channeled information reveals some very important information about the way our thoughts can create different realities. As a result of this, I included verbatim information received from her during this trance because I felt it was very relevant to the way we view our lives. The information channeled through these regressions serves as a font of wisdom to be followed for a more fulfilled, informative life. She brought back a lot of useful information that we should all try and heed.

Two Stranger DescribeTheir Multiple Lifetime Travels in a Joint Regression Session

I finally spoke with Alicia, and she instantly felt that she could be one of the people Courtney was talking about. I had been working with Courtney for a few years, while I had only worked with Alicia two to three times. As I was walking to my office, I reminded myself that I had to contact Courtney and Alicia about the upcoming meeting to discuss Courtney's experience. I had spoken with Courtney, and now I had to talk to Alicia. At the second I said that to myself, a truck with the name of the restaurant in which Alicia and I had lunched went by. I like to think that my spirit guides are having fun and reminding me that they are around.

So, finally, one year later, we finally met; yes, that's how long it took for the three of us to be able to arrange our schedules. The energy that flowed during that encounter was overwhelming. When Alicia told Courtney that she felt they were together in an Egyptian lifetime, for the first time, I saw Courtney hesitate. She said she couldn't acknowledge that and said that she was being kept from going there by her spirit guides. This was the first time in all of the regressions we had worked on together that she reported that her spirit guide was keeping her from any experiences. And for me, I had never experienced the powerful interchange and flow of energy in my life as I did during the following past life regression between these two women who met for the first time.

Courtney and Alicia:

A: I feel like I'm in Egypt. Not sandy—very lush. The healing temples are there. I know I see Courtney.

C: I'm in the Pacific Northwest and a lot of medicine men and we're still around the fire and we're Blackfoot.

A: I think that's later. There's something that's important about crystal and Egypt and pyramids. There are places on earth known as power spots and they hold an energetic grid-work-like a geometric construct. These lines run through the earth.

C: Are you near Alaska?

A: Mt. Shasta. There's a road that takes you to New Mexico to the four corners—the Agnizes.

C: There's a pulse. I feel a pulse. I hear the...I can feel the pulse in my sacrum. Like the pulse of the earth. I feel so bound to the earth and it's a very visual kinesthetic feeling. To think that one day man would feel so out of it. From this place I hear the drum too.

A: I see you there and we're talking about…and we talk about the crystal matrix.

C: Is more localized. Like priestly cults in Egypt were not universal. I have a headache as if I'm in some resistance about remembering this. It comes from a fear. I thought I knew then this would happen now. If I go too deeply into this it would get too confusing a feeling of….

A: My present body is giving me a headache…

C: I'm…

A: You're a boy hmmmmm and I'm a man.

C: Yeah I see you.

A: The ability to travel into other world(s), so easy and we had a gift. Like others—hunting or—has a very respected place in the community it seems like …

C: Shape shifter.

A: Not the—sense of—being able to travel with just consciousness and what would be helpful for the present.

C: It's for teaching I see. They're magic.

A: You can travel on their call—they have a great sense of call.

C: The way the whales do.

A: Northwest—whales there is great numbers off the way to…feel them in my…

C: They are my brothers. Long memory….In the water, wash over me.

A: Let the energy--- from sacrum rise up and warm.

C: There are dolphins there too.

A: Fishing is easy when you call and ask who…

C: All life is connected and is...and we knew when we ate something we blended with its energy.

A: I'm under the water now. It's almost like there's a city under there. Not like a city it's...something in the water...important that it's the Pacific... different from Atlantic.

C: More clarity.

A: Fire in the water power runs like electricity and carries the energy—has different quality. The whales have something to do with it. Can you leave the...

C: Goes through the body.

A: And a stillness because there is motor...

C: We're supposed to go somewhere else. I'm in the sky. We built a cruise observation of the dog man.

A: There?

C: Yes.

A: Certain people in the tribe took care of our bodies while we were traveling.

C: In case anything happens.

A: Not us—we're the travelers and we know there's a big disaster going to happen to our tribes. The coming of the White man, a lot of fighting. I feel like I'm traveling back into time so fast when the earth was new.

C: I've dreamt when the continents were jumbled together and the place that I am was the Russian steppes. Human, one-half human and one-third animal that didn't quite make the transformation into human.

A: Egypt-temples to help. Like the Centaurs that were half-human half-animal.

C: Almost as if the...from the star beings and they got trapped going in and out of the bodies and they could...

A: Now I'm in China. Someone with a long white beard and he's a venerable teacher. Cold and mountainous but there's energy there that reminds me of Tibet?

C: Not more of a continuum of conscious from life to life?

A: The importance of the continuity of consciousness and allows us to use the mind not as a weapon but to have control—it's a natural religion but learning to use the mind I feel like I'm being taught this and there is great physical hardship how to heal our body with our minds. Go with the power of the energy and use the one like Martial Arts of the mind discipline. I see little. Being schooled I seem to be wearing black-quilted robe with a red sash. I feel that the point of this is that we remember how much history how much energy has gone in. Feel awareness of present in the past and despite....Now an enormous shift happening. Watch and be aware that this is so—it is real no headache.

C: Headache to front of head—diamond—like third eye.

A: Sacred to the Indians.

C: Goes back into time before that it's recognizing, remembering and recovering skills. Indians had the...and so much ahead.

A: We're being called to open the doors again and it will all unfold and next steps will be clear. At the moment it is important to recognize the importance of these guides who are here and will always help.

C: And they laying hands on you.

A: If you ask us to, if you do, when you go and stop a minute we will help you. Do your work and in your relationship and allow the...to come. Don't have to be forced—is changing hologram—double helix and spiral within spiral and don't need to know it or see it all it will...in bite-size pieces.

This past life regression between Alicia and Courtney was one of the most powerful experiences I had ever witnessed. Here were two women, totally unknown to each another before this meeting, who were obviously together in other lifetimes. The only common factor was my introducing them to each another. They felt an immediate connection when they met. Courtney was hesitant to explore the Egyptian lifetime since she believes there is something there that she is not ready to explore at this time.

As I listened and wrote and taped their exchanges, I had no interaction except briefly as noted above. The consensus is that we all come in for a reason, and we have a mission to accomplish. Each of these women is involved in practices of spirituality and works with others through their personal participation in making the planet a more peaceful place. This includes working with and teaching others to evolve to their highest level of ability. The experience was a personal validation of our interconnectedness. It encouraged them to continue their work.

I hope you, the reader, can allow yourself to "listen" to these regressions and peoples' experiences and let them resonate within yourself. I believe that all of us have the ability to tune into the world and our own life purpose. The range of these experiences should be heard from within and not judged. Hopefully, the inclusion of all of these reenactments may provide a springboard for your own spiritual journeys.

13

Conclusion

"The purpose of life is not to be happy. It is to be useful, to be honorable, to be compassionate, to have it make some difference that you have lived and lived well."

~RALPH WALDO EMERSON

Emerson was a 19th century philosopher, poet, and essayist. He had a tremendous influence on the American Transcendental movement influencing Walt Whitman, Henry Thoreau, William James and Friedrich Nietzsche, and other great thinkers. He said at the time, "Perhaps the Buddhist is a Transcendentalist." He was ahead of his time in relation to his life purpose view. The Dalai Lama's belief that we are all here to contribute to the world in our own particular way is a beautiful message for everyone. He teases out the boundless, unlimited strands of consciousness. I have found that as a result of PLRT, many seekers who found themselves stuck in long-term therapy and unable to find the crux of their chronic problems made immediate life changes as they took responsibility for all dimensions of their lives.

In addition, they were strongly affected by the reports of others' regression experiences that I recounted. People applied the spiritual implications gleaned from those reports into their own lives. Those suffering from the death of a loved one felt hopeful that these souls were freed up and that they would meet with them again. Others described a greater appreciation for their own individual contribution even in a world that seems to reward self-focus and materialism. This therapy is not widely used, but I believe the findings warrant increased exploration in the psychological community.

After working as a psychotherapist for more than 39 years, I continue to be amazed at the immediacy of this work and the rapidity of each person's personal growth that is experienced within a short time. Through PLRT, I found that people were at ease as they were able to talk about their emotional difficulties. They told me that they were able to solve problems that had not been addressed nor helped within their traditional psychotherapy or by taking antianxiety and antidepressant medications. The most important outcome was that individuals were able to gain a new awareness of their current life situations and how to change them. People learned how to reframe situations of their life view and to determine what they could gain from each experience, instead of being self-punitive (e.g., bad things are happening to me now because I was a bad person in another life). Many have moved toward a greater awareness of their spiritual connection in the universe, and these changes have helped them to transform their life experiences. This is what prompted me to document their experiences, resulting in this book.

Some people found immediate relief from their phobic symptoms. However, for those with severe panic attacks and phobia problems, suffering from chronic, crippling fears or with phobic reactions in place for many years, it took multiple sessions for change to occur. These people usually needed more time using PLRT and psychotherapy to overcome their emotional paralysis. In fact, in these instances, the importance of working through these experiences using the psychotherapeutic process is emphasized. This work serves to enhance people's interpretations by simultaneously integrating the findings into their daily lives.

What has become quite clear for me and the hundreds of patients I have worked with individually using PLRT is that current life events are one brief light in the broader picture of our life purpose. It is important for us to become more conscious, understand our life's experiences, and make unique contributions to society. Our souls have lived before during different time periods in different countries throughout the world—both rich and poor, male and female, from all religions, races, and ethnic groups. We are part of and not separate from the rest of the world. Issues can no longer be viewed from the narrow scope of one country.

We are here with souls we have lived with before. People from other cultures may have been our spouses, parents, siblings, and close friends. All people must be treated with respect as if we are family, ensuring everyone's civil rights. If we learn to love each other as our family, then we will become outraged when people are denied their civil rights. Respect should be extended to peoples throughout the world and cut across race, gender, religion, and national origin. We should have a universal belief system whereby each person contributes something to the planet to help it heal before we experience the ultimate meltdown and deterioration as services continue to decline. People should have an opportunity to aspire to the greatest they are capable of being and be encouraged to make a difference in the world. We are all here for a reason. Events happening in the world have a broader and deeper meaning than external experiences or stereotyped materialistic values. We can become more fulfilled, and then our souls can move on.

It is imperative that we determine our purpose and life goals during this lifetime. If we decide that it is to gain more humility, we may choose to be reborn into a family where that experience could be lived through to our broader purpose. We might realize that some of our "soul mates" or deep friendships are with people we have chosen to be reborn with to help each other work through the patterns together. Many have chosen to be reborn with soul mates in deep friendships to work through behavioral lifestyle patterns together. We must all become stewards of the world *in the family of man.*

Life purpose explorations affirm the importance of spirituality in our lives, which is an integral part of this book. It is critical for a person to determine his or her life purpose during this lifetime. People should understand that illness and other conditions may be lessons to evolve their soul's purpose for themselves and others. During their explorations, people began to question their current world views: beliefs that we are supposed to live as long as we can without illness, look young, and be happy, and "whoever dies with the most toys wins." The premature death of someone young, good, successful, or attractive with "everything going for them" is seen as tragic: "They went before their time."

Perhaps a soul incarnates with the purpose of providing insights or maybe to serve as a lesson for another person or groups of people. Viewed from these perspectives, the soul's hidden goal may not be to stay on earth as long as the body holds on but only as long as the individual is of service to humanity. Someone with a prebirth goal of gaining more humility may have chosen to be born into a family living in a part of the world where that experience could be lived through to the person's "broadest purpose." Current experiences should force us to reexamine our need for labeling perceptions and adjust them accordingly and accept that there are other belief systems to explain life experiences.

Some choose to believe that no matter what happens, good or bad, it is for their highest good. It is hard to make sense of tragedies like the senseless death of a loved one, the loss of a home during a catastrophe, or the loss of a career. Life is not a neat package following the good rule's paradigm: "if I'm good and pay my dues, nothing bad will happen." Recognizing this has been an integral part of my work with individuals who chose to search for their own meaning and life purpose. We are all concerned about our mortality. It is comforting and reassuring to know that not only does our soul live on, but that we will meet our relatives and loved ones once our soul moves on.

Through my constant searching as well as my work with the people who chose to use PLRT, I can say I do believe in reincarnation. I cannot prove it beyond a shadow of a doubt, since no one can prove what happens after you die. I simply allowed people who explored this work the freedom to find their own answers. Many did not believe in reincarnation and their past life regression experiences simply opened that up as a possibility. For those who stated that they did believe in reincarnation, they described their regression experience as an affirmation of their belief. So as you can see, there are a variety of ways these techniques can work.

The question, "Why must little children suffer?" started my journey and spiritual search, which has totally transformed my beliefs. Now I believe that souls come in of their own choice to serve as lessons for others. Some may choose to come in for a brief period of time as a child or a miscarried fetus or as a young person or good person. The goal is not to stay in this body for 100 years. The broader message is to come in for our own soul evolution and the greater purpose of humanity. Many people who have died in catastrophic events are often souls who may have chosen to reincarnate for a broader universal contribution. They are the soldiers who lost their lives to show us the greater societal problems that need to be addressed. Unfortunately, we do not pay attention until someone is tortured, dies, leads a severely dysfunctional life, is abused, or murdered. Perhaps some evolved souls have chosen to come into this lifetime only to serve as an example to bring the world to a higher purpose.

As I prepare this book for publication, I would be remiss if I did not mention the Paris terrorist attack of November 13, 2015, and the early December 2015 San Bernardino, California attack. It is hard to understand why people would intentionally kill innocent people. Ironically, while ruminating over this situation, I was working with Courtney, who discussed her prior past lifetime during the Holocaust in chapter 8, "And Some Gave All." In this regression, she saw herself as an eight-year-old girl being fed by the nuns in a Catholic church along with other Jewish people in 1939, war-torn France on the border of Germany. She hid the fact that she was Jewish.

The scene shifted, and Courtney saw herself excited at the thought of being taken to a "work camp" and being able to work. She said the camp was Bergen-Belsen and described many people wearing jackets with yellow stars affixed, marching to the camp. Her next vision was being taken out of the building and marched around to the back. She saw an open pit with dead bodies and she knew what was about to happen to her—she was already out of her body as she was shot—and she never felt a thing!

She reincarnated into this lifetime, as most of us have, to continue to evolve her soul.

Many people who believe in reincarnation know that their souls made a choice to reincarnate into each lifetime with a goal of further soul growth. Through this process, they learned unconditional love, compassion, and acceptance of all people. They continue to reincarnate until they reach a level where they are so evolved that they do not have to reincarnate further.

It has become evident to me and others that our presence on earth is like being in a classroom of learning in order to change the world and evolve our souls to their highest level. So, perhaps it's your lesson, my lesson, our lesson to see how far we have evolved our souls. Some people have specifically made a prebirth decision to come into this lifetime and serve as a lesson for broader humanity. They often don't know what that is, but they have asked to come in and serve. So, when people are born, their service may entail dying in an event of which they have no knowledge but will serve as a lesson to help people further evolve their souls. Or, they may have died on 9/11 or in Paris or in San Bernardino to bring the world together to fight Al Quaeda or ISIS as part of their growth to create acceptance for all peoples. Above all, we must thank the souls that gave their lives for humanity. Sometimes, more evolved souls have chosen to reincarnate for a short while to serve a higher purpose.

Some people have validated their distorted belief that their religion is the only one by killing and pillaging those of a different faith. Ironically, while our horror in the United States at the ISIS attack in Paris or the ISIS-inspired San Bernardino attack is justified, statistics reveal there have been 294 mass killings and 1264 killed or randomly injured by gunfire in the United States in 2015 alone!

Many believers in reincarnation think that world events often happen as a test for all to evolve to their highest level of consciousness. Will we rise to the occasion and evolve our souls to the next level?

The test is, do we join the murderers or do we fight for the rights of people of all races, religions, and belief systems to practice their beliefs as long as they do not infringe on the rights of others?

Can we have compassion for the Syrian refugees fleeing from their war-torn country by embracing them the way our ancestors were welcomed at a time of need? Can we help them find solace and welcome them? Waves of immigration are what have made our country great. In order to survive and to continue to be great, we must continue to embrace a diversity of ideas and cultures.

Empathy for others is hard to develop within people who have not learned how to love, how to be loved, or have grown up in an emotionally impoverished environment. They have the choice to evolve to a higher level or follow their base instincts. So they have to learn from others who do not take the path of least resistance and earnestly strive to do the right thing.

The Statue of Liberty, which stands at the entrance of New York harbor, a gift from the French people, has stood as a symbol of freedom and democracy for decades. Its inscription: "Give me your tired, your poor, your huddled masses yearning to be free" has served as a cornerstone and reflection of our nation's belief.

As Mother Teresa said, "If we have no peace, it is because we have forgotten we belong to each other." The key is to grow in a spiritual and creative way, to advance our soul and that of all life on earth. We must learn how to stand back and examine our life situations from different vantage points with an understanding that everything happens for a reason even though we may not understand it at the time.

But the questions of who we are and why we are here remain timeless for us all. Exploration of who you were in a past life can clarify the work you choose to pursue in this lifetime. It can help you to understand your life purpose as you find greater understanding of life's meaning. Everyone has a unique contribution to make. We all have to give back. It's up to each of us to give direction to our soul and decide what our distinctive contribution will be this time around.

I hope that these writings reflect the stories of individuals' life changes, which resulted in a greater appreciation for their own personal contributions. This includes a reexamination of their values, especially in a world that seemed to reward self-focus and materialism. These stories highlight the fact that all people are interconnected and must take more responsibility for the path they walk. They should fully recognize the universal consciousness.

The universal search for a life purpose affirms the importance of spirituality in life and is an integral part of this book. As people read about the regression experiences, I hope they will be encouraged to begin their own search for their life purpose. According to Lois, "You can't change a life, but you can change your actions anytime. Even with a past you're not happy with, you can make a switch today."

One night as I was returning home, the following information came through me as I spoke into my recorder:

"Remember this, that you and all of the people that you have been doing the past life regression work with have come in with the soul group, and they decided to come in and help you, and you help them when you brought messages into the world about life purpose and the knowledge that we are all here to make a life purpose. This will be the next section for you to think about."

During the past few years, an increasing number of people have begun their search for solutions to their problems through PLRT. My work with those seekers who traveled from abroad and throughout the United States for this unique therapy was very enjoyable to me. Now, I want to share their stories and my insights derived from this very exciting therapy with a broader audience. I believe this book is very timely; it can show how PLRT can help us understand ourselves, our problems, and our broader life purpose. But perhaps a simpler reason is just to help people focus on *who* they are and *why* they are here, now.

Appendix 1

Individuals Describe
Their PLRT Experiences

"And the man whose inner vision is bathed in conscious-
ness at once realizes the spiritual unity which reigns over
all racial differences, and his mind no longer stumbles
over individual facts, accepting them as final."

~RABINDRANATH TAGOR

Tagor captures the essence of unlimited spirituality through a universal unity of all individuals' experiences. Many people were profoundly affected by the past life regressions that I facilitated. I wondered if the regression experiences had long-term effects on people, whether the changes were enduring. So I mailed the following questionnaire to some people I had worked extensively with. I would like to share their replies with you. The following are responses from some participants in the past life experiences narrated in this book. Claire responded first. (Her experiences are reported in chapter 4 as the barn burner and in chapter 10 as the gunslinger.)

1. What prompted you to do PLRT?

I had read Brian Weiss's *Many Lives, Many Masters* and found it very moving. I was really curious to see if I could have a past life experience, and I have always wanted to understand myself better, to feel better about being me. When I called Brian Weiss's office in Miami to ask for a referral in New York City, you were the only name he gave out. I was so excited when you were able to fit me into your schedule.

2. How did you feel when you had a past lifetime experience?

I wasn't really sure it was a past lifetime at first. I felt more like I had simply let my imagination run wild. After the relaxation part of the hypnosis, I remember you started asking me to envision myself on a path, and so I simply imagined a path and went on from there to see how I felt and what I thought I might look like. It was like a game.

There were only two times out of about a dozen past life sessions that I really felt I was being taken somewhere completely surprising, that something other than my imagination was taking over. In both of those experiences, I was the opposite gender from my current life, and I had been the agent of great violence, also the opposite of my current life. Both of these experiences really jump-started my understanding of myself.

3. Did the experience change your views about reincarnation?

I find the concept of reincarnation extremely comforting—much more so than any other concept of what happens after you die. I love the idea that we get to keep working on ourselves, that we come back to improve what we got wrong last time, that the people who really loved us will find us again, and the people who we hurt will present themselves again for us to do better this time around (or not). After having my past life experiences, I felt so much more serene about wanting to believe in reincarnation.

4. Did the experience effect life changes for you, and if so, what are they?

I was in therapy on-and-off with you for about nine years. Speaking to you on a regular basis and learning from your positive outlook on life did effect life changes for me in the sense that it made me feel much less anxious and insecure about myself. That has been sustained up to the present, and it's been almost a dozen years since we first met.

5. Did this experience make you aware of your own life purpose?

No. I'm not sure that we have one life purpose—we interact with so many people in so many different ways. It made me feel a whole lot better about being here, but as for feeling this is it, here is my one true life purpose, and I have now found it for sure—no.

6. What do you think would be important to include in any writings about PLRT?

I think it's important to realize that around 40% of people cannot be fully hypnotized, but everyone can benefit from this therapy. If you let your mind wander and go freely into imagining yourself in a different place and time, you uncover aspects of yourself that have been troubling you. Ultimately, it makes no difference whether these lifetimes "really happened" or whether you needed to envision yourself in another way to understand yourself. You also have a terrific library in your office of the books that have been written about PLRT and the people who see spirits from other lives. I loved borrowing books from you and immersing myself in that spiritual world. These were all books that I would never have spent money on or taken the time to read otherwise. Coming from a family of atheists, it was really refreshing to read about people with complete faith in a spirit that continues. Thank you!

The next participant's responses:

1. What prompted you to do PLRT?

Originally, there was a natural curiosity that I believe we all have. The question about why I was drawn to or repelled by things, places, and people was never answered satisfactorily, so my "instinct" told me there has to be more to it. I had heard a former partner talk about a "trance" session he had with a shaman where he had seen me in a previous incarnation, which at that point I dismissed as hocus-pocus...or did I? I was certainly intrigued and years later was exposed to the books of Shirley McLaine, then later Dr. Brian Weiss (the forerunner in terms of this work), which appealed to me and increased my interest. Through him, I found Barbara Pisick, who helped me let go of my last doubts before embarking on a journey that lasted many years. And I wouldn't want to miss one second of it!

2. How did you feel when you had a past life-time experience?

I can't give a general answer, just because every time was different. However, I *can* say that once I was completely "in it," meaning I was fully relaxed and open, and I didn't censor the images, words, or feelings that were coming up, that I felt totally alive. It was a full-blown sensory experience, almost like you would imagine a "virtual reality" experience. I could see, smell, hear, taste, touch, and feel everything that was pertinent to the situation. Furthermore, it seemed that my "higher self" was so smart that it skipped to the moments that had important information or lessons. Like a fast-forward button on a remote. My emotions were alive and vivid, corresponding to what was happening during the regression, and at the same time, my mind was fully alert and discriminating.

3. **Did this experience change your views about reincarnation?**

Most definitely! It confirmed what my gut was already telling me. Since I didn't know anybody who had done this kind of work or could answer my questions about life after death or where we come from or the separation of body and soul, I felt so lost up until I did this work. And the church I grew up in was completely silent on the subject as well, which didn't help.

4. **Did the experience effect life changes for you, and if so, what are they?**

Absolutely! It helped me release phobias, heal relationships, clear old negative habits, improve my health (reduce stress levels, for one, which affected other health issues), and opened my heart to a "better" me. My self-esteem improved, which helped me to change careers and created a new platform to explore new venues which I hadn't dared to pursue before. I am convinced that this work has ultimately encouraged me to be the one I had always dreamed of, as it removed layers of old, previously "unseen" parts of me that kept holding me back, as well as putting me on a more spiritual path.

5. Were these changes sustained over a long period of time, and if so, how long?

I did this work for several years, on-and-off, starting on a more irregular basis, then increasing the sessions. The intensity of the responses to my regressions varied, and I noticed that the changes were increasing over time. The reasons for this are in my estimation: a) my willingness to look at the situation in depth in the first place; b) my ability to see patterns or themes of the various regressions (was there a "type" or story or lesson that kept repeating?); c) my desire to truly learn from these regressions, and yet allowing myself the necessary time and space to do it at my own pace; and d) to draw parallels between the different lifetimes and the present, making an effort to applying the understanding to the here and now.

I also think the effects are cumulative. The changes I have experienced have been sustained for years now, and I have a hard time remembering sometimes how I felt "before." It has definitely improved my life, made me calmer, saner, happier, and nicer.

6. Did this experience make you aware of your life purpose?

I truly hope to say that this is true. But what I can say is that I have found sides of myself that made me glimpse all the potential that I seem to have. And that life purpose has nothing to do with my ego-driven career goals I used to have, but rather with a life of service and giving to others. Healing yourself is key to being able to serve, and it brings with it a tremendous amount of gratitude and humility. But this awareness didn't come overnight, and it does not mean that I have to stop doing what I was doing before. It changed how I am doing it. I am fully aware, though, that this may not be true for everyone, as everyone's life purpose is different. We're each here to do our job, even though we forgot what it was. The regression work opens the door to remembering it.

7. What do you think would be important to include in any writings about PLRT?

In my many conversations about this work I have had with people of all walks of life—young, old, skeptics, and believers alike—the two things I often clarify is that you a) are fully aware of what you are saying and you can remember it afterwards, and b) hypnosis is not some crazy hocus-pocus that one should be afraid of. I don't remember how many regressions I have had, but there were many, and there was not one single instance where I didn't feel in control.

The next participant, Courtney:

1. What prompted you to do PLRT?

About 15 years ago, I went with a very good friend of mine to a past life workshop at the Open Center in New York. The hypnotherapist leading the group was trained by Brian Weiss, author of *Many Lives, Many Masters*, a book I had read a year before. I attended out of curiosity and to support my friend. Several years later, another friend had visited a therapist and began to tell me of her experiences with past life regression. At the time, I could not afford to indulge my curiosity. It was not until after the 9/11 attacks and completing a feature film did I feel compelled to seek out the past life work. Suffering from anxiety and symptoms of post-traumatic stress, I decided to make my first appointment to try and decipher patterns and behaviors that seemed to repeat and cause physical discomfort.

2. How did you feel when you had a past lifetime experience?

The first time I was brought back to a past life experience I remember feeling the sensation of rocking gently in a boat. Then the vivid memories began to open up for me. I felt awe and deja vu and realized what a potent tool this kind of work could be to untangle some of my current issues as well as issues stemming from the past.

3. Did this experience change your views about reincarnation?

As a child growing up in the Deep South, I had been told and taught by religious teachers that reincarnation is not part of the Christian belief system. Somehow my intuitive self told me that was not true. I had a very vague belief in reincarnation. I did not really understand how it fit within the culture I was brought up in, but I could not ignore my intense interest in Native American culture. As a kid, I knew how to make a bow and arrow without instruction. I knew instinctively how to approach certain plants in my environment and what they would do and if they were dangerous or medicinal. And I knew how to respect animals and the land.

4. Did the experience effect life changes for you, and if so, what are they?

The past life work helped me to identify patterns particularly within relationships and intimacy. It also helped me to release self-defeating beliefs and behaviors. When self-confidence is low, even when one is brought up in a supportive atmosphere, there is the determination of keeping everyone at arm's length so that one cannot get hurt. It is very hard to ask for help. For me, I have always been self-reliant for everything. But when it comes to love and relationships, there must be some openness and willingness to be vulnerable otherwise love cannot flourish. On the flip side, one must also have the empowerment and self-respect to create boundaries and stand up for oneself. That is something I had to learn from the ground up.

5. Did this experience make you aware of your life purpose?

My work with PLRT started in 2004 after a mild breakdown. My relationships and self-confidence have improved markedly over the course of almost three years. There is still more work to be done. I feel I have awakened to the possibilities within myself. And the amazing experiences awaiting me in life and love. The work has most definitely made me aware of my life purpose as an artist, actress, and film maker. Those scary places of true self-expression can only be achieved by plumbing the depths of the soul.

6. What do you think would be important to include in any writings about PLRT?

I think one of the most important things to be mindful about in this type of work is the energy that is the universe. There are so many other dimensions hidden from us in our waking state. It includes spirit guides, angels, the subtle energies of the body chakras, and the powers of manifestation. There is so much that we do not know perhaps on a conscious level, and yet we are beings of light in our perfect state. We know all of it in our most wise, higher selves. It is accessing that primordial knowledge that helps to free us all and humanity as a whole.

Courtney has worked with me both within the traditional psychotherapy model as well as using PLRT. You can read her experiences as a Northwest Indian in chapter 6, her multiple regressions as a young Jewish girl living in France during the Holocaust beginning in chapter 8, and as a Greek priest in chapter 11. I believe that these multiple reenactments enhanced each other and resulted in healing her chronic fear and anxiety problems in a shorter period of time than traditional psychotherapy would.

The next commentary was written by Debra, whose regression is included in chapter 9.

1. What prompted you to do PLRT?

I had a problem that I had to deal with, which was the death of my mother whom I was really close to. I am an only child and was her primary caregiver, although I lived in another state.

2. How did you feel when you had a past lifetime experience?

Better, much better. Your (Barbara's) stories of people hovering over their bodies at their deathbeds and at their funerals rang true with me, and in one regression, I saw my mother and me as a little child, and how happy we were together. In another regression, I saw myself as a Viking, male, lost at sea in a horrific storm.

3. Did the experience change your views about reincarnation?

Although my views of reincarnation were sketchy at the time and not very well formed or informed, it gave me the hope that this current life isn't all there is—or wasn't.

4. Did the experience effect life changes for you, and if so, what are they? Were these changes sustained over a long period of time, and if so, for how long?

Yes, very much so. I was able to heal from the loss of my mother—I still feel her spirit around me even today at times—and now I understand why I have an irrational fear of the water—even calm waters!

5. Did this experience make you aware of your own life purpose?

I think so. I think my life purpose has to do with letting go of old attachments and having the faith and trust and courage to form new ones. To have faith and trust in your fellow travelers. To be brave in everything. No matter what this life may bring you.

6. What do you think would be important to include in any writings about PLRT?

Other people's experiences. It's always interesting to hear how other people experienced PLRT.

Alison's regressions are included in chapters 5 and 8.

1. What prompted you to do PLRT?

I had read Dr. Brian Weiss's book, *Many Lives, Many Masters*, and then attended his weekend workshop at the Omega Institute in upstate New York. It made so much sense to me to accept the notion of past lives because too many "signs" I was getting pointed in that direction, whether it was deja vu, having instant rapport (like or dislike) to places and people, or weird coincidences. So I was curious and thought it could unravel some stuff I was grappling with.

2. How did you feel when you had a past lifetime experience?

It always felt like I had opened a door that had been shut for many, many years. Sort of like, I was remembering something that on an emotional level I "did" know before but couldn't put my finger on. After a regression, it was somehow feeling like I was connecting the dots, putting a more complete picture of who I am back together, like puzzle pieces finding their way home onto the big canvas of my life.

3. Did the experience change your views about reincarnation?

Yes, for sure. In my teens, I had heard about reincarnation, but it was not part of my upbringing or what people would talk about.

Having had many, many sessions, some of which had surprising stories, I could not deny that I would never make this stuff up, but that it had to come from a vast pool of memories that I now started to have access to.

4. Did the experience effect life changes for you, and if so, what are they? Were these changes sustained over a long period of time, and if so, for how long?

Absolutely! I am so grateful to have done this work because when I started, I was grappling with some issues that regular "talk" therapy was not able to address because it would only consider my current life experiences. However, so many layers of my being and my consciousness are affected by experiences that happened before that time. I used to suffer from panic attacks, anxiety, depression, anger issues, and overall feelings of inadequacy, shame, and guilt. Now I am calm, peaceful, feeling free and joyful, and this has been like this for many years now. I did add other things into my life—like yoga and holistic bodywork—but I believe that was a result of having done all this preliminary work.

5. Did this experience make you aware of your own life purpose?

It's an interesting journey discovering one's life purpose to begin with. With my regression work, however, I started seeing a red thread throughout many of the lifetimes I saw, and that gave me pause. I noticed that over and over again, I was "shown" lifetimes that had to do with a similar theme. If I hadn't seen this, I might have chased a path that would have prevented me to see that and meet all those amazing people that I was apparently supposed to meet in order to manifest and clarify that life purpose. So, yes, I can definitely say that this work has contributed to that discovery process.

6. What do you think would be important to include in any writings about PLRT?

I think it's really important to understand that it absolutely does not matter whether you can verify the "past lives" you see in regression. Why? Because there are millions of souls in the universe, and many of our sometimes very mundane lives have not been documented. What really and only matters is the fact that we have emotional attachments to our past lives, which is why we still carry that energy within us here and now. Hence, these past lives still affect us, unless and until we go through a regression, experience the death in that life (to return to the place where we know and remember everything, our Higher Selves' home). After that transition, we have access to the lesson, the complete understanding of our karma in that life, and the key to how we can heal ourselves. So, have no expectations, but be open and receptive to what comes through to you and what is of your highest good to know and see "right now." Another thing to consider is something that came to me in a very vivid dream during the time of my active regression therapy. In the dream, I was given a very loud and clear message that "time isn't linear," over and over again. It made no sense to me in my Western-trained analytical mind because I was taught that you read time from left to right (on a timeline)—the past being on the left, the future on the right. However, that concept is only in place to cater to our limited minds. So I think it's important to think outside of the box, even in regard to PLRT, because I believe once we do, we can access even more amazing concepts, realities, and lessons to help us become the best versions of our selves/souls/spirits.

The following responses are from Lara, whose experiences are recounted in chapter 6, "Spiritual and Religious Universality."

1. What prompted you to do PLRT?

I was in such a difficult place and felt that by doing a regression, I might have a greater understanding as to whether or not this was a pattern that I was repeating time after time.

2. How did you feel when you had a past lifetime experience?

I thought it was an amazing and enlightening experience. As a matter of fact, I had several regressions.

Barbara made me feel so comfortable in the beginning and very easily brought me down into relaxation and back to past lives. All of them had relevance to my life now.

3. Did the experience change your views about reincarnation?

I had hoped that by doing a regression into a past life that I would have a bigger picture of what was happening to me in this lifetime. It certainly did that and my experiences were so real, I could hear, feel, see, and experience all of the period I was in, and I could not imagine such things by myself. I think I have always believed in reincarnation, but actually having the experience convinced me that it was true for me.

4. Did the experience effect life changes for you, and if so, what are they? Were these changes sustained over a long period of time, and if so, how long?

These regressions had a tremendous effect for me. I had a belief that it wasn't safe for me to speak up. It was alright to have a voice and that I wasn't going to be pierced with a sword by doing so. I also understood my relationship with my ex-husband and that certain patterns were being released and would no longer be brought forward. This was a big one for me. I think that by having the regressions, my life turned 360 degrees in my own life journey. I am certainly not in the same kind of space I was in before this was done.

5. Did this experience make you aware of your own life purpose?

Having this experience led me to making life changes that opened possibilities in other areas of my life. These possibilities would not have taken place had I not made them (changes in my life). I am not the same person I was and I do understand how magnificent our physical bodies are.

6. What do you think would be important to include in any writings about PLRT?

Past life regression allows you to have a much bigger picture of your life. I discovered that we all carry patterns through lifetimes until we do something about changing them, otherwise they will continue. For me, it was all about building more consciousness within myself. It was one of the best things I had ever done.

These questionnaire responses highlight the powerful, long-standing effects of this work. I feel that people's personal responses enhance this work. As I read people's comments on the way the PLRT helped them in their lives, I was so touched at the long-term effects of this work.

These are just a few examples of people's responses to the questionnaire and are just small glimpses of the effect that PLRT has had on their lives. Hopefully, it can help you understand the dimensionality of this work.

Acknowledgments

My heartfelt thanks again for these spiritual travelers and their stories they shared with me. They allowed me to share their experiences with you, the reader. Hopefully, I was able to highlight the poignancy of their experiences

Thank you to Stephen Adolphus, who provided me enormous help by reading my manuscript and giving me invaluable advice.

Also, thanks to Patricia Martinez, whose grammatical focus and encouragement helped move this book forward.

Thank you to Ardon Kessler, Karen Murtaugh, and Anne Liguori for their recommendations and support.

The book cover design by Rami Efal brings a wonderful dimension to this work. Words are not enough—seeing is believing. Thank you so very much.

I am so deeply appreciative to my editor, Madalyn Abrams. Her hard work and patience, her insightful and thoughtful recommendations and corrections, especially to my comma-challenged writing, helped to clarify and elevate my writing to a higher level.

Bibliography

Almundsen, C. (1998) *Insights from the secret teachings of Jesus: The gospel of Thomas.* (Master's thesis). Fairfield, Iowa: Sunstar Publishing Ltd.

Andersen, G. (1999). *Lessons from the light.* New York: Berkley Books.

Eliot, T.S. (1991). *Quartets. A harvest book.* New York: Harcourt Brace & Company.

Frankl, V. (1959). *Man's search for meaning.* Boston: Beacon Press.

Hanser, R. (2012). A Noble Treason:*The story of Sophie Scholl and the white rose revolt against Hitler.* San Francisco: St Ignatius Press.

Kolata, Gina. (June 20, 2005). "PSA Test No Longer Gives Clear Answers." *The New York Times* Health Section.

Kubler-Ross, E. (1969). *On death and dying.* New York: Simon & Schuster/ Touchstone.

_____ (2000) *The cocoon and the butterfly.* (2000). Barrytown, N.Y.: Barrytown/Station Hill.

Mehrota, R. (Ed.). (2006). *The essential Dalai Lama: His important teachings.* New York: Penguin Books.

Moody, R. (1975). *Life after life: The investigation of a phenomenon—survival of body death.* New York: Mockingbird Press.

Pagels, E. (1979). *The gnostic gospels.* New York: Random House.

Ring, K. (1998). *Lessons from the light: What we can learn from the near-death experience.* New York: Insight Books.

___(2008). *Mind sight: Near-death and out-of-body experiences in the blind.* (2nd ed.). New York: iUniverse, Inc.

Schwartz, G. E. (2002). *The afterlife experiments: Breakthrough scientific evidence of life after death.* New York: Atria Books.

Stevenson, I. (1974). *Twenty cases suggestive of reincarnation.* Charlottesvile, Va.: University Press of Virginia.

Weiss, B. (1988). *Many lives, many masters.* New York: Touchstone.

Made in the USA
Middletown, DE
27 July 2021